MW00774206

Creating a Buddhist Community

In the series *Asian American History and Culture*, edited by
David Palumbo-Liu, K. Scott Wong, Linda Trinh Võ, and
Cathy Schlund-Vials. Founding editor, Sucheng Chan;
editor emeritus, Michael Omi.

Also in this series:

A list of additional titles in this series appears at the back of this book

Creating a Buddhist Community

A THAI TEMPLE IN SILICON VALLEY

JIEMIN BAO

TEMPLE UNIVERSITY PRESS
Philadelphia • *Rome* • *Tokyo*

TEMPLE UNIVERSITY PRESS
Philadelphia, Pennsylvania 19122
www.temple.edu/tempress

Copyright © 2015 by Jiemin Bao
All rights reserved
Published 2015

Library of Congress Cataloging-in-Publication Data

Bao, Jiemin, author.
  Creating a Buddhist community : a Thai temple in Silicon Valley / Jiemin Bao.
    pages cm. — (Asian American history & culture)
  Includes bibliographical references and index.
  ISBN 978-1-4399-0954-6 (hardback : alk. paper) — ISBN 978-1-4399-0955-3
(paperback : alk. paper) — ISBN 978-1-4399-0956-0 (e-book)   1. Wat Thai of
Silicon Valley.   2. Buddhism—Social aspects—California—Santa Clara Valley
(Santa Clara County)   I. Title.
  BQ6377.S382W383 2015
  294.3'650979473—dc23

                                                              2014040345

♾ The paper used in this publication meets the requirements of the American
National Standard for Information Sciences—Permanence of Paper for Printed
Library Materials, ANSI Z39.48-1992

Printed in the United States of America

113015P

For Wat Thai of Silicon Valley,

whose future practitioners may someday read this book

Contents

Preface

The seeds of this project took root in 1993 while I was in Berkeley writing a doctoral dissertation on identity formation among first- and second-generation ethnic Chinese in Bangkok. As the dissertation developed, I began to wonder about the Chinese Thai who had subsequently migrated from Thailand to the United States. Eventually, the fruit of my research was published as *Marital Acts* (Bao 2005), which examined the competing effects of ethnicity, gender, sexuality, and class in shaping the cultural identities of three generations of Chinese Thai in succeeding waves of migration. In the course of my research, I connected with Wat Thai of Silicon Valley (hereafter referred to as Wat Thai), the Buddhist temple that became the focus of this book.

Wat means temple in Thai; however, the temple's name is somewhat misleading in that its community includes many non-Thais of various ethnic, racial, class, and religious backgrounds. The making of the temple and its community fascinated me as a participant and as a scholar. After leaving Berkeley for the University of Nevada, Las Vegas, I stayed in contact with temple-goers and became increasingly intrigued by how the participants engage with local and transnational networks to articulate who they are while building the temple. As I developed closer relationships with community members through phone calls, e-mails, and visits, I saw the potential for a study of a single middle-class temple to dispel commonly held stereotypes about Buddhism, monks, and immigrants.

During nine consecutive years (2004–2012), I spent part of my summer or winter break in the field. My ability to speak Thai, Lao, and Mandarin Chinese and the cultural knowledge gained from previous fieldwork sensitized me to the respondents' points of view and helped me to comprehend the subtleties of their stories. My language skills often served as an icebreaker and made it relatively easier for me to conduct interviews.

I conducted interviews with 112 Thai and non-Thai participants in Silicon Valley and Thailand. I interviewed some respondents more than once, with the length of interviews varying from forty minutes to more than twenty-five cumulative hours. My selection process varied, as well, with some people interviewed at random at the temple and others recommended by previous interviewees. Sometimes Luang Pho, the head monk at Wat Thai, introduced me to potential respondents by saying, "Khun Latsami [my Thai name] is Chinese, but in a previous life she was Thai." On other occasions, he introduced me as "Dr. Jiemin Bao."

The people I interviewed at Wat Thai can be divided into six broad categories: white-collar professionals (including engineers, nurses, teachers, computer programmers, retired U.S. Navy and Air Force officers, artists, architects, a bank manager, and a lawyer); Buddhist monks; Farang (White people), most of them men with Thai partners; college students who shuttle back and forth between Thailand and the United States; homemakers, hairdressers, and factory workers; and entrepreneurs.

When I was doing my research in Silicon Valley, I roomed with others at Wat Thai. Sometimes, three or four of us shared a small room and slept side by side on the floor and used the same shower. Over the years, sharing a tiny space with nuns, teachers, a brain tumor survivor, widows, and sleepover volunteers provided unexpected learning opportunities. For example, I watched a roommate practice the Buddhist principle of refraining from taking the life of a living being by capturing an annoying mosquito and releasing it outdoors.

A temple is a social theater where people act out their roles and identities; as such, it is an ideal place to participate and to observe. Over the years, I attended every annual Buddhist ceremony, event, and festival held at Wat Thai more than once. These communal affairs demonstrate what the community values most, what meanings they ascribe to these activities, where connections exist among temple members, and the politics of these events. Activities I attended ranged from participating in meditation sessions to chanting in Thai; raking leaves to preparing food; washing dishes to arranging flowers; attending wedding rituals to attending funeral ceremonies; observing the ordinations of novices to observing disrobing rituals; offering alms to the monks to taking the precepts as a nun; and observing language, dance, and music classes to recycling bottles and cardboard boxes. Sometimes it was physically and mentally exhausting to conduct interviews and take field notes in a day already filled with participating in activities, but these experiences proved crucial to my understanding of the community. Without living at the temple, I would not have insight into how the monks and volunteers spend their time before visitors and practitioners arrive and after they leave, and my understanding of their practices, perspectives, and goals would have been more limited.

Sometimes Luang Pho invited me along when he and the other monks went out to conduct rituals or visit the sick and dying. During those outings, I observed the monks blessing the grand opening of a new business and the anniversary of a restaurant, and I watched as they expressed compassion for elderly and terminally ill patients in their homes and at assisted-living facilities. Taken together, these excursions disclosed the interconnections among spiritual practices and economic activities.

During the time that I conducted interviews and observed participants both inside and outside the temple, I was granted access to Wat Thai's records, including newsletters, brochures, and photograph albums. The publications and photographs captured many important moments in the temple's history. I also shot thousands of photographs of my own. Some of the photographs helped me to grasp the community's complexity with respect to regional, ethnic, gender, and class dynamics. Sharing copies of the photographs gave me an opportunity to reconnect with people and revisit events.

In addition to doing research in Silicon Valley, I conducted fieldwork in Bangkok and Roi Et, Thailand, during the summer of 2007 and the winter of 2011. I interviewed monks at three royal temples that have close relationships with Wat Thai; the vice-president of the National Council of Social Welfare, who sponsored Thai American youth groups who went to Thailand to give dance and music performances for more than twenty years; professors at Chulalongkorn University who provided training to Thai language, music, and dance instructors before sending them out to teach at temple schools overseas; founding members of Wat Thai who had retired and returned to Thailand; and villagers, primary school teachers, and monks who were the beneficiaries of Wat Thai's financial support. This multisite fieldwork compelled me to attend to the interconnection among ideas, money, events, and people who live far apart.

Following the ethical practices of cultural anthropology, I do not identify either Wat Thai or my respondents. The name of the temple and the names of all participants used herein—with the exception of public figures such as members of Thailand's royal family—are Thai, Chinese Thai, and English pseudonyms selected to correspond to the original names. According to Thai custom, Thai sources are cited in the text and listed in the references by the author's first name. For Thai terms, I follow the system in *Romanization Guide for Thai Script* (Rātchabandittayasathān 1968), with the exception of a few conventional name spellings. Frequently used Thai words and Buddhist terms are included in the Glossary.

Social and religious categories and titles are not just labels; they also have a political component. I capitalize the terms "Black," "White," and "Farang," just as I capitalize "Cambodian," "Lao," and "Asian." I translate the Thai word *Bhikkhuni* (fully ordained, female Buddhist monastics who follow 311 rules of discipline) as "female monk" rather than as "nun." In Southeast Asian Theravada Buddhist societies, the term "nun" has the negative connotation of a brokenhearted, poor, uneducated woman. In addition, nuns do not receive the support and privileges that the state grants to monks (Muecke 2004: 224–227; Sanitsuda 2001: 188, 204, 295). Bhikkhunis, who are cognizant of the distinctions between nuns and monks, tend to refer to themselves as female monks (Tsomo 2009: 156). Against this social backdrop, equating Bhikkhunis with nuns would serve to further marginalize the handful of female monks who are already situated at the periphery. The term "nun" among Thais refers to *maechi* and *chi pharm*, who follow the Eight Precepts or the Ten Precepts. "Novice" usually refers to young men between eight and nineteen who are ordained by following the Ten Precepts. "Monk" refers to those who obtain full ordination at twenty and observe 227 rules of discipline. In the United States, Thai monks are sometimes referred to as "missionary monks." However, I refer to Thai monks as transnational monks, as Sangha, or simply as monks, because in English "missionary" implies someone who goes door-to-door trying to convert people, a practice Thai monks do not follow.

I use several terms related to the status and rank of monks throughout the book. *Than* is a term of respect used to refer to a monk who has yet to obtain expertise in the first three (of nine) levels of Pali, the ancient scriptural and liturgical language of Theravada Buddhism. *Maha* is an honorific indicating that a monk has passed at least the first three levels of expertise in Pali. Some prefer to use *Achan* (teacher) to refer to monks, regardless of their level of expertise in Pali. Although *Achan* can be applied to both laypeople and monks, *Maha* applies to monks only. *Somdet* is a royal title granted to the nine highest-ranking monks who make up the Supreme Sangha Council of Thailand. *Chaokhun* is a title granted by Thailand's king to 704 distinguished monks. These terms and titles, which have no English counterparts, embody the connections among Thai Buddhism, the social order, and the monarchy.

I spent many years learning about the Wat Thai community. Community development and identity formation are best studied through long-term participant observation. In both subtle and overt ways, the monks and laypeople taught me that spiritual and mundane practices are deeply intertwined. I strive to present the multiple facets of this dynamic community and convey the members' weblike interconnections by providing detailed, in-depth descriptions of their everyday practices. Some of the information I gathered did not make its way into the final version of this book but deepened my understanding of the community and sharpened my focus. My academic inquiries and analyses are framed not only by current perspectives in anthropology, Asian American studies, and American Buddhist studies but also by my fieldwork. Thus, ultimately, my representation of Wat Thai is a "partial" truth, at best (Clifford 1986: 7). To borrow from Stuart Hall (1990: 222), I "write and speak from a particular place and time, from a history and culture which is specific. What we say is always 'in context,' positioned."

Acknowledgments

First and foremost, I thank Wat Thai of Silicon Valley. It was a humbling experience to see participants practice what we call Buddhism and to observe the compassion and commitment monks and volunteers showed while serving the community, teaching classes at the temple school, cooking at the food court, and maintaining the facilities. I am indebted to the temple participants I interviewed for sharing their stories and insights, for telling me what really matters to them, and for showing me what they do at the temple. I owe a great deal to Luang Pho, the abbot, for his enduring openness and patience in answering my questions and for giving me unfettered access to Wat Thai, his home village, and associated temples in Thailand. This support greatly helped move the project forward.

I am also grateful to the monks who showed me how they differed from monks depicted in the movies. I owe a big thank-you to the women and men who fed me delectable dishes and helped me to understand the connections among food, Buddhist practices, fundraising, and ethnic identity. I am indebted to Amdee Vongthongsri for editing and polishing the lyrics to two Thai songs that I translated and for making them sound like songs again. Thanks also go to the participants at several Thai temples in Las Vegas who welcomed my students and allowed me to conduct research there. Although I do not divulge the real names of the people I write about, I hope that the stories and experiences depicted in this narrative ethnography capture the dynamics of the community. I dedicate this book to the community in honor of their commitment and the compassion they have taught me over the years.

Second, I thank my colleagues. I appreciate the intellectual exchange with Deborah Boehm, Oona Paredes, and Heidi Swank, members of our writing group, at the chaotic beginning stage of manuscript development. Heartfelt thanks go to Alyssa Crittenden and Barbara Roth for their generous and critical feedback on the entire manuscript. I appreciate their labor of love. I am also indebted to Aihwa Ong, my mentor, for her inspiration, encouragement, and friendship. I owe profound thanks to Emily Chao and Lindsay French for their unfailing support and consultation and to Nancy Chen, Qianjing Wu, and Xiaojian Zhao for their warm friendship and conversation.

Third, I thank my undergraduate students, who helped me see the urgent need to study middle-class Southeast Asian Americans. I am indebted to my former graduate students Danielle Axt, Aaron Hockman, and Rayette Martin. I deeply appreciate the assistance they provided at different stages of the project.

Fourth, I am grateful for a Social Science Research Council Research Fellowship in 1996–1997; University of Nevada, Las Vegas (UNLV), SITE Research Grants in 2002, 2003, and 2005; a UNLV College of Liberal Arts Summer Fellowship in 2007; and a UNLV Faculty Opportunity Award in 2012–2013. This funding was essential to the support of research that endured more than a decade.

Fifth, this book greatly benefited from the attention of Janet Francendese, former editor in chief at Temple University Press, who nurtured the project from the beginning and provided me with instructive feedback throughout the process. Insightful questions, critique, and suggestions from Linda Trinh Võ, co-editor of the press's *Asian American History and Culture* series, inspired me to strengthen the manuscript. Many thanks go to Joan Vidal for her efficiency and professionalism in shepherding the book through production. Many thanks also go to Dr. Paul Numrich and several anonymous reviewers, whose insights I took to heart. I express my gratitude to Leo Van Munching for his friendship and expertise in digital photography, which helped me when I most needed it, and to Joshua Nelson for his efforts on my behalf.

Finally, I thank my mom and dad for the gift of life and for tolerating my living far away. Profound appreciation goes to Minmin and Sansan for taking good care of our dear parents and for keeping my heart at peace. Last but certainly not least, I am grateful to Jerry for loving the bird and for loving her nest.

Creating a Buddhist Community

1
Introduction

A Community in the Making

Nestled in the heart of a tranquil Silicon Valley neighborhood, a Thai Theravada Buddhist temple glistens in the bright morning sun. Tiers of glazed green terra-cotta tiles with orange trim adorn the roof, echoing the amber foothills nearby.[1] Eight birdlike golden "sky hooks" affixed to the curling roof finials add a dash of exotic flavor. More than fifty thousand two-inch squares of gold leaf gild the chapel's architectural highlights. Above the south doorway, the emblem of Thailand's Queen Sirikit is inscribed at the center of a triangular gable. On the gable above the west doorway is an imaginative rendering of a hybrid bird: a mixture of the American bald eagle and the Garuda bird, Thailand's national emblem. Two thirty-foot-long gold, green, and red railings, fashioned to resemble guardian serpents, flank the chapel. Boundary stones, white on the bottom and gray on top, encircle the chapel to mark the division between mundane and sacred space. A few feet from the driveway, five flags—the national flags of Thailand and the United States, the California state flag, the Buddhist flag, and the temple flag—fly side by side. Trees planted through the years by Queen Sirikit, three princesses, a former prime minister, and high-ranking monks, each memorialized with a plaque, catch the visitor's eye.

This temple—Wat Thai of Silicon Valley (hereafter referred to as Wat Thai)—was founded in 1983 by a small group of professional men and women, Thais and non-Thais.[2] Today, the temple community includes Asian migrants from Burma, Cambodia, China, India, Laos, Malaysia, Sri Lanka, and Vietnam, as well as a considerable number of White Americans and a handful of Latinos and African Americans. Although most regular temple participants are Theravada and Mahayana Buddhists,[3] Christians, Catholics, Jews, Sikhs, Hindus, and Muslims take part in a variety of temple activities, crossing religious as well as ethnic and racial boundaries.

Many regard Wat Thai as the anchor of the community. I repeatedly heard: "No temple, no community." This ethnography examines how the participants—regardless of their cultural, religious, ethnic, racial, and gender differences—practice Buddhism in building a temple and creating a middle-class community in Silicon Valley. A temple provides cultural space for people to socialize and gain a feeling of solidarity, especially for those who feel that their numbers are small and that they are widely scattered. Thais and those associated with them use the temple as a platform to raise Thai cultural visibility, display class respectability, and forge alliances with White Americans in Silicon Valley and elites in Thailand. Building and maintaining a temple have become ways to practice their American citizenship and perform their spiritual and cultural existence with dignity.

These Thai and non-Thai, Buddhist and non-Buddhist, immigrant and non-immigrant Americans *do* have different reference points, practices, and preferences. They often see themselves and others through multiple lenses—ethnicity, race, class, and gender—in both local and transnational contexts.[4] They are not intimidated by competing cultural ideas and practices. Encountering and intermingling with people of different backgrounds at the temple—just as they do at work or school—has become routine. Despite confronting misunderstandings, negative stereotypes, and discrimination in daily life, many realize that they are more alike than different as they share numerous interests, concerns, and dreams for themselves, their children, and the world.[5]

When I first visited Wat Thai in 1996, the chapel was still under construction. A bevy of monks and volunteers worked feverishly, adding final touches to the decorations and preparing the temple for the mid-June 1997 demarcation rituals. The chapel changed day by day, week by week. On June 14–15, 1997, seventy Thai monks from temples throughout the United States and eighty-one monks from Thailand, headed by His Eminence Somdet Phramaharajamangalacarya, gathered at Wat Thai. The demarcation rituals they performed transformed Wat Thai into the first Theravada temple in Northern California qualified to conduct all Buddhist rituals within its purified chapel space. These rituals have historical and symbolic significance, reproduce Buddhist consciousness, and transplant Buddhism to the United States.

During these demarcation ritual days, the temple attracted a variety of visitors. A Thai woman who had traveled from New York to participate in the rituals said to me: "In Thailand, it is hard to see big monks. In the United States, big monks come to visit us." This is so because the Thai state regards overseas Thai as a potential resource and Thai temples as *the* institution for reaching out to migrants and their descendants.[6] Another woman expressed gratitude to the city for not prohibiting the building of the temple. A number of White men joined in the rituals with their Thai spouses. Mothers and grandmothers assisted children and grandchildren in gilding boundary stones and placing money in donation boxes to make merit (*thambun*), whereby they transfer economic capital into religious capital and display moral worth. Some visitors enjoyed seeing the photographs that recounted the temple's history; others remarked on the short essays written in Thai by students at the temple school. Men, young and old, took advantage of this auspicious opportunity to become ordained temporarily as novices or monks. Women took the Eight Precepts to be ordained as nuns. People used the word "happy" and the phrase "feel good" over and over. Happiness can mean different things to different people. However, at this moment, the participants expressed a shared sense of happiness from seeing the chapel acknowledged as legitimate by local authorities and the Supreme Sangha Council of Thailand.

Inside the chapel, the hall was full of monks and laypeople chanting, meditating, and listening to Somdet Phramaharajamangalacarya's Dharma talk. Outside, under white awnings, people purchased offering packages, Buddha statues, and pendants blessed by the monks. Improvised donation boxes of all sizes and shapes were everywhere. Luang Dae, the head monk at Wat Thai of Los Angeles, the first Thai temple founded in the United States, who was known as one of Wat Thai's most diligent advocates, did some spontaneous fundraising after the rituals were completed. He grabbed a donation canister, sat it next to himself, then passed out miniature Buddha images and blessed individuals by sprinkling them with a few drops of water. Luang Dae visually reminded participants that giving matters when it comes to practicing Buddhism. Giving is often interpreted as a way to cultivate detachment from the material world. A crowd of men and women gathered around him, some with money in hand to donate.

The Buddhist practices described herein are dynamic, minute, sometimes unpredictable, and, above all, far more complex and interdependent than we have imagined. These two days of celebrations can be viewed as an allegory for building a Theravada temple and establishing a dynamic community. The flow of people, including monks in the United States and from Thailand, as well as the flow of symbols, money, and Buddhist practices significantly contributed to Wat Thai's very existence. Moreover, what the temple members did for these two days—feeding monks and visitors, cleaning and maintaining the temple, raising money for the temple, meditating, participating in rituals, and articulating their cultural identities—is what they do here throughout the year.

Today, Buddhism is one of the fastest growing religions in the United States. The generally agreed on estimate of the number of American Buddhists is 2.5 million–4 million.[7] A majority are Asian Americans.[8] Nearly every Buddhist school and sect can be found in cosmopolitan cities such as Los Angeles and New York (Tanaka 2011: 4). Los Angeles has become "the most complex Buddhist city in the world" (Eck 2001: 148). In *A New Religious America* (2001), Diana Eck argues that America has been transformed into the most religiously diverse nation in the world.

Although American Buddhism has been characterized as diversifying the American religious landscape (Queen 1999: xviii), most popular literature on American Buddhism focuses narrowly on meditation, self-help, and "white converts" (Jones 2007: 217–219; Kapleau 2000; Morreale 1988, 1998; Pirsig 1974; Prothero 1996; Suzuki 1970; Watts 1957). For a long time, articles in *Tricycle: The Buddhist Review*, the Buddhist periodical with the largest circulation in the United States, contributed to this tendency but more recently has broadened its scope (Tweed 1999: 76). In this country, meditation alone among Buddhist practices seems to have captured people's attention; the idea that spiritual practices are internal and superior privileges meditation. To date, little has been written about how temple communities engage in a varied array of activities, including how they build their temples through the *joint* efforts of Asians and non-Asians; what monks do besides teaching meditation and conducting rituals; how temples orchestrate spiritual practices through materiality and physical labor; or how participants forge class alliances. Furthermore, no study has examined how a diverse assemblage of participants at a *single* Buddhist temple crosses ethnic, racial, and religious boundaries.

To fill these gaps, this ethnography focuses on what participants *do*—how they practice Buddhism—and the meanings that they assign to their conduct. All activities—meditating or attending rituals, carving out cultural space, merit making, teaching the Thai language, cooking at the food court—are regarded as Buddhist practices. Many believe that *everything* they do influences their spiritual trajectory.

Participants at Wat Thai are both active agents and subjects of hybrid cultural principles and socioeconomic forces. How they engage in self-making and are being made as they build a multifaceted community constitute the heart of this book. Self-making refers to how people negotiate with regulations and institutions in working toward individual and shared goals based on particular circumstances. Being made refers to the ways in which people are informed and shaped by various regulations, ideologies, and socioeconomic conditions. The activities they organize and participate in, what they say, and their multiple identities are deeply informed by their family, schools, the larger society, and the localities where they live and work, a crucial aspect of being made. Throughout this book, self-making and being made are always in dialogue and in process and demonstrated in multiple configurations instead of a singular one. The actors at Wat Thai need to be understood within, not outside, structural constraints, market operations, and cultural forces.

Participants often refer to Wat Thai as a diverse temple. Diversity is a modern concept. The notion of "human diversity"—"the variety of human life" (Hannerz 2010: 544)—suggests that difference is informed by history, religious beliefs, sex/gender, rights, practices, and interpretations. "Diversity" is a fuzzy term. There is no general agreement about what it means. The diversity discourse "generally exclude[s] whites" (Doane 2003: 15). Scholars, however, do agree that it is not enough to see diversity in relation only to ethnicity, race, languages, religion, and other variations (Eisenlohr 2012; Hershock 2012; Jindra 2014: 324; Lamphere 1992; Sanjek 1998; Vertovec 2007). Steven Vertovec (2010: 1) suggests that we have to explore "the relationships between how diversities (and the groups within a varied social array) are imagined, how they related to social, economic and geographical characteristics, how such depictions reflect or influence social interactions, and how political systems of diversity governance themselves utilize or create depictions of diversity." Put simply, diversity is not just differences but the differences that involve power relationships informed by politics, social structures, public discourse, and access to resources.

I call special attention to the differences informed by power relationships and the *interconnections* that underscore such a notion of diversity. Many people at Wat Thai conceive of their experiences, both transnational and local, through the lens of interconnection. All things, similar and dissimilar, are seen as in a state of flux. Something occurs because other things have changed or ended; everything is believed to be connected. For example, intermarriage by itself does not carry social significance in relation to the formation of a Thai temple. Nevertheless, when these women involve their husbands and children with the temple, they are affecting and being affected by the ongoing interplay of racial/ethnic, gender, and class relationships. Intermarriages, like diversity, are knotted within a cluster of power relationships and involve complex social interactions and webs of connections. Therefore, my analysis of the making of the temple and its community focuses on interactions, inclusion, and interdependence grounded in daily engagement with translocal forces and a range of circumstances. (I used the term "translocal" to emphasize the intermingling of transnational and local power relationships, networks, and flows.) By paying attention to the juxtaposition of different cultural principles and multiple entangled networks, I write from the position that differences are relative, temporary, and continuously being renewed in response to new conditions and power relations.

Although this book is about Buddhism as practiced in the United States, it is also about connections and relationships between and among Thai Americans, the United States, and Thailand. Thai Americans identify with the United States and Thailand because they are informed by past and current events in both countries. In the age of transnational migration, it has never been more important for us to understand how migrants engage with translocal networks and with different cultural logics. In the process of temple building, Thai immigrants not only *become* Thai Americans but also *reproduce* Thai and American culture, make their middle-class identity visible, and make the community and the physical existence of the temple felt locally. They, in fact, challenge the discourse on Americanization—how immigrants are assimilated into American society—and call our attention to what they have contributed to American society. In the remainder of this chapter, I situate this study within the current academic discourse on American Buddhism, the middle class, transnationalism, and gender relationships.

Reimagining American Buddhism

In the twenty-first century, Buddhist concepts and meditation have been integrated into American popular culture to an unprecedented degree. Many people, however, may not be aware that during the past 150 years in the West, the Buddha and the Buddhism we know about were greatly influenced by a Parisian Frenchman, Eugène Burnouf, who never visited Asia or met a Buddhist but who interpreted Buddhism on the basis of his translations of random Sanskrit Buddhist manuscripts (Lopez 2013: 3–5).[9] Moreover, a monumental number of texts that recorded the Buddha's teachings, some written thousands of years ago in Pali, Sanskrit, Tibetan, classical Chinese, and other languages (along with archeological objects), remain unstudied (Schopen 2009). Many texts we do know about are copies of copies of copies that cannot be traced back to the original. However, people seem to think they know what Buddhism stands for.

It is important to keep in mind that Buddhism is an organized religion. As Gregory Schopen (1997, 2004, 2009) shows, even two thousand years ago, Indian Buddhist monks engaged with socioeconomic and legal systems, politics, cultural norms, art, mathematics, literature, and even eroticism. In *Prisoners of Shangri-La*, Donald Lopez (1998: 3) reminds us that, in the eighteenth and nineteenth centuries, Tibetan Buddhism was sometimes described as "the most corrupt deviation" from the Buddha's teachings. Ironically, many Westerners today have developed a romantic fascination with Tibet and Tibetan Buddhism. Tibet before 1959 is portrayed as a utopian society ruled by a god-king in which Tibetans, located in an isolated and ecologically enlightened land, lived a happy, peaceful life, willingly following the Dharma (Lopez 1998: 11). In this simplistic view, all of the inequalities, power struggles, and politics among Tibetans and within institutional Tibetan Buddhism have somehow vanished. Such a formulation, as Lopez so eloquently states, attempts to "[deny] Tibet its history, to exclude it from a real world of which it has always been a part, and to deny Tibetans their agency in the creation of a contested quotidian reality" (Lopez

1998: 11). Clearly, Buddhism needs to be analyzed in relation to history, ideologies, and socioeconomic systems.

In Thailand, Buddhism is the majority religion. The monks there have long been involved with national discourses, political and economic activities, and national identity formation (Anderson 2012; Fuengfusakul 1993; Keyes 1989; Kirsch 1978; Kitiarsa 2012; McDaniel 2011; Morris 2000; Reynolds 1978; Sanitsuda 2001; Tambiah 1970, 1976, 1978, 1984; Zehner 1990). For example, in 1973, Kittivuddho, a well-known Thai monk connected with right-wing military extremists, claimed that killing communists was not killing people "because whoever destroys the nation, the religion, or the monarchy, such bestial types (*man*) are not complete persons" (Keyes 1978: 153). Buddhism, in various forms, continuously has been incorporated into Thai national ideologies, national identity, and everyday life.

In the United States, Buddhism has also absorbed nationalistic ideologies, such as assimilation and Americanization. Moreover, American Buddhism is influenced by the notion of individualism and by the association of culture only with ethnic minorities, not the majority; in addition, it continues to be classified along ethnic and racial lines.

The Politics of Classification

American Buddhism has long been divided into two categories: "immigrant Buddhism" and "white [convert] Buddhism"—or, as it is referred to in the literature, the "two Buddhisms" (Layman 1976: 262–263; Prebish 1979: 51, 1993: 187). Constructing categories has become the core of the two Buddhisms discourse (Table 1.1). Immigrant Buddhism or ethnic Buddhism is described as ritual-centered and is largely practiced by Asian immigrants and their descendants who were born into the faith (Nattier 1998: 188–190). Convert Buddhists tend to be depicted as well-educated, well-traveled, elite and middle-class White Americans whose primary interest is meditation (Coleman 1999: 95–98; Fields 1994, 1998; Fronsdal 1998: 178; Machacek 2001: 69; Morreale 1998; Nattier 1998: 190; Numrich 1996, 2003). In contrast, the class status of Buddhist immigrants often is assumed to be working class or is simply ignored.[10]

The two Buddhisms paradigm has been refined for decades, reducing social complexity to a set of simple contrasts and erasing the vigor and diversity of practices. Classification schemes are informed

TABLE 1.1. TWO BUDDHISMS PARADIGM

Immigrant Buddhism	White Buddhism
Immigrant Buddhists	White converts
Ritual-oriented	Meditation-oriented
Working class	Middle class

by power relationships (Hacking 1990), and attempts to map Buddhism are no different. As Rick Fields (1994: 55) pointed out, "It is mainly white Buddhists who are busy doing the defining. . . . [T]hey're defining it in their own image," and through such a discourse meditation becomes the "real Buddhism." These binary categories are bred from asymmetries of power and reinforce the existing racial stratification. Helen Tworkov, former editor-in-chief of the Buddhist magazine *Tricycle*, exemplified this propensity when she stated, "The spokespeople for Buddhism in America have been, almost exclusively, educated members of the white middle class. Meanwhile, even with varying statistics, Asian-American Buddhists number at least one million, but so far they have not figured prominently in the development of something called American Buddhism" (Tworkov 1991: 4). Tworkov not only positioned herself as a spokesperson for American Buddhism but also denied the contribution of Asian Americans in reterritorializing Buddhism by building temples and by introducing Buddhism to America. Such a discourse, as Joseph Cheah and Wakoh Hickey point out, reflects ethnocentrism, White privilege, and racialization (Cheah 2011: 129; Hickey 2010: 1). The line between interpreting behavior informed by social systems and suggesting that one kind of behavior is superior to others may be fine, but it is not insignificant.

Sometimes a simple omission misrepresents a diverse community. For example, Paul Numrich (1996: 65) chose to "exempt" the husbands of Thai women, most of them White, from his study because these men did not practice meditation. Such an omission reinforces the assumption that meditation is the key marker of American Buddhism and excludes the demographically significant number of Whites who go to the temple with their wives to participate in activities other than meditation. According to the 2010 U.S. Census, half of Thai American women and the majority of Thai immigrant women are married to non-Thai men (Hidalgo and Bankston 2011: 88). More important, intermarriage between Thai women and Farang men creates cultural space for interactions and conversation, and works with and against racial/ethnic ideology. Thus, taking intermarriage into account is crucial for illustrating the formation of Thai American Buddhist temples.

The categories "White convert" and "immigrant Buddhist," therefore, fail to capture the ambiguity of practitioners who cross the boundaries between Christianity and Buddhism. Luang Pho, the abbot, often said to visitors of different faiths that "Buddhism is just a brand name. . . . [O]ne does not need to be an American to eat a hamburger." From his perspective, one does not need to be a Buddhist to practice Buddhism. Some White Americans are also unaware of the connection between meditation and Buddhism; those who do know the connection often are ambivalent or even afraid of being stigmatized by openly self-identifying as Buddhist (Cadge 2005: 24, 165–169). Others practice both Christianity and Buddhism. According to a survey conducted by the Pew Research Center's Forum on Religion and Public Life in 2009, a large number of Americans attend worship services of more than one faith or denomination; about 24 percent of them attend services weekly and about 59 percent attend services monthly.[11]

Some scholars have resisted these binary categories. Thomas Tweed (1999: 71–75) suggested paying attention to hybridity and the ambiguity of Buddhist identities. He proposed the category "sympathizer" or "night-stand Buddhist" to include those who read books about Buddhism and practice meditation but do not identify with Buddhist organizations. In a similar vein, Jeff Wilson (2009a: 840–841) used the metaphor "purple" America instead of an America broken down into blue states and red states to problematize the two Buddhisms dichotomy. Despite these new perspectives, we have little firsthand knowledge about how a heterogeneous community is established and how hybrid cultures and identities are constructed at a temple.[12] For that reason, a book that does justice to a diverse community is needed.

Multifaceted American Buddhism

Buddhist temples serve as multifunctional centers and play an important role in engaging with political, cultural, and socioeconomic activities in American society (Ama 2010; Asai and Williams 1999; Cheah 2011; Chen 2008; Nguyen and Barber 1998; Seager 1999; Suh 2004; Van Esterik 1999; Williams and Queen 1999; Wilson 2012). To date, more research has been conducted on Mahayana than on Theravada Buddhism. Mahayana Buddhists came to the United States much earlier and outnumber Theravada Buddhists. Chinese and Japanese migrants have been bringing Mahayana practices and beliefs to the United States for more than a hundred years. In contrast, most Theravada Buddhists— Burmese, Cambodian, Laotian, Sri Lankan, and Thai—arrived in the United States after 1970. Within Mahayana and Theravada Buddhism, there are many schools and lineages. Some are mentioned below. These existing labels are used as shorthand to echo historical, geographic, and cultural differences.

Numrich published the first book about immigrant Theravada Buddhist temples in the United States in 1996. He compared a Thai Buddhist temple in Chicago with a Sri Lankan Buddhist temple in Los Angeles. Numrich (1996: 66–68) argued that immigrant Buddhists and American converts within the same temple formed "parallel congregations" that "intersected" but did not "interact," because the immigrants were ritual-oriented and the converts were meditation-oriented.

After Numrich, Wendy Cadge (2005) compared a Thai immigrant temple in Philadelphia with an insight meditation center in Cambridge, Massachusetts, composed largely of White participants. Instead of focusing exclusively on the differences, the crux of the two Buddhisms paradigm, Cadge mapped out some of the *similarities* between the two groups. She showed that immigrant and White practitioners draw on Theravada history and share a commitment to meditation and the Dharma (Cadge 2005: 46, 101) and that each group has been influenced by different interpretations of what it considers Buddhism to be (Cadge 2005: 5, 98–102). Emphasizing what White meditation practitioners and Thai immigrants share becomes Cadge's strategy for problematizing the premise of the two Buddhisms schema.

In comparison, Jeff Wilson (2012) illustrates how five groups, which identify with separate lineages, practice at a single temple, Ekoji Buddhist Sangha of Richmond, Virginia. He calls our attention to regional characteristics by showing that the members of different lineage groups, predominantly White, use the same temple space, in part because of limited resources, opportunities, and the small number of Buddhists in the South (Wilson 2012: 5, 119, 126). Although each group maintains its distinctive Buddhist lineage and practices, the members mingle, learn from one another, and find something they all share. The story that unfolds at Ekoji is, as Wilson (2012: 7) points out, "one of intersecting, not parallel lines."

Most scholars have focused on Buddhism practiced by *a single ethnic/racial group.* Their work shows the complexity within the group. For example, scholars have found that Zen *centers* tend to focus on meditation and Buddhist studies, but Zen *temples* tend to focus on memorial and funeral services and cultural events (Asai and Williams 1999: 20). Although Japanese Zen meditation has become increasingly popular in the United States, Japanese Shin Buddhism, which rejects meditation and the precepts, has declined (Bloom 1998: 45). Nichiren Shōshū and Soka Gakkai Buddhism have developed into something quite different in the United States from the forms they take in Japan (Hurst 1992). Meanwhile, a noticeable number of Soka Gakkai participants are African and Hispanic Americans (Tanaka 2007: 116).

Cultural differences also appear in the few studies of Theravada Buddhist practitioners. Some scholars have observed that Thai immigrants are noted for respecting monks' leadership and knowledge (Cadge 2005; Numrich 1996), whereas others observe that Cambodian migrants have tended to distrust monks, in part because monks with spiritual standing were massacred during Pol Pot's regime (Douglas 2003: 164; Smith-Hefner 1999: 50). More recently, new kinds of relationships have developed between Thai and Cambodian laypeople and monks in the United States. Many Thai Buddhists are not afraid to challenge a monk's authority, while new Cambodian monastic leaders have tended to earn the trust of the community through their deeds.

Whereas most recent scholarship focuses on Buddhist practices within an ethnic group, a few scholars have compared Buddhist and Christian practices within the same ethnic group in different locations. Okyun Kwon (2003) maps out the socioeconomic and religious characteristics of Christian and Buddhist Korean Americans in addressing questions such as, Why do more Korean Protestants than Buddhists immigrate to the United States? Carolyn Chen (2008) wrote a rich ethnography about how Christianity and Buddhism differently enable Taiwanese immigrants to adjust to life in America. Taiwanese Buddhists make more conscious effort than do Taiwanese Christians to prove themselves in order to gain social acceptance in a predominantly Christian society (Chen 2008: 79–81). In studying senior Nisei (second-generation) Japanese Americans, Peter Yuichi Clark (2003: 61) notes that Buddhist Nisei and Christian Nisei share compassion despite their different faiths. In the same spirit but in different ways, Cambodian Americans cross the boundaries between Christianity and Buddhism

(Douglas 2003: 171; Ong 2003: 228). Indeed, boundary crossings occur not just between Buddhist branches and schools but also between religions. Nevertheless, there is a dearth of knowledge about Buddhist and cultural activities conducted by different ethnic, racial, and faith groups within the same institution. People of many different backgrounds live under the same roofs, study together in the same classrooms, and work together at the same job sites because the United States is made up of migrants from all over the world. Social interactions and collaboration among people of different backgrounds are part of everyday temple life. Nevertheless, scholars tend to focus on temples along ethnic lines and associate ethnicity with a reified culture. The dominant discourse, as Gerd Baumann (1996: 17) pointed out, "reduce[s] all social complexities, both within communities and across whole plural societies, to an astonishingly simple equation: 'Culture = community = ethnic identity = nature = culture.'"

It is crucial to pay attention to those who join the temple by crossing racial boundaries and those who are members of more than one religious community. In this book I treat the differences among Thais as seriously as the differences between Thais and non-Thais. Having the same country of origin may mask some significant distinctions. At Wat Thai there are members of three major ethnic groups who come from Thailand: the ethnic Thai, ethnic Chinese, and ethnic Lao of northeastern Thailand (Isan). People have different statuses, experiences, and educational attainment within each ethnic group. Some have had many more transnational engagements than others because of their economic capital or legal status. The members of different ethnic groups may bond with one another in one context and reinforce negative stereotypes against another ethnic group in another context. Participants from other ethnic and racial groups also bring their history, faith, and practices to the community. Heterogeneity within a community plays a crucial role in a study such as this one.

Whiteness

The rich literature on Whiteness asserts that White Americans enjoy certain privileges and are projected as worthy citizens (Bonilla-Silva 2012; Lipsitz 1998; McIntosh 1989; Ong 2003; Rothenberg 2002; Sacks 1994; Wildman 1996). Long ago, Ruth Frankenberg (1993: 15, 147) pointed out that *not* talking about color-consciousness is a White privilege; seemingly neutral color-blindness actually supports White racism by refusing to acknowledge the links between racial ideologies and socioeconomic structures. Whiteness carries symbolic capital, standing for American and middle class. Asians, regardless of their American citizenship and socioeconomic status, do not automatically possess the same measure of symbolic capital. As Toni Morrison (1992: 47) has observed, "Deep within the word 'American' is its association with race. . . . American means white."

Like skin color in the United States, skin shades in Thailand are etched with specific meanings. In Buddhism, the "color of one's mind" is considered much more significant than the "color of one's body" (Wiyada 1979: 118). Black-minded people are bad; white-minded people are good. In between is a variety of people with "other colored minds" (Wiyada 1979: 118). The color of one's mind, or moral worth, is depicted in temple murals by means of skin color. The hierarchical order descends *vertically* from the Buddha, who is "whiter than white," to angels, monks, laypeople, and those in hell (Wiyada 1979: 118). Because lighter skin shades impart higher status, people with lighter skin are located in the upper part of a mural; those with darker skin are considered of lower status and are located in the lower part. The cosmic world and the social world intersect in the painting. Such a belief is further reproduced through the idea of karma in Thai popular culture. Those with light skin are perceived as having more positive karma than those with dark skin (Weisman 2001: 234).

Although Thailand was never a colony, in the first half of the twentieth century, the Thai nation-state introduced Western manners, modes of dress, hairstyles, and family surnames so its Thai subjects would appear "modern" (Reynolds 1991: 7; Thongchai 1994: 4-5; Van Esterik 1996: 213, 2000: 96–108). Light skin is further associated with beauty and is a sign of being modern in Thai society (Mills 1999: 106). Historically, "Thai nationalists," as Jan Weisman (2001: 232) notes, have "denigrated Black people as models of behavior that is to be avoided by Thai, while presenting Whites (whose phenotype is also greatly preferred) as models to be emulated." Thai national ideologies generate a racial continuum similar to that in the United States, with White at the top and Black at the bottom.

The legacy of colonialism and of associating Whiteness with modernity has had a profound impact on how Asians and Asian immigrants view Whites and America. Today many Filipinos still "equate

American with white and often use these two terms interchangeably" (Espiritu 2003: 159). Burmese, too, equate "American" with "white" (Cheah 2011: 76). Thai people use a special term, "Farang," to refer to White people without distinguishing their ethnicity. I adopt the term "Farang" to reflect this notion. I argue that Thai transmigrants are subject to both Thai and American ideologies when deciding whom to marry, with whom to forge alliances, and whom to include in the temple power structure.

"A Culture of No Culture"

Once while teaching a class on Buddhism, I asked my students, "Why can one find Buddha statues but no statue of Jesus at Whole Foods?" One answered, "Buddha is cheerful and pleasant, not miserable or suffering like Christ." Buddha is perceived as a kind of free-floating image untouched by culture, politics, and history. Romanticized Buddhism exists not only in popular culture but also in academic discourse. Janet McLellan (1999: 26–27) claims, "The development of non-Asian Buddhism has had no historical links to western culture, government, power, or politics. . . . Among Asian Buddhists, the transmission of and belief in traditional doctrines and scriptures are expressed as part of their cultural heritage." She applies the concept of culture to "Asian Buddhism" but takes "non-Asian Buddhism" for granted. In fact, Western culture and politics have had a profound impact on modern Buddhism. As Edward Conze (1975: 146) pointed out a long time ago, "Until Europeans wrote about them, the 'Buddhists' were happily unaware that they were 'Buddhists.' What they were preaching, practicing, and meditating about was not Buddhism but the 'holy dharma.' . . . Buddhism was an abstraction, coined by unbelievers for their own convenience." Today, the prevailing prejudice toward Buddhist rituals is, to a certain extent, underscored by the Protestant prejudice against Catholic ritualism and superstition (Snodgrass 2009: 29, 40; Yang 2008: 18). When meditation is idealized, few scholars pay attention to the confluence of commerciality and materiality on meditation practices (Padgett 2000).

Schopen warns against romanticizing meditation. On the basis of his examination of the archeological evidence and the rarely studied and voluminous Mulasarvastivda Vinaya—Buddhist legal texts for governing monks in northern India in the early medieval period—

Schopen noted that the Buddha, as recorded by Mulasarvastivda monks, was more than just a wise man; he was also a shrewd business-man and a sophisticated lawyer. Consequently, Mulasarvastivda monks neither gave up their personal property nor renounced money (1997, 2004, 2005, 2009). Schopen contends that the Sangha, or community of monks, at that time meant something closer to an economic corporation than a monastic community. In his 2009 UCLA Faculty Research Lecture, Schopen pointed out, "In short, we are not normally aware that the same Buddha who taught 'all things are impermanent' also taught his monks how to use and service a permanent endowment." In other words, from the beginning Buddhism has been subjected to time-specific socioeconomic systems and norms, just as it is today, although in different forms.

Denying the impact of culture on non-Asian Buddhism and meditation is similar to what Sharon Traweek (1988: 162) diagnoses as "a culture of no culture." Drawing from her study of high-energy particle physicists, she shows that these elite intellectuals believed that they revealed the secrets of nature, so that neither their science nor they themselves had anything to do with culture (Traweek 1998: 78). However, these scientists, as she illustrates, *do* have a culture. They share notions of time, space, and the social order.

The physicists are not alone. Larry Rosenberg, founder of the Cambridge Insight Meditation Center, regards breathing meditation as "an ideal way to teach Buddhism in the West, because it does not carry the 'cultural baggage' other methods do" (Cadge 2005: 96, citing Rosenberg and Guy 1998). Accordingly, "cultural baggage" refers to the religious beliefs, rituals, ceremonies, and cultural identity—but not meditation—that immigrants carry with them to the United States (Cadge 2005: 29; Nattier 1998: 190). Jack Kornfield claims that "insight meditation" is free of "the complications of rituals, robes, chanting and the whole religious tradition" (cited in Fronsdal 1998: 167; Prebish 1999: 152). Kornfield is known for making a great effort to combine meditation and psychotherapy (Cheah 2011: 67; Fronsdal 1998: 167–170). Nevertheless, combining meditation with psychotherapy is taken for granted because meditation is assumed to be free of cultural baggage and psychotherapy to be scientific. Furthermore, the category "baggage Buddhism" or "ethnic Buddhism" refers to Buddhism as practiced by Asian immigrants (Nattier 1998: 190). Through such a discourse, "culture" equals "ethnic minorities." Meditation is romanticized as "real"

Buddhism; rituals are marginalized as cultural baggage. The former becomes spiritual and natural, and the latter religious and cultural. It is true that breathing is natural, not cultural. It is also true that meditation does not involve monks, candles, incense, kneeling, and bowing. However, the moment one connects breathing with understanding one's body and mind or with low self-esteem, fear, or anger, breathing and looking inward become cultural acts. Meditation is appreciated and preferred because it fits neatly into the cultural fashions of America—psychology and individualism. Individuals, nevertheless, are impossible to be separated from, but rather constantly communicate with, social systems and ideologies (Scheper-Hughes and Lock 1987: 6, 13).

Thus, Buddhism is cultural. Culture is not a kind of inherited property but "a dynamic and potentially oppositional force which stands in complex relationship with the material conditions of society" (Brah 1987: 44). As such, a culture permeates the mutually constitutive relationships between people of Eastern and Western backgrounds, the intertwining of spiritual and mundane practices, and the interplay among different forces in the process of temple building and community-making. What Thai Americans (the majority of regular participants) and White Americans (the majority of regular non-Thai participants) do and say at Wat Thai help us see how they perceive and practice Buddhism. Therefore, the terms "cultural forces" and "cultural principles" apply to each of these groups to capture how they are influenced by different norms in certain contexts and by the same values in other contexts and how they continuously reproduce Buddhist culture.

The Middle Class: A Cultural Struggle

As mentioned earlier, in the dominant discourse on American Buddhism, Whiteness is viewed through the category of class, but immigrants are viewed through the category of race, with a hidden class message. Indeed, as many scholars have noted in a variety of contexts, American society is marked by a Black-White continuum of status (Franklin and Moss 1994; Hale 1999; Harris 1993; Makalani 2003; Omi and Winant 1986; Ong 2003). In this line of thinking, White Anglo-Saxons often are assumed to be upper class; Jews are assumed to be middle class; and African Americans and ethnic minorities are assumed to be lower class, regardless of their actual socioeconomic status (Ortner 1998: 7, 2003: 51).

Many Thai immigrants were middle class before they came to the United States. The middle class, for them, means having a comfortable lifestyle, a stable income, a good education and owning a home. Collectively, they perceive themselves as educated, affluent, urban professionals who enjoy living a more cosmopolitan lifestyle than many Cambodians, Laotians, and Vietnamese. They nevertheless suffer cultural and class "invisibility" (Thongthiraj 2003: 102).[13] Especially before the 1990s, few Americans knew much about ethnic Thais or Thai culture. Mary's experience was typical: "When I say, 'I am Thai,' they say, 'Oh, Taiwanese.' I say 'Thailand,' and they say, 'Oh, Taiwan.'" Among those who did know about Thailand, Thais were often associated with the "land of smiles," the sex industry, and spicy food (Thongthiraj 2003: 102). In addition, Thais were often mistaken for refugees because their economic capital was masked by skin color, a foreign accent, and immigrant status. Thus, some have found that belonging to the middle class is not enough to gain *group* cultural and class visibility.

Therefore, this book is not so much about how an individual achieves socioeconomic upward mobility as about how these individuals work together *collectively* to gain class respectability, acquire cultural visibility, accumulate social and religious capital, resist racialized profiling, and develop new gender relationships. When a temple thrives, the individuals associated with that temple are dignified. Their middle-class practices include pooling resources from Thailand and the United States to build a multimillion-dollar temple, welcoming everyone to that temple, making class alliances with those who support the community, and fostering a younger generation that is bilingual and bicultural. As Mark Liechty (2003: 265) points out, "Middle-class practice is about carving out a cultural space in which people can speak and act themselves into cultural existence." What middle-class members *do* is more important than what the middle class *is*. Class is neither a "thing" nor a "category"; it is a "cultural practice" and a "process" (Liechty 2003: 20–21, 255).

Before Liechty, Pierre Bourdieu (1984) emphasized that class is not just an issue of money. It is also a matter of taste. He pointed out that just as a common taste may disclose class, gender, and educational differences, taste serves as an important social marker and is part of the process of forming boundaries and identities. Taste is embedded in the process of accumulating capital; taste shapes what types and quantities of capital individuals accumulate. Bourdieu (1987: 3–4) shows us that people accumulate and convert different types of economic, cultural, social, and symbolic capital: "In a social universe like French society, and no doubt in the American society of today, these fundamental social powers are . . . firstly *economic* capital, in its various kinds; secondly *cultural* capital, or better, informational capital, again in its different kinds; and thirdly two forms of capital that are very strongly correlated, *social* capital, which consists of resources based on connections and group membership, and *symbolic* capital, which is the form the different types of capital take once they are perceived and recognized as legitimate." Capital is a form of power: Different kinds of capital indicate different kinds of power and resources and are interconnected and convertible.

Nevertheless, there is more than one set of criteria for potential convertibility in a heterogeneous society—a point that Bourdieu failed to recognize (Ong 1999: 89). People, especially transmigrants, encounter "*a perceived mismatch* between the distinction of their symbolic capital and their racial identity" (Ong 1999: 91; emphasis added). Two kinds of incompatibilities were evident at Wat Thai: the Thai identity of White people and the middle-class identity of the Asian immigrants. Due to this perceived mismatch, racial ideologies, and the asymmetrical power relationship between Thailand and the United States, Thais and Farang experience different kinds of structural constraints. Thai Americans come to realize that it is difficult, at the least at the present time, to convert their religious capital into symbolic capital in American society. Nevertheless, the *temple* can provide cultural space where they gain access to this kind of convertibility. At the same time, Farang come to realize that their white bodies are perceived as incompatible with a Thai identity. They are racialized because of the mismatch between their Thai cultural capital and racial identity. Indeed, identity is articulated not only through self-identification but also through how they are perceived by others (Barth 1969; Eriksen 2010). The temple becomes a platform on which Thais and Farang perform and articulate their identities situationally.

Interlocking Local and Transnational Circuits

This ethnography pays special attention to translocal movements and encounters that intensify interaction and diversity. Analyzing the intermingling of different forces helps us to see how Buddhism is produced and reproduced in the United States. "Awareness of multilocality," as Vertovec (1997: 282) points out, helps one connect "oneself with others, both 'here' and 'there,' who share the same 'routes' and 'roots.'"

Some scholars have tended to focus on nationalistic Americanization or assimilation in the discourse on Asian American Buddhist organizations and practices (Cadge 2005: 11, 39, 202; Machacek 2001: 71, 74; Numrich 1996: xxiii, 80, 140; Prebish 1993: 193).[14] Their underlying message is that immigrants and their descendants gradually lose their distinctiveness over successive generations, transforming from non-Americans into Americans. The emphasis on Americanization is not new. Asian Americans have long been conceived as both "a racial 'problem' and a racial 'solution'" (Yu 2001: 7). In practice, Americanization is never complete.

The Thai Americans at Wat Thai, for example, participate in at least two *mutually* influential cultures: one by birth and the other by choice. At the local level in Silicon Valley, these Thai Americans connect with their neighbors, other Buddhist communities, schools, park officials, and city authorities via education, jobs, intermarriage, Buddhist activities, and community building. Silicon Valley, which has a distinctive history and demographic, to some extent shapes Thai Americans and the temple; they, in turn, influence Silicon Valley through their cultural performances and construction of cultural space. At the transnational level, they bond with their kin, high-ranking monks, royal family members, Thai government officers, teachers, and the places where they were born. Many maintain an array of associations with temples in Thailand, the United States, and elsewhere. They stretch their cultural life and activities beyond national borders, to borrow Anthony Giddens's words, "in such a way that local happenings are shaped by events occurring many miles away and vice versa" (Giddens 1990: 64). Simultaneously engaging with translocal networks and with two clusters of cultural codes, I argue, has defined Thai Americans as transnational subjects.

Cultures are linked to one another even without direct personal contact (Appadurai 1991, 1996; Hall 1995; Liechty 2003). Yet as Jonathan Inda and Renato Rosaldo (2002: 11) point out, culture often "has been seen as something rooted in 'soil.'" Actually, culture is *not* some "bounded entity that occupies a specific physical territory"; instead, culture travels (Inda and Rosaldo 2002: 11). Thus, we need to see that culture and beliefs are simultaneously being "deterritorialized" and "reterritorialized" (Inda and Rosaldo 2002: 10–12). However, many have not recognized this. As Akhil Gupta and James Ferguson (1997: 40) note, "Even anthropologists still talk of 'American culture' with no clear understanding of what such a phrase might mean, because we assume a natural association of a culture ('American culture'), a people ('Americans') and a place ('the United States of America')." I agree with Tweed (2011: 23) that we need to "trace the flow of people, rituals, artifacts, beliefs, and institutions across spatial and temporal boundaries" in the study of American Buddhism.

My strategy, therefore, is to study both "where they come from" and "where they are at" (Gilroy 1991: 3). I focus on how Thai transmigrants are largely conditioned by the materiality and ideologies of the United States, the country in which they now dwell, and by those of Thailand, the country they left behind. Just as Thai migrants are pressured by nationalistic ideologies to become Americanized, Thai authorities expect Thais and their descendants to adhere to culturally constructed khuam pen thai (Thainess) regardless of where they live. Such a public discourse normalizes and naturalizes an essentialized notion of Thainess—for instance, equating it with being Buddhist (Ishii 1968: 865; Keyes 1971: 567). To achieve a reification of Thainess, youngsters learn the Thai language, dance, and music and often are reminded that they have full Thai blood (sailuat khuampenthai tempiam),[15] which makes their Thai identity "natural" and obligates them to identify with Thailand. The temple school becomes the most important institution for Thai heritage and identity-making and remaking, both concealing the intricacies of cultural politics and creating a narrative advantageous to the agenda of the Thai state. Thus, examining a temple's institutional role enables us to see how the cultural identity of Thai migrants and their descendants are reconstructed by two nation-states.

Ethnic identities often are articulated in contrast with others and in relation to what they are not (Eriksen 2010: 1–4, 34). Nevertheless, in some contexts, a combination of different cultural symbols is used to highlight two interconnected identities. For example, the architect, artists, abbot, and the board of directors at Wat Thai creatively used diverse cultural symbols to highlight Thai American identity via spatial forms. Many participants see themselves as Thai and American without contradiction. Thai Americans, like the members of the diaspora Stuart Hall (1995: 206) discussed, belong to more than one country. They "have learned to negotiate and translate between cultures, and . . .

because they are irrevocably the product of several interlocking histories and cultures, have learned to live with, and indeed to speak from, *difference*." Identity is constantly changing in response to different power relations that are "never complete, always in process, and always constituted within, not outside, representation" (Hall 1990: 222).

If we focus exclusively on Buddhist practitioners within the city or region in which they live, we miss some of the complex interplay of regional, national, and transnational circumstances. Therefore, I use the term "Thai American" to highlight that these people are informed by both Thai and American cultural principles. The term "transmigrant" emphasizes mobility, and "immigrant" conveys their legal status. I use the term "migrant" in a much broader sense, without distinguishing between those who are documented and those who are not. I also pay special attention to gender relations and gendered practices among people of different backgrounds.

Gender Games

Thai women are structurally prohibited from becoming monks but are expected to visit temples and provide monks with food and other provisions. In 1928, the Supreme Sangha Council of Thailand passed a rule prohibiting Thai monks from ordaining women. The few women who have tried to become monks have met with limited success, most being ostracized and some even jailed (Falk 2007; Nissara 2005).[16] Women often are advised that they should just practice Buddhism the best they can. Motherhood, nurturing, and contributing daily necessities to monks are regarded as moral actions that lead to improving a woman's karma (Andaya 2002: 7, 29; Keyes 1984: 228–230; Kirsch 1977: 251; Muecke 1984: 462; Whittaker 1999: 47). More recently, a few women have been able to circumvent the Thai Sangha and receive full ordination overseas. Nevertheless, Thai Bhikkhunis (female monks) and nuns still struggle to "achieve formal legitimation as religious persons" (Falk 2007: xi).

In comparison, Thai men are expected to enter a Buddhist monastic order as novices or monks as a rite of passage. Thailand's government encourages male civil servants to become ordained by granting them a leave of up to three months with full pay (Keyes 1987: 36).[17] The monkhood, nevertheless, does not serve as the primary means of obtaining higher education and social upward mobility, as it once did.

In the United States, few Thai immigrant men or their sons ordain for the long term.

At Wat Thai, most volunteers are women; yet more men than women serve on the board of trustees and the board of directors, the temple's governing bodies. In contrast, the temple school is largely led and run by women. At the temple's food court, the women do most of the preparation and cooking, whereas the men, including the monks, do all the heavy lifting—emptying the trash cans, taking down the awnings, rearranging tables and chairs, and so on. Collectively, the men and women tend to divide labor along gender lines. Similar gendered arrangements can be found at other Buddhist temples and meditation centers (Cadge 2005: 187–188; Suh 2004: 82). To a certain extent, gendered immigration patterns—*pioneer migration*, led by middle-class, urban, male Thai and Chinese Thai students, and *marriage migration*, dominated by working-class Thai women who married Farang—have shaped the power dynamic and composition of the community. Collectively, more Thai and Farang women practice meditation than Thai and Farang men. These gender differences trump constructed racial differences, such as White converts being meditation-oriented and immigrants being ritual-oriented.

There is an implicit assumption that Asian immigrant women enjoy greater gender equality in the United States than women generally do in Asia. However, no simple criterion of high versus low status can measure the social status of women across cultures (Atkinson and Errington 1990: 7). Gender relationships cannot be captured just by counting the number of men and women in authoritative positions or by noting how labor is divided, because power relationships are mutually constitutive. Thai American gender relationships often are expressed in unpredictable, inconsistent, and disruptive ways. An account that follows the twists and turns of two women's life experiences sheds light on how, despite constraints imposed by new socioeconomic conditions and gender ideologies, these women made use of every available opportunity.

Thomthong, born into a middle-class ethnic Chinese family in Bangkok (her grandparents immigrated from southern China to Thailand), earned a bachelor of arts degree from Chulalongkorn University, Thailand's oldest and most prestigious university. She taught English as a second language at a medical school in Bangkok before joining her husband, an engineer, in Silicon Valley in 1987. Despite her education and teaching experience, she could not find a comparable job in the San Francisco Bay Area. She decided to stay at home to take care of her children; she volunteered to teach the Thai language and do bookkeeping for Wat Thai. Some of her Thai friends thought she was wasting her talents. However, Thomthong told me, "I am 100 percent really proud of myself. I am proud of the work that I do with my children [one graduated from the University of California, Berkeley, and another from Yale Law School]. You don't need to have lots of things to be happy but just learn to be content with the things that you have."

Like Thomthong, Kamala is an ethnic minority, a Phunoi. Compared with ethnic Chinese, the "trading minority" (Wertheim 1965), Phunoi suffer greater marginalization through stereotyping as a backward hill tribe. Whereas Thomthong was born into a middle-class family in a cosmopolitan city, Kamala was born into a poor rural family in Isan. Kamala married a Farang and immigrated to the United States in 1972. With just four years of primary school education and limited English-language skills, she could find work only as a hairstylist. However, after two years, she opened her own salon and eventually became an entrepreneur, operating four beauty shops and supervising twenty employees. Because she worked long hours six days a week and volunteered on Sundays at Wat Thai, Kamala was often absent from home. Her husband eventually divorced her. Kamala does not fit the stereotype of a Thai woman who is always smiling, pampering her husband, and sacrificing for her children. When the hair salon business became too competitive, Kamala sold her shops and reinvested her money in real estate. A wave of rising home prices made her a millionaire. She retired at forty-eight but continued to donate money, time, and labor to temples and schools in the United States, in Thailand, and in India during her pilgrimages.

Each woman made what seemed to her the best available decision in her new circumstances. Thomthong, a former career woman who spoke fluent English, became a stay-at-home mom and accepted the socioeconomic downward mobility that resulted when her previously accumulated educational capital failed to convert in the United States. She devoted herself to her family and her temple, redefining success. In contrast, Kamala, who had very little education, saw business as a path to upward class mobility. Nevertheless, her work ethic, leadership, and the resulting income that testified to her success threatened her husband, who valued her domestic caretaker role far more than her other accomplishments. Indeed, immigration changed these two women's life trajectories in ways that no one could have predicted.

The Organization of the Book

This study is situated in both a historical and a translocal context. Chapter 2 focuses on the establishment of Wat Thai, its new power structure, its leaders, and its key participants, as well as on various practices and boundary crossings. I argue that inclusion is a communal practice and that the formation of the temple community is informed by Thai gendered immigration patterns, the regulation of nonprofit organizations in the United States, the demographics of Silicon Valley, and the effects of intermarriages.

The remaining chapters are organized at the intersections of community building, the construction of cultural space, merit making, and the reification of Thai culture and Thai American identities. Although the spiritual, educational, social, and economic realms are distinguished from one another for the convenience of analysis, and even though one facet might stand out more than another in a particular context, all of the activities that take place within these different realms are intertwined.

Chapter 3 focuses on the social sphere—the process of temple building and carving out distinctive religious and cultural space. The Wat Thai community constructed a chapel by negotiating its way through American building codes and Thai Buddhist beliefs and notions of sacred and secular space. I argue that spatial forms are consciously employed as a mechanism for place-making and community-making and for conveying identities and classed taste. Such space has made an imprint on the Silicon Valley landscape.

Chapter 4 highlights the religious realm. I focus on Thai and White monks who dwell at the same temple but meet different challenges. Their social interaction and collaboration allow us to explore how they reinterpret monastic codes in Silicon Valley to get work done; how they deal with cultural differences and gender politics; and how they perform and negotiate between spiritual and mundane activities. The monks' physical labor is vital for the community and for their own spiritual growth. What separates the Thai and White monks is neither cultural differences nor racial categories but gender.

Chapter 5 looks at the economic sphere—the ways in which capitalist activities are inextricably linked with Buddhist activities. Just as Schopen (2004: 1–15) shows that a "good" monk in ancient India was the one who knew how to handle money, I suggest that a Buddhist temple in good standing in America is the one that knows how to raise and manage money. Merit making is the key apparatus for fundraising at Theravada Buddhist temples. Monks perform the role of middlemen between the material and the spiritual world, converting money and materials into symbolic capital for merit makers. Generosity has become an important marker for being perceived as middle class and a good Buddhist. In addressing the meanings, strategies, and dynamic practices of merit making at Wat Thai, I suggest that merit making is conflated with class making and that it is a translocal enterprise.

Chapter 6 emphasizes the educational realm: The temple has revived a lost "tradition" in Thai society, a civic school inside the temple, to invest in the identity formation of young Thai Americans. The teachers and the students negotiate with two social bodies: the American body politic, which is typified by individualism and equality, and the Thai body politic, which is typified by expressing gratitude to seniors and conforming to the hierarchical order. These youth learn to perform their cultural identities, not only in the United States, but also in Thailand, and both onstage and offstage.

In short, this ethnography addresses large social issues in a small temple. It first suggests that dismissing socioeconomic ties and transnational connections, and essentializing ethnic and racial differences are cultural constructions of American Buddhism. Isolating spiritual practices from the existing social, economic, and political forces and movements tells us more about the Buddhism that has been reimagined than about the Buddhism in practice. Seeking happiness or well-being is the most frequently stated reason for practicing Buddhism. Nevertheless, happiness is more than a state of mind. A spiritual journey takes place at the vortex of chaotic multiple social forces and tangible material conditions. This journey is entangled with history, inequality, and ideologies. People are not able to remove themselves from the social formation of race, ethnicity, gender, and class, which contribute to who they are and what they do. Failure to acknowledge an American Buddhism that has absorbed cultural meanings, ideologies, and socioeconomic and global impact would serve to further romanticize Buddhism and marginalize ethnic minorities.

Second, Americanization is not a natural process. It needs to be analyzed in the context of power relationships between the state and the minority and between the United States and other countries that have political, economic, and religious ties with immigrants here. Moreover, Americanization is an illusion, because immigrants act selectively on cultural principles and perform their identities contextually, sometimes conforming with and sometimes resisting it. Through such performances, they not only become *integrated*, in part, into American society; they also *enrich* and *transform* American society through what they do.

Finally, people today, regardless of color, creed, or ethnic identity, are far more connected to and dependent on one another than we have realized. Intermarriage, kinship, friendships, and professional relationships connect people through visible and invisible webs as they share fundamental beliefs, interests, and positions, despite the existence of inequality and racism. People often cross boundaries while simultaneously maintaining their ethnic/racial and religious identities. We have to go beyond a linear way of thinking and recognize how everything— race, class, gender, faith, culture, and the past, present, and future—is interconnected. To understand American Buddhism in practice, we must recognize that what a practitioner *does* often is more important than who counts as a Buddhist; that spiritual pursuits can hardly be separated from materiality; that immigrants should not be equated with "working class" or "non-American"; and that the temple community is neither enclosed nor homogeneous but, rather, cuts across ethnic, racial, religious, and national boundaries.

2
Creating a Temple Community

"This temple is open to everyone, including cats and dogs," said Suwanna, who twice immigrated via intermarriages: first from Thailand to Britain and then from Britain to the United States. Transnational migration, intermarriage, and job mobility have increased the cultural, religious, and demographic diversity of the United States. The participants break down the imagined wall—between immigrants and Whites, between Thai and American culture, between meditation and ritual, even between humans and other species.

This chapter focuses on the establishment of a middle-class temple community through the practice of inclusion. Dan, the Farang vice-chair of the board of directors, said to me in 2005, "We sometimes think about the temple in terms of marketing. Like a business. Marketing. What communities do we attract?" The communities Dan refers to are largely middle class. In this regard, inclusion is both a communal and a class practice. As Mark Liechty (2003: 265) put it, "Class practice *locates* people (either inside or outside the collectivity) and creates *locations*, conceptual and material spaces of, for, and by class." Class practice at Wat Thai is informed by how the board of directors projects the image that Thais are *not* people who, to use the words of Luang Pho, "come from jungles."

Class-consciousness is expressed in various contexts. On the basis of an examination of why Thais immigrated to the United States, how Wat

Thai came to be founded, and how it locates and includes people, I argue that inclusion at Wat Thai is informed by distinctive Thai immigration patterns, the demographics of Silicon Valley, the regulation of temples as nonprofit organizations, the impact of intermarriages, and the agency of temple participants. The formation of the temple and its community can be read as a long-term struggle for class and cultural visibility.

From Thailand to the United States

Thai immigration to the United States has been driven by individuals seeking family security, educational opportunities, and socioeconomic upward mobility. The following history of Thai immigration is deeply inscribed with ethnic, class, gender, and regional differences.

The first Thai who migrated to the United States for whom we have records were Chang and Eng, the famous conjoined twins, who arrived in Boston on August 16, 1829. Despite being perceived as biologically and racially alien, the twins became popular entertainers and successful entrepreneurs, met with crowned heads of states, and inspired scores of literary works as varied as a satirical sketch by Mark Twain and a contemporary monologue by Garrison Keillor. After retiring from show business, against all odds, they became gentlemen farmers, married sisters, and fathered more than twenty children.

In Siam (Thailand's name before 1939), Chang and Eng were known as the Chinese Twins because they were born to an immigrant Chinese father and a Chinese Siamese mother (Wallace and Wallace 1978: 15). In the United States, however, Chang and Eng called themselves the "Siamese Twins," emphasizing where they came from instead of their ethnicity. They had different connections to China, Siam, and the United States. China was the home of their ancestors. Siam was where they were born and grew up. The United States was where they settled.

After Chang and Eng, few Thai or Chinese Thai migrated to the United States through the first half of the twentieth century. However, a student, whose Thai name was Phraya Sarasin Sawamiphakh and whose Chinese name was Huang Tianxi, graduated from New York Medical College in 1871.[1] The pioneer migrants from Thailand were ethnic Chinese, not ethnic Thai. Under the shadow of a Thai nationalist movement in the 1940s and throughout the Cold War, when most Chinese schools were forced to shut down, wealthy ethnic Chinese sent their Thailand-born sons and grandsons to college in the United States as part of a family strategy to escape discrimination and gain a foot-hold abroad. According to a survey conducted among Thai students in Los Angeles, 50 percent "had at least one Chinese parent" (Desbarats 1979: 308). Although ethnic Chinese made up only about 10 percent of Thailand's population at that time, the number of ethnic Chinese among Thai migrants was disproportionately high.

The number of foreign students in the United States nearly doubled from 1960 to 1968 (Niland 1970: 13). The fact that 29.9 percent of the students from Thailand received financial support from their fami-lies, a rate much higher than that for students from India (5.1 percent), China (4.6 percent), Japan (1.9 percent), and Korea (10.3 percent), shows the extent to which elite Thai and wealthy Chinese Thai families in-vested in their children's education. A degree from the United States carried not just educational but also social and symbolic capital for the students and their families. These students, overwhelmingly males from wealthy families, made up the majority of Thai migrants before 1962 (Desbarats 1979: 305).

Over the years, many graduating students and those who dropped out of school chose to stay in the United States to seek socioeconomic upward mobility. According to U.S. consular offices in Bangkok, in 1975, 75 percent of the Thai students remained in the United States, a complete reversal from ten years earlier, when more than 90 percent re-turned to Thailand (Desbarats 1979: 307). Some did not want to go back to live under the Thai military regime, especially after the Massacre of October 6, 1976, in Bangkok.[2] Many found jobs and climbed corporate ladders, joining the professional and managerial class. Some opened the first Thai restaurants in cities across the country. Chonan, a former restaurant owner and later a bank manager, recalled that in the 1970s, a $10,000 investment in a restaurant was enough to acquire permanent residency. Others started import and export businesses, hotels, print shops, gift shops, gas stations, travel agencies, and jewelry stores. A few even started banks. Thus, white-collar professionals and an entrepre-neurial class have quietly but steadily emerged from the former student body. With new jobs and new businesses, they were transformed from foreign students into permanent residents and American citizens.

The proportion of skilled professionals among the Thai immi-grants grew from the 1960s through the 1980s. By 1967, 29 percent had professional or technical occupations, a much higher percentage than that of immigrants from Korea and Japan (Niland 1970: 3). The Immigration and Nationality Act of 1965 abolished the quota system and established seven preferences for immigrants, including one for professionals, one for skilled or unskilled workers in occupations for which labor was in short supply, and one for family reunification. The act did not fully take effect until 1968 (Chan 1991: 145–148). In response, thousands of Thai female nurses seized the opportunity to come to work in metropolitan areas with a high density of hospitals and medical facilities, such as Chicago and Houston. Many later became U.S. citizens. While the United States was easing restrictions on immigration, Thailand was unable to absorb many of its own highly trained people into nonagricultural jobs, despite a booming economy (Mason 1999: 14). High inflation and low salaries in Thailand during the late 1960s and 1970s led many doctors, scientists, and engineers to leave (Lewis 1997: 883). By the early 1980s, there were about 1,000 Thai physicians practicing medicine in the United States (Kangvalert 1986: 140–141).

In contrast to young professionals who gained class upward mobility, Thai immigrants in their forties and older tended to suffer downward mobility. For example, Samnuan, a police colonel, was so fearful of a communist takeover in Thailand after the Vietnam War that he brought his entire family to the United States. However, he could find a job only as a security guard. His wife, a distant relative of Thailand's royal family, worked as a cook in a Thai restaurant. Having to settle for blue-collar jobs was something they had never anticipated.

Whereas the pioneer Thai immigrants were predominantly male college students and urban professionals, those who immigrated because of marriage, especially during the Vietnam War era, were predominantly rural-born working-class women. From 1968 to 1977, 14,688 Thai women immigrated as wives of American military personnel.[3] Most were ethnic Lao from northeastern Thailand, or Isan, the poorest region of the country. A majority came from peasant families and had only a primary or middle-school education and basic English skills. They met their future husbands at U.S. Air Force bases, tourist destinations, hotels, bars, dance clubs, or brothels in Thailand. For some Thai women, especially young single mothers who had suffered abusive or unfaithful relationships (Footrakoon 1999: 74–76), marrying a GI was regarded as a means of escaping their current situation and lifting their natal families out of poverty. Based on the Thai bilateral kinship system, the daughter, not the son, is expected to support the parents (Knodel 2012: 27; Potter 1977: 20, 99). Todd Perreira (2008: 168, 173–178) suggests that Thai women without a college education tend to "marry up" because they are motivated to accumulate money to help their natal family, but well-educated Thai women are more likely to marry Thai men who have a similar educational background. Due to gender expectations, Thai men tend to immigrate for reasons other than marriage; they also tend to marry Thai women (Hidalgo and Bankston 2011: 91).

The conjugal ties between Thai women and American military personnel must be understood in the context of the United States–Thailand defense alliance. The Thai government permitted the United States to build and staff military bases in Thai territory from 1961 to 1975,[4] and signed a treaty in 1967 allowing U.S. troops to visit Thailand for "rest and recreation." From 1967 to 1975, about 700,000 U.S. military personnel poured into Thailand on leave (Altman 2001: 11). The money spent on rest and recreation leaped from approximately $5 million in 1967 to $20 million in 1970 (Truong 1990: 161). In 1976, among all Thai immigrants, 42 percent had visas in the category "wives of U.S. citizens" (Desbarats 1979: 305). The percentage of Thai women married to non-Thai military veterans remains high.[5]

In 2010, about half of all Thai American women, regardless of birthplace, were married to non-Thai men.[6] Due to marriage immigration, the number of Thai women quickly surpassed that of the men. In 1976, almost three-quarters of the immigrants were women (Desbarats 1979: 305). From 1980 to 2010, Thai women have consistently outnumbered Thai men by 22.4 to 18.9 percent.[7] This trend has continued to this day.

Among the intermarried couples, a majority of Thai women married White men: 63.1 percent in 1980, 51.6 percent in 1990, and 50.7 percent in 2000 (Hidalgo and Bankston 2011: 88). In 2010, the proportion of Thai women who married White men was about 53.3 percent.[8] Thai women who marry African American men experience societal and family pressure. These women, including Kutilda Woods, Tiger Woods's mother, often are regarded by other Thais as being "of suspect morality" (Weisman 2001: 231). Therefore, it is inadequate to view the preference of spousal choice simply from the perspective of economic standing, Thai kinship expectations, or cultural norms. As others have argued, "Increasing intermarriage could also be reflective of inequality rooted in the complex articulation of racial and sexual hierarchies" (Shinagawa and Pang 1996, as cited in Omi 2001: xi).

After immigration, many Thai women who married military personnel lived on or near Air Force bases, and some continued to move with their husbands from base to base within the United States and overseas. In 1976, a majority of these women (83 percent) did not hold income-producing jobs (Desbarats 1979: 305). In addition, they had to overcome culture shock, the language barrier, and isolation, as well as a lack of spices, herbs, and other ingredients used to cook Thai dishes.

The Thai women who relocated to Silicon Valley tend to live differently from those women who live on a military base. Their husbands tend to have high-paying jobs. At Wat Thai, according to Luang Pho, about 70 percent of the White men who married Thai women were engineers. Some of these women had no financial pressure to work outside the home. Others found low-paying jobs. Some worked only to send remittances back to Thailand. A few gained upward mobility through their own jobs.

Thai authorities estimate that about 160,000 undocumented Thai migrants live in the United States, especially Los Angeles.[9] Thais call these undocumented migrants "Robin Hoods." In her doctoral dissertation, Jirah Krittayapong (2012: 5, 230) claimed that the fifteen Robin Hoods she studied came from affluent families and had a bachelor's or master's degree from Thailand or the United States; most had restaurant jobs that they never would have considered taking in Thailand. She argued that since the 1990s, being a Robin Hood has become a lifestyle and a battle with an "addiction" to make money and purchase luxury consumer goods and the desire to live a "happy life" in a "free" land (Krittayapong 2012: 74–75).

In short, most early migrants were male students, soon followed by female nurses and white-collar professionals. This eventually shifted to female marriage migration, commencing a new trajectory that has become a distinctive characteristic of Thai immigration: more female than male migrants. Class, ethnic, gender, and regional differences play a significant role in terms of how one gains access to immigration, higher education, and a good job. Such a gendered immigrant history has had a profound impact on the formation of the Wat Thai temple community.

After Immigration

Thai Americans are among the fastest-growing Asian ethnic groups in the United States. A majority of Thai Americans are foreign-born.[10] The statistics on Thai Americans for 1960–1980 included only immi-

TABLE 2.1. THAI AMERICAN POPULATION IN THE UNITED STATES, BY YEAR

	1960	1970	1980	1990	2000	2010
Number of Thai Americans	458	5,256	45,279	91,360	150,283	237,583

Source: U.S. Department of Justice, Immigration and Naturalization Service, *1984 Statistical Yearbook of the Immigration and Naturalization Service* (Washington, DC: U.S. Government Printing Office), 4; U.S. Census Bureau, 1980 Census of Population, vol. 2, subject reports, PC80-2-1E, Asian and Pacific Islander Population in the United States, January 1988; U.S. Census Bureau, 1990 Census of Population, Asian and Pacific Islanders in the United States, August 1993, Table 1: General Characteristics of Selected Asian and Pacific Islander Groups by Nativity, Citizenship, and Year of Entry, 1990; U.S. Census Bureau, Census 2000, Demographic Profile Highlights, using American FactFinder, http://factfinder.census.gov (accessed July 22, 2012); U.S. Census Bureau, Asian Population: 2010, Census Briefs, Table 6: Asian Population by Detailed Group: 2000 and 2010, 14, http://www.census.gov/prod/cen2010/briefs/c2010br-11.pdf (accessed July 22, 2012).

grants. Since the U.S. Census of 1990, however, the totals have included those born in Thailand and those born in the United States who self-identify as Thai. In just twenty years (1990–2010), the population increased by more than 160 percent (Table 2.1).[11]

The largest Thai population outside Thailand is in the United States. California has the greatest concentration of Thais;[12] the first Thai Buddhist temple and Thai Town were founded in Los Angeles. Los Angeles is sometimes called "Thailand's 77th province."[13] After California, the most Thais dwell in Texas, Florida, and New York.[14]

The average Thai American is better educated than the average American adult. In 2010, the percentage of Thai Americans age twenty-five years and older who hold bachelor's degrees or higher was much greater than that for Americans as a whole: 41.9 percent compared with 28.2 percent.[15] Thai Americans also tend to dwell in suburbs and exurbs (Cadge 2005: 162–163; Numrich 1996: xx). In addition, a correlation exists between educational attainment and the distribution of skilled labor. For example, the number of Thai Americans in Silicon Valley and Las Vegas is about the same.[16] Nevertheless, the percentage age twenty-five years and older who hold bachelor's degrees or higher in Silicon Valley is nearly twice the rate of educational attainment in Las Vegas: 47.8 percent compared with 25.2 percent.[17] Accordingly, there are more white-collar Thais in Silicon Valley than in Las Vegas, where many work in the service industry, especially in casinos.

Demographics of the Silicon Valley

Wat Thai is affected by its location in the Silicon Valley.[18] A global technology hub, Silicon Valley is relatively suburban in character with diverse demographics. The face of the suburbs has changed significantly. "Back in the 1950, the suburbs were distinct in terms of their demographics," Bill Frey, a demographer at the Brookings Institution pointed out. "You could say you were from the suburbs and people would conjure up that you are white, middle class, had a family and lived in a single-family house."[19] Silicon Valley attracts highly educated workers from all over the world. Doug Tinney, one Silicon Valley resident, put it well: "I didn't need to travel the world, the world came to me."[20] In particular, many well-known high-tech companies, including Yahoo, Cirrus Logic, Juniper Networks, and Lam Research Corporation, were founded or co-founded by Asians.[21] As of 2000, Asian American "entrepreneurs were operating 29 percent of the technology firms in Silicon Valley" (Choi, Chen, and Lee 2010: 356; Pellow and Park 2002: 39–49). The large number of Thai engineers at Wat Thai reflects this distinctive characteristic of Silicon Valley.

According to the 2012 Index of Silicon Valley, the Asian population is second in size only to the White population and larger than the Hispanic population. In contrast, African Americans make up just 2 percent of the total.[22] Approximately 43 percent of the adults in Silicon Valley have a bachelor's degree or higher,[23] but that rises to 58 percent among Asian adults (Figure 2.1).[24] In other words, the Asian population

Figure 2.1. Educational attainment: four-year degree or higher, 2012. (Illustration by the author.)

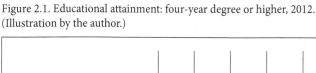
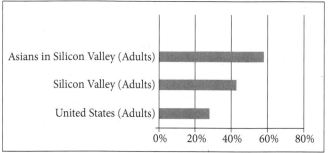

in Silicon Valley is large and possesses comparatively more educational and economic capital.

Most of Wat Thai's regular participants live in Alameda, San Mateo, and Santa Clara counties. The geographic boundaries of Silicon Valley are notoriously difficult to define. However, the region can be characterized roughly as beginning about thirty miles south of San Francisco, extending through San Jose and Santa Clara County and from Palo Alto to San Mateo County in the north. It encompasses about 1,850 square miles and contains approximately 2.9 million people, of whom approximately 36 percent are foreign-born (Cohen and Fields 2000: 192; Lee et al. 2000: 4). Wat Thai enjoys a geographic advantage: Four of the highest-earning Zip codes in the country (based on the number of households earning $100,000 or more) are within driving distance.[25] As Achan Prem, the second monk (Luang Pho was the first) to serve at Wat Thai, put it, "The demographics of the temple members are underscored by geographic issues."

The Founding of Wat Thai and Its Power Structure

In the United States, a Buddhist temple is, legally, an incorporated nonprofit religious organization. Like a profitmaking corporation, a temple must comply with federal and state laws and often has a board of directors that sets policy. Officers, typically a president, vice-president, and treasurer, oversee day-to-day operations. Power, ideally, is shared rather than exercised by an individual. In comparison, in Thai society, temples typically have a lay committee, which includes a treasurer and an accountant, to help organize rituals and festivals and conduct fundraising (Tambiah 1976: 295, 366). In principle, the key difference between a lay committee in Thailand and a board of directors in the United States is that the former only assists the abbot, who legitimately has absolute authority, whereas the latter makes decisions on the basis of consensus and can overrule the abbot.

Nevertheless, in practice the conventional Thai management style still applies at many temples throughout the United States. Having a board of directors does not guarantee that decision making is shared.[26] At the Bay Area (BA) Temple, the abbot abolished the board of directors for objecting to his decision to purchase a piece of property.[27] In response to this exercising of monastic authority, Sombun, a mechanical engineer, and others decided to split from the temple. Harvey, a

Farang Jew and longtime member of the BA Temple (his spouse was Thai), tried to mediate a compromise. As he saw it, the BA Temple was like a Catholic church in which the clergy make the decisions. He tried to persuade the abbot "to let the people have a say and not to feel that 'this is my temple. You do what I want you to do, and that's it.'" Harvey, however, underestimated the resistance of an autocratic abbot.

Breaking apart one temple to form another was not unusual. Buddhist temples, like all institutions, must cope with tension and conflicts. In Chicago, a group of Thai physicians broke off from their temple and established a meditation center (Numrich 1996: 30, 36). Splits have also taken place in Los Angeles, Denver, Las Vegas, and other cities. Sometimes conflict arises between two camps that can trigger a rupture between those who follow the abbot and those who prefer the temple to be run by an elected collective body.

Soon, Sombun led a group of BA Temple members and established an association that developed into Wat Thai. These founding members already had established successful careers before launching Wat Thai. Among the women were a banker, an architect, an accountant, and an instructor who taught solar energy classes for the National Aeronautics and Space Administration. Among the men were engineers, bank managers, a real estate broker, and a restaurant owner. Most of them had experience working for a corporation. Before coming to the United States, several also had earned bachelor's degrees from Chulalongkorn University, known informally as "Chula." (A degree from Chula, Thailand's top-ranked university, carries social prestige in Thailand and in Thai American communities. So many Chula alumni attended Wat Thai that they hosted an annual reunion there.) Collectively, they valued education, emphasized efficiency, and were well-aware of their class status.

The first task they took on was drafting bylaws. Thais and Farang—Sombun and Harvey in particular—worked together as a team. The bylaws granted final decision-making authority to an elected board of directors and a board of trustees. Having two boards was a deliberate attempt to check and balance power to prevent the recurrence of what had happened at the BA Temple. (Most Thai American temples have only a board of directors.) Wat Thai's bylaws stipulate that each board consist of the abbot and fourteen others. Directors are elected by the membership; trustees are selected by the board of directors. Only the abbot is appointed to both boards. The board of directors meets every month, and the trustees meet once a year, unless something exceptional occurs. The board of directors administers day-to-day policy and creates subcommittees to carry out specific tasks in finance, religious affairs, and maintenance. The board of trustees focuses on policy making and overseeing the general direction of the temple. Both boards have access to attorneys for legal advice. Sombun made the point that "the monks and lay people interface with each other, support each other, and *balance* each other, controlling each other to make the organization work more effectively." For thirty years (1983–2013), the boards have consisted of monks and lay people, men and women, Thais, other Asians, and Farang.

Like a neighborhood Silicon Valley startup hiring a chief executive officer, the founding members conducted a search to find an abbot who would share their vision. They chose Luang Pho because they regarded him as a hardworking, open-minded, and well-educated monk. More important, they knew him personally because he had served at the BA Temple before he transferred to a temple in Houston.

When the temple community was small, Luang Pho spent much of his time visiting Thai American families; Sombun recruited new members among his friends in the engineering association. However, when seeking volunteers, Sombun said, "We are looking for friends who understand us and we them. We are *selective*. When they volunteer, if they are no good, they are not desirable." A commitment to the temple is regarded as more important than skin color or faith. Sombun and Harvey, one a Buddhist born in Thailand and the other a Jew born in the United States, have forged a long-term friendship in the course of serving the Wat Thai community.

In short, the creation of Wat Thai has to be understood in relation to the impact of state and federal regulations for nonprofit religious organizations, the new power relationship between monks and lay people, and the inclusion of non-Thai professionals on the boards. Finally, the lessons learned from the BA Temple and the vision of the two boards have continuously shaped Wat Thai's goals, management style, and strategies for locating collaborators.

Working Together Regardless of Color, Creed, and Culture

Even though many Thais had worked and forged friendships with non-Thais, practicing inclusion met resistance in the beginning. A few people suggested that the temple be run by Thais, for Thais. However, one board member, Thongchan, a design engineer with a doctorate who had come to the United States in 1968, disagreed, saying,

> The temple is in America, not in Thailand, so we don't know that much about American culture. To bring Thai culture here 100 percent is not good. You have to be willing to listen to the Farang, their opinion. So how do you listen to them? You have to give them a say. . . . We find that we discriminate. We discriminate against Farang. We discriminate against the Cambodians. We discriminate against people with no degree. We discriminate against people who have no money. We are always nice to the rich people. If you drive a Mercedes, then "Ohhhh. Wow." But if you drive a Volkswagen, like me, then they look down on you.

By insisting on including non-Thais at the temple, Thongchan tried to avoid reproducing the prejudice and discrimination that he and many other Thais had experienced. He could never forget what he and his family had suffered simply because of their skin color. He and his wife had purchased a house in Chicago, but their neighbors did not welcome them. Their house was vandalized; someone kept throwing rocks through the windows. After living there for only three months, Thongchan had sold the house and decided to take his traumatized daughters back to Thailand. "I went to my boss and said, 'I am not living in this country anymore. I am going back home to Thailand,'" he recalled. "My boss went bananas: 'We have many branches. Take your pick.'" The company could not afford to lose Thongchan, and he was transferred to Silicon Valley. He turned his painful experience into something productive: working against racism. At the same time, like many others, he regarded Farang as his frame of reference for being American. So Farang who are committed to Wat Thai have been included in the power structure.

Over the years, Wat Thai's overarching mission—serving the community—has persisted; nevertheless, ways to achieve that goal have changed over time. Wat Thai initially presented itself as "a forest temple" with an emphasis on meditation. "Thai Buddhism doesn't have the same charm as Tibetan Buddhism," Achan Prem explained. "It doesn't have many things that attract Americans except the meditation. But meditation is still just for a certain group of people." As the word spread, more Thais started coming. In response, the boards decided to shift from a focus on meditation to serving as a community center, conducting Buddhist rituals, and teaching the Dharma, as well as meditation, the Thai language, music, and dance. Meanwhile, in response to new needs, more projects have started up, and more sub-committees have been created, including those for the school, festival affairs, the food court, construction, and special events.

The boards, to a certain extent, symbolize how members of diverse backgrounds work together at the temple. A Chinese Laotian and a Vietnamese American have served on the board of directors at different times. Most board members are Thai American men, but sometimes as many as one-third are Thai American women and one-fourth are Farang. Although Farang are a minority, they are visible in public forums. In 2012, Sulak, the president of Wat Thai, told me that "we let the Farang do the talking [to the public], especially when the temple was first founded. They have much broader networks than we do." Sulak was not "color-blind" but, rather, conscious of racial politics. The board has consciously tapped into the larger social power structure. Before a meeting, board members may speak Thai and English or mix the two. However, when the meeting begins, as Alan, a Farang Hispanic, said, "We're speaking English. Everybody is from a different background. You get different ideas all the time. That makes us special." Differences are inscribed with positive meanings in this context.

However, the boards are not conflict-free. At times, some board members try to insist on their own ideas. In one interview, Luang Pho commented, "They are very successful in their own careers. However, the temple is for all, not just the topmost." As the abbot, he tried to make the best use of each member's strengths. "Five fingers. Each is different, but they work together," he said. "Five fingers" represent the differences—each finger functions a bit differently, but all of the fingers are mutually dependent.

Despite disagreements, tension, and a hierarchical order based on seniority, the board of directors and board of trustees strive to maintain a professional working relationship to do their best for the community. The abbot, board members, and regular participants make a great effort to convey Wat Thai's goals, needs, and accomplishments to the public. Their perspectives and experiences shape the trajectory of the temple.

Expanding Horizons: The Abbot and Key Players

Luang Pho, an ethnic Lao, is of medium height and slender. Born in rural Isan, he was ordained as a novice at eleven. As he looked back on his life, Luang Pho said, "I grew up with the Thai Sangha [community of monks]." His temples—the ones in his village and in Bangkok—became the homes he knew best. In 1968, before he turned twenty-one, he received full ordination as a monk. He attained level-seven Pali expertise, and earned a master's degree in ancient Indian studies and Asian studies at a university in India. Before he came to the United States in 1982, he had traveled in Japan and Laos. "Traveling and living abroad helped me become open-minded," he reflected.

What Luang Pho does each day, how he prioritizes work, and how he interacts with people reflect who he is. In part due to the unpredictable nature of daily happenings, he organizes temple activities around a few scheduled events—chanting and meditation at 6:00 A.M., cleaning the temple at 7:00, serving lunch for the monks at 11:30, evening chanting and meditation at 7:00 P.M. He conceives of his role as meeting people's expectations and making people happy. "What does happiness mean to you?" I asked. He said, "For me, it means to be empty of everything. Just open. Don't go too far up or too far down. If I got a $2 million donation, I would not get excited or become a big mouth."

Luang Pho spends most of his time and energy dealing with whatever comes through the door that day. Sitting meditation and chanting take up only a fraction of his time. He shifts effortlessly among different kinds of work. One afternoon, for example, after returning from conducting a birthday ritual for the owner of a restaurant, Luang Pho blessed a car with "holy water," then talked to a female documentary filmmaker who sought his support in making a video against domestic violence. Then he taught meditation to a drop-in visitor who was having trouble sleeping; later, he juggled the accommodations for overnight guests among the temple's limited number of rooms. Around 5:00 P.M., he took three monks to console an intermarried couple who had just lost a family member and returned just before 7:00 for night chanting and meditation.

On weekends, Luang Pho sits in the lotus position on a platform with his back ramrod straight for hours, meeting visitors and conducting rituals. When crowds of people come to make offerings to the monks, he goes out to the line and groups people together to shorten the waiting time. He connects with people by remembering everybody's name. He rarely makes a long speech and tends to use everyday examples to teach the Dharma. When he sees young children come to the temple school, Luang Pho greets them with joy. If they arrive early, he might turn on the television and find cartoons for them. "If there are no children running around the temple, there is something wrong with that temple," he said. Than Gabriel, a Farang monk at Wat Thai, put it well: "With some people, he's a big brother. With some people, he's an uncle. With some people, he's grandpa. For some people he's a dad. But they all respect him because he has the teaching and the practice of a Buddhist monk, so he has that something extra in the way that he relates to them."

Depending on whom he is speaking with, Luang Pho switches among Thai, Lao, and English. In Thai society, the Lao language is branded as vulgar (Keyes 1987: 203). Luang Pho is aware of this prejudice. However, he said, "When I see another Isan, I speak Lao. I am never afraid of saying that I am from Isan. It is my roots. Some central Thai discriminate against Isan. I am proud of it." Besides speaking face to face, he communicates with people though phone calls and his iPad.

Luang Pho understood what he could and could not do for templegoers. Once, after blessing a Cambodian family and saying good-bye to them, he said to me, "They should see a lawyer rather than get holy water from me. But I can make them feel happy." In interacting with Farang, he consciously takes their background into consideration. To help Jennifer, a pious former Catholic nun, concentrate on her walking meditation steps, Luang Pho told her to chant "Jesus, Jesus, Jesus" instead of the usual "Buddha, Dharma, Sangha."

In addition to teaching, conducting rituals, and interacting with people, Luang Pho pays great attention to the upkeep of the temple. He tells newly arrived monks, novices, nuns, and volunteers that it is much more important to keep Wat Thai clean and tidy than it would be to keep a temple clean and tidy in Thailand because "Americans care about this." Once he gave me a lecture: "When you visit the office of a big company, their windows are shining. We need to *match* that. Cleanness and greenness make people happy. People start to calm down when they enter the temple." Then, looking around the chapel, he said, "We do not hang pictures here. Pictures are beautiful for us [in the chapel] but not beautiful for Americans [*laughs*]." He was actually talking about culturally informed middle-class taste, although he did not use the term.

Luang Pho habitually makes sure that the water for flowers on the altar has been freshly changed; the flowerpots have been cleaned; the bathrooms are spotless; the tables and benches at the food court are wiped clean; the trash containers are rinsed; and the bottoms of the fountains are scrubbed and free of debris. If these things are not done to his standards, he does the cleaning himself. So the monks and longtime volunteers know that it is important to do a thorough job. His reputation for keeping the temple neat and clean is even known in Thailand. In an interview, a monk in Bangkok said to me, "Luang Pho has a good heart. But he is very picky in America." Perhaps being a stickler for cleanliness is part of Luang Pho's effort to project an image of the temple as middle class.

Wat Thai, for Luang Pho, is a vital institution. In 1997, he told me, "The temple is at the center of belief. It is at the heart, and in the blood, of the people. . . . People support the temple more than any club or association because the temple helps people not only in this life but in the next life, as well." Meeting the daily needs and expectations of such a varied constituency for thirty years requires unshakable commitment and compassion. His approach and his subtle way of teaching are compatible with the vision of the temple's key founding members. Reminiscing about Luang Pho during an interview in 2011, Sombun said, sighing with relief, "We have a *good* leader. God sent him to the temple."

Luang Pho reminds me more of a chief executive officer than the stereotypical "otherworldly" monk. He has become perhaps the most influential figure at Wat Thai, and his accomplishments have been recognized in Thailand. In 2001, Thailand's king gave Luang Pho the title "Chaokhun," a monastic title granted to 704 distinguished monks. He became one of only five out of the approximately three hundred Thai monks based in the United States to be awarded such a title at that time. The Supreme Sangha Council of Thailand honored him with a new name. On the king's behalf, the crown prince presented Luang Pho with a new *phatyot* (long-handled ornamental fan), which represented his new status. His *phatyot* signifies symbolic capital because it marks his ranking as one of the top 660 monks among the more than 290,000 monks in Thai society.[28] His religious capital (from having built Wat Thai, taught Buddhism in Silicon Valley, and renovated his village temple); his social capital (from serving as vice-president of the Council of the Thai Bhikkhus in the United States, as an abbot, as the chairman of the board of directors, as the president of the board of trustees, and as an associate abbot for his temple in Bangkok); and his educational capital (from attaining expertise in Pali, a master's degree, and a recent honorary doctorate from Chula) are converted into symbolic capital at Wat Thai and in Thai society. He is invited to participate in major events at Thai temples throughout the United States. Luang Pho visits temples in Las Vegas a few times a year, lending his support and offering his advice, just as the late Luang Dae did for Wat Thai years ago. Nevertheless, his monastic name, *phatyot*, and title can neither be precisely translated into English nor converted into religious capital in larger American society.

Luang Pho's leadership is important to the process of community formation. However, without the contributions of key constituents in the community, he would never have been able to sustain the temple. Sombun has been a leading figure since Wat Thai was founded. Because of his father's prestigious civil service job, Sombun traveled extensively in Thailand during his youth. He was also ordained as a monk for three months. Later, he studied and worked in Japan, Laos, and the Philippines before immigrating to the United States in 1969. While he worked as an engineer for the Bay Area's subway system, Sombun earned a master's degree. These experiences helped him to become a respected leader of the temple community.

His wife, Apinya, whom Sombun introduced to me as his "boss at home," was born into a distinguished entrepreneurial family in Thailand. She was an architect and a Chula graduate. Like Sombun, for decades she had volunteered at Wat Thai. When she served as the temple school's first principal, Apinya wrote the first textbook and made good use of her drawing skills. "I was a teacher, and I was a janitor, too. I did everything," she said. Besides teaching the Thai language, she taught the students to sing Thai songs and Christmas carols. She did not regard singing Christmas songs as conflicting with her Buddhist identity. (Because of her beautiful voice, she was invited to sing the national anthem at the Oakland Coliseum and was regularly in demand to sing at churches during Christmas.)

Apinya and Sombun treat the temple as an extension of their home. When Wat Thai lacked the space to lodge volunteer teachers from Thailand, the couple opened their home to them for months at a time. Every morning they drove the teachers to Wat Thai, then picked them up in the evening. They did the same for visiting monks. In 1985, when

Wat Thai had no line of credit, the couple co-signed a $290,000 loan to buy the property where the temple now stands. Other board members told me that Sombun had served in every position on the board of directors, doing whatever the temple needed most at the time.

Dedication to the temple is highly valued. Kamala, the Phunoi who had just four years of formal education, gained respect through her business success and contributions of time, money, and labor to the temple. She served on the board of directors for ten years and volunteered at the food court for eight years. I asked what motivated her. "I want the temple," she replied. "For Thai people, when they are sick, when they are hurt, when they are miserable, they come here [to the temple]. When I see the kids walk or run around, I'm happy." In 2005, she added that she wanted to help Luang Pho. "Some people from Bangkok do not respect him," she said. "He would scratch his head and pick at his nose in public. You look at Achan Prem, he always sits still, talks well. He gets much more respect." Kamala expected Luang Pho to perform as a sophisticated cosmopolitan monk. She was concerned that his manners might undermine his authority and reinforce negative stereotypes about ethnic Lao. Kamala apparently internalized these notions of middle-class manners by which she evaluated Luang Pho.

Sutsinee, who was much younger than Kamala, was born into a well-connected, affluent family in Bangkok. She came to Los Angeles in 1985 to attend college. Later, she married Dan, a Farang computer software consultant. After resettling in Silicon Valley, the couple began offering food to the monks every Sunday. Sutsinee also volunteered to teach Thai, networked with officials in Thailand to take the students to perform in Bangkok, and made the arrangements whenever Thailand's princesses came to visit. She served on both boards at different times. When she became too busy with her importing business to keep up her service at Wat Thai, Dan increased his involvement with the temple. Dan serves as vice-chair of the board of directors to this day.

Alan was the only Farang Hispanic on the board of directors. He and Kob, his Thai wife, had met in Italy. Alan and Kob were not rich: Alan worked at the Post Office, and Kob worked in a factory. Nevertheless, when they learned that the temple wanted to purchase property, they offered to co-sign the loan with Sombun and Apinya. They are known for having compassion for others. Kob has volunteered to sell offering items at temple events for almost thirty years. When she thought someone might not have much money, she charged less, saying, "Give whatever you can." Although Alan was Catholic, he volunteered to perform all kinds of work at Wat Thai, from directing traffic to selling soda and barbequing pork at the food court. During an interview, he said, "I still say I am a Catholic, but I do not remember the last time I visited my church. I am doing good things at a Buddhist temple." By doing good things at Wat Thai, Alan believes, he is practicing his Catholic faith.

Some Farang, like Alan, describe themselves as "Thai in a white body." Dan, Sutsinee's husband, once joked that for him to become a "real" Thai, he would have to have surgery to change his skin color, hair, and the shape of his eyes. He referred to himself as "quasi-Thai," or a "dishonest Thai," in contrast to a "real Thai" like his wife. "I am Thai in the sense that I have been involved in the community for so long," he said. Achan Prem, indeed, introduced Dan to the audience as "a Thai with an American face" at a big event I attended in June 2006. Everyone applauded.

Dan was sometimes asked to say things at board meetings that one Thai might feel uncomfortable saying to another. "That's fine, because we can also hide behind the fact that we're not Thai," he remarked. "If they get upset with us, we can [say], 'Hey, I'm sorry. I didn't know' [laughs]." Dan and Alan sometimes had to act as the bad guys when visitors double-parked their cars. "For those kinds of jobs, I think it is better that Farang do it," he said, "because [Thais] can blame us, and we don't know what they're saying about us" [laughs]. Dan and other Farang sometimes represent the temple by talking with neighbors, the Fire Department, and local officials when there is a conflict. His playful performance is the way he negotiates his Farang and Thai identities.

When Farang identify themselves as "Thai," they are not rejecting their American or Christian identities. Harvey, who sometimes wore a Star of David together with an image of Buddha, said in an interview in 1996, "I am accepted as part of the community. I conceive of myself as an insider. The abbot said to me, 'You only look like an American, but you are a Thai.' The abbot is my counselor, and I am his adviser." Harvey often played the role of mediator between Farang and Thais. He said that Farang board members tended to like making plans and setting goals, but their Thai counterparts often altered those plans. This created tension. Harvey reminded his frustrated colleagues that "the reason to make a plan is so that you can make changes."

Like laypeople, monks bring their experiences to the temple and engage with many different challenges. Achan Prem was ordained as a novice at eleven and attained level-nine Pali expertise at twenty, becoming only the thirteenth novice in two hundred years to achieve such a feat. After coming to Wat Thai, in addition to his regular duties, he led the creation of the temple school. At the same time, he also earned a master's degree from the University of California, Berkeley, because he loved to learn and to teach. Another monk, Maha Aphai, was known for his ability to repair anything. He was ordained as a novice at fourteen, achieved level-eight Pali expertise, and earned a master's degree from Thammasat, Thailand's second best university.

The life trajectories of these key participants have changed over the years. Sombun and Harvey, together with their wives, retired and moved to Thailand, where they became neighbors. Maha Aphai returned to his temple in Bangkok and was promoted to abbot. However, all three still serve on Wat Thai's board of trustees. Living in Thailand marks a new phase: providing service to Wat Thai from abroad. Maha Aphai's temple has become a gathering place for those who travel back and forth to Thailand. Maha Aphai has also returned to Wat Thai annually to raise money for the education of young monks at his temple. Harvey often used his connections at the U.S. Embassy in Bangkok to help solve visa problems for instructors who came to teach at Wat Thai. A few years ago, he received a prestigious Thai national award in recognition of his contribution to propagating Buddhism.

Achan Prem took a different path: He disrobed. (A Theravada monk can leave the monastic order any time and return to lay life, an act known as disrobing.) "When I disrobed, some people got very angry," he recalled. "They said 'Why did you do it?' They could not accept it. Some even stopped coming to the temple for a while. I continue to come to the temple. I stayed the same. Only the clothes changed. All my training was to be a monk. It was difficult to change." He now works as a computer programmer. Nevertheless, he provides service as a layman, at times leading the chanting and explaining the meaning of rituals to the public at the big events.

Wat Thai's most valuable asset is its participants. Each of the participants presented here has expanded his or her horizons in the process of creating Wat Thai and sustaining its community. Despite many differences, one thing they all share is their commitment to the temple. Together they form the bedrock of the community.

The Multifaceted Wat Thai Community

At Wat Thai, there are more middle-class homemakers, white-collar professionals, engineers, nurses, restaurant owners, and college students than factory workers, hairdressers, and waiters. Because of the explosive appreciation in home prices in Silicon Valley, it is possible for someone to work in a blue-collar job and own a million-dollar house. According to Luang Pho Wat Thai today has approximately two thousand members who come from an array of class, ethnic/racial, and religious backgrounds. About three hundred people visit the temple on a typical weekend. The line between visitor and member is blurred. A visitor can become a member; a member can disappear for a few years and then reemerge.

The temple's physical space mirrors religious heterogeneity. A magnificent bronze statue of Buddha cast in Bangkok stands at the center of the chapel. In the garden is a larger-than-life-size statue of Guanyin, the Mahayana goddess of mercy and compassion; donated by a Chinese Thai family, the Guanyin statue rests on an elegant, dark brown, wooden pedestal built and donated by a Vietnamese entrepreneur. Next to Guanyin is a small statue of the Hindu goddess Durga. These statues symbolize Wat Thai's commitment to inclusion.

Wat Thai has many Asian and Farang participants. The number of African American participants, by contrast, is tiny, corresponding partly to the small African American population living in Silicon Valley. Over the years, I have known only two African Americans who regularly visited Wat Thai. Big George, a security guard, studied the Thai language and practiced meditation for about eight years. Linda, who suffered from a chronic illness, sometimes came just to sit quietly in the chapel.

Most temple participants are Thai transmigrants, more women than men. In Thailand, men typically make merit and pay back their parents by becoming monks. Most men offer alms only on special occasions, such as birthdays and important Buddhist holidays (Kirsch 1975: 184). Women typically make merit by taking care of their parents and by regularly supporting Buddhist temples and monks. In the United States, however, a Thai man can no longer afford to take his Thai or Buddhist identity for granted. He confronts questions about his faith, or being mistaken for a refugee or Taiwanese, something that would never happen to him in Thailand. A temple is one of the few places where he can mingle with other Thais, speak his mother tongue, share common concerns, and act out his Thai cultural identity. Instead of regarding temple visiting as a women's activity, some men now go with their wives as a social endeavor. Some go to combat homesickness or seek relief from stress. Some take their children with them. Tongchai, an engineer, said, "I do not expect that my sons will be a Thai like me, but they have to learn about where I come from." Thus, one may see more Thai men at Buddhist temples in the United States than in Thailand. However, women still outnumber the men.

Some men are as dedicated as any of the women. For years, Mr. Chen, a Chinese Thai restaurant owner, prepared breakfast for the monks. Sometimes he would arrive at 5:30 A.M., and sometimes he would stay overnight at Wat Thai. As he explained to me, in Chinese, "Working at the temple gives me peace of mind. No one asks for anything. It is not like my restaurant." The temple environment helped him gather his strength to deal with the stress of running a business.

While a majority of Wat Thai's participants are Thais and other Asians, about 20 percent of the regular temple members are Farang. Based on my observations, Thai Americans rarely pay much attention to a Farang's ethnicity. For example, three Farang lawyers have donated their services for many years. No Thais have ever mentioned these lawyers' ethnicity to me, but they do talk about their legal specialties, their faith, their spouses, and the paths that led them to Wat Thai. Farang lawyers, as Luang Pho explained to me, "have no language problem, and they know the system" inside out. It is their Whiteness, their expertise, and their commitment—not their ethnicity—which carry social significance at Wat Thai. White ethnicity tends to surface when a Farang talks about his or her family history or when a Thai woman talks about her Farang husband. Indeed, ethnicity does not always carry social significance; it depends on circumstances (Eriksen 2010: 16).

Among the intermarried couples, especially those age fifty and older, the Farang men tend to have more education and higher-paying jobs than their Thai spouses. Nevertheless, these Farang, similar to the American men who married Filipinas and the Chinese women about whom Nicole Constable (2003: 66–67) wrote, often do not care about their wives' educational attainment and earnings but value a stable marriage that makes them happy. Constable points out that liberation and freedom have different meanings to women of different backgrounds. For some, liberation is being independent and working outside the home. For others, liberation is finding a foreign husband, working at home, and being a devoted wife and mother (Constable

Figure 2.2. Blessing an infant, 2008. (Photograph by the author.)

2003: 65–66). Constable provides us with new ways to think about women's power and different expressions of agency.

Among the Farang, more men than women visit the temple, exactly the reverse of the Thai participants. Most of the men have Thai spouses. Only a handful of Farang women visit Wat Thai. They tend to go to the temple alone rather than through a spouse. Some Farang men participate in rituals with a Thai partner or a friend or visit simply to enjoy Thai food sold at the food court. A few take Thai language classes. Some bring new babies for a blessing or to obtain a name derived from cosmology (Figure 2.2). Some regularly volunteer; others help fix things as needed. If a stray cat the temple adopted got sick, Phillip, an engineer, would take it to a veterinarian and pay, sometimes hundreds of dollars, out of his own pocket. These Farang men, nevertheless, seldom take part in meditation retreats at the temple, although a small number—Harvey, for example—practice meditation at home.

In contrast, Farang women tend to go to Wat Thai to practice meditation and study the Dharma. A few long-term members participate in a wide range of activities. For example, Sabrina, a Farang schoolteacher, attended all the activities—meditation, rituals, offering food to the monks—and viewed these endeavors as complementary: "I like to bring meditation into my daily life. Ritual helps me do this. The rituals are a way to make the meditation a way of moving and to incorporate it into speech. . . . I see ritual and meditation as integrated, as part of the same thing. This is a way of participating in a community."

Practicing meditation and performing rituals are seen as reinforcing each other; the individual and the community are interconnected. Furthermore, Sabrina believed that certain aspects of ritual carry universal symbolic meanings. In referring to part of a ritual in which participants pour water into a cup and then sprinkle it on a plant, she said, "Yes, it is a cultural activity that originated in Thailand, but it still has meaning for me, because the symbolism is universal. We are sending our *metta* [loving kindness] to the plants, to the animals, and out into the world. So pouring the water on the plants is the symbol of sending that *metta* out. So if you understand the symbolism, then the cultural stuff is just like the clothing, but the practice and the meaning behind it is the body, the solid part of the practice."

Similar to Sabrina, Beth, another Farang woman, is an active member of the temple. Whereas she self-identifies as "a scientific person," she meditates, joins in the rituals, and occasionally teaches the temple students and young novices the Dharma. She does not think that being White hinders her from being part of this community. She states that she attends the temple for the same reason that Asians have visited temples and supported monks for centuries. It nevertheless has taken her more than twenty years to become who she is today. She first learned about Buddhism through meditation and listening to audiotapes of Dharma talks by Achan Sumedho, one of the most famous Farang Theravada monks in the United States. To attend a three-month retreat in England, Beth resigned from her job as vice-president of a billion-dollar company. This happened at a time that she really wanted to "piece together what it means to be a human being on this earth," she said. The retreat became a turning point in her life. There she saw everyone bowing to a Buddha statue and to the monks. As Beth recalled in an interview, she said to herself, "I'm not going to bow. I can't bow." One senior participant understood what she was thinking, she said, and told her, "'You know, by the end of this [retreat], you'll be bowing to the *cockroaches*.' And he was right. It took me a while, but I came around [*laughs*]. Bowing is just a form. It just transcends what people think it is. As the Dharma starts taking hold and gratitude starts in, even the form becomes a practice, an expression of gratitude and an expression of community."

Now Beth conceives of chanting as a way to learn the Buddha's teachings. She differentiated singing Protestant Christian hymns from Buddhist chanting. "Hymns were written to venerate God," she said. "It was a way of showing faith and veneration. And that is true here also, but it is not the same. Really, the foremost reason for chanting is to preserve the teachings." When she chants, she said, she feels the power of the words; the power of the Dharma; the power of history; and the power of rhythm, flow, the sound, and repetition. This is how she explained it to me:

> Words are only approximate. But these words have been venerated for more than 2,500 years, have been carefully preserved for the love of the Dharma and for the love of those people who might come to hear it and become free from suffering. The words have become smooth, powerful, and beautified, just like the constant repetition of water on a stone. It is like the flow of life, the flow of spiritual attainment, the flow of the love and the compassion in the Dharma, moves in and around these words. It creates this bedrock of smooth and beautiful words so that we can use our minds, and, if I was still a Christian, I would say, our God-given minds.

Sabrina and Beth see connections between ritual and meditation and between chanting and learning the Dharma. Their experiences reveal that Farang are as flexible and dynamic as Thais. In other words, neither Farang nor Asian immigrants fit into the two Buddhisms paradigm. This multifaceted community becomes a site where people of many different backgrounds intermingle. Over time, the temple community has become more diverse.

Performing Religious Identities

The Wat Thai community is anything but homogeneous. Yung, for example, identified herself as a Buddhist and a Christian. She was born in rural Isan to a Thai mother and a Cambodian father and completed only four years of formal education. She was a divorcée with two children before she married a Farang Christian, a chemical engineer and a patent attorney. The couple attended both a Buddhist temple and a Christian church. In June 2006, she told me, "[On Sundays] we go to church in the morning, and then in the afternoon, we come to the temple. At home I have a Buddha statue, and we have a cross, too." After enrolling her two American-born daughters in Wat Thai's temple school, Yung did whatever she could to help, including cleaning the kitchen and assisting at the food court. On Christmas Day of 2006, Maha Sandi and I were discussing what it meant to be a Buddhist when Yung happened to pass by. He pointed to her and said, "She is a good Buddhist. She is loving and kind to her children and to the temple." Being a Buddhist was identified as doing good things and showing compassion toward others; Yung's affiliation with a Christian church was not viewed as contradicting her Buddhist faith.

Like Yung, a few Thais who self-identified as Christian, Muslim, or Sikh visited the temple for Thai New Year or on other occasions. As Yui, a Thai Muslim who regarded the temple as her "home away from home," explained, "This is the only place where Thai people hang out. I want my daughter to learn about where I came from." Non-Buddhist Thais are not shy when it comes to talking about their faith. I once witnessed a Thai Christian tirelessly propagate the virtues of Christianity in Wat Thai's dining room. The monks just smiled and walked silently by.

Sometimes a Thai changes his or her religious beliefs for socioeconomic reasons. Lingling, a Chinese Thai woman, converted to Mormonism while living in Korat Province, Thailand. Converting allowed her to attend college at no cost. However, after she married a Farang Catholic husband and immigrated to Silicon Valley, she switched back to Buddhism and took her husband with her to Wat Thai. This phenomenon has also been observed in other Asian American groups. Thomas Douglas (2003: 174) has noted that selectively engaging with Christianity and Buddhism became part of Cambodian American identity.

To ensure that they get a good education, some devout Buddhists send their children to Catholic schools. They know this may be confusing to the children and that some might convert to Catholicism, but they do it anyway. Natee, a registered nurse, volunteered at the temple for over a decade, sometimes going to cook at the temple food court on Sunday mornings after working the graveyard shift. Yet her commitment to the community did not prevent her and her husband, a Hong Kong Chinese physician, from sending their only daughter, Muay, to a Catholic school. Muay attended Catholic school during the week and the temple school on weekends. During our interviews, Muay, then a college student, recalled how she had tried to make sense of it all.

"Catholics believe in one God," she said, "and I thought, 'Oh, I've got Buddha, too.' When I prayed to God, it wasn't like I felt like I was betraying Buddha. I just felt like, 'Oh, well; this is what everyone else is doing. I should do it, too.'" Chuck also went to a Catholic school. Unlike Muay, Chuck converted to Catholicism but continued to practice Buddhism. "During the day, we learned about God, how to be a good Catholic, and eventually [I chose] to be baptized," Chuck said. "At night, at home, and on the weekends, we were Buddhist. Needless to say, those were very confusing years for me. Heaven and hell . . . Rebirth and enlightenment . . . Sin and penance. . . . [W]hat a mess! As I grew into adulthood, I would come to appreciate my two faiths. I discovered that this was not a burden but a gift."[29]

Just as attending a Catholic school involves performances and interactions, so does intermarriage. Some couples hold two wedding ceremonies—one at Wat Thai, and the other at a Christian church. These wedding ceremonies create a chain of opportunities for interaction. Some regard switching between a church and the temple, between the Buddha and God, as "cool" and being cosmopolitan. Tanaphon, who married a Farang, said, "I go to church, but I pray to the Buddha before I go to bed." She sought protection for her family and herself from both God and the Buddha. Alan and Kob have a Buddha room in their house. "We have Buddha on one side and God on the other side," said Alan. Sometimes when a Farang spouse passes away, the wife invites monks to conduct a funeral ritual. Terry, a White Catholic, was ordained as a Buddhist monk for a month at Wat Thai. He explained to me that practicing Buddhism made him "a better Catholic." After he disrobed, Terry continued going to the temple. He is one of many who articulate the contemplative dimension of Christianity.

The monks also interact with religious figures from a variety of faiths and from different countries. Every year, they attend a Thanksgiving celebration organized by an interfaith organization, together with other Buddhist, Christian, Jewish, Sikh, Hindu, and Islamic groups. On Buddha's Day in 1997, I witnessed Sri Lankan, Vietnamese, Korean, and Japanese monks gathered at Wat Thai. The groups took turns chanting in their mother tongue. For a big event, a Farang monk, such as Achan Pasanno, might be invited to give a Dharma talk in English. More recently, a Farang monk was invited to teach a weekly meditation class. Flexibility and transcending religious boundaries have become distinctive characteristics of this diverse community.

No Wall between Meditation, Ritual, and Culture

Whereas sitting meditation tends to be conducted alone or with a group silently in a quiet place, rituals tend to be practiced in a crowd of lively and noisy family and community members, relatives and friends, at the chapel, in the host's living room, at a Thai restaurant or another public setting. Sitting meditation is a process of looking inward; ritual practice is a form of acting and sharing with others. For many, practicing meditation and attending rituals share a goal: freedom from suffering.

In May 2008, I attended a six-day meditation retreat at Wat Thai led by Luang Da, an eighty-three-year-old monk from a Thai temple in Washington, DC, who has been practicing meditation for more than half a century. Eighteen people—ten Thai women and men, six Farang women, one Sri Lankan man from Australia, and I—took part, not counting others who dropped in to participate for a day or two. Farang participants included Sutama Bhikkhuni, a female monk; Amber, who had practiced meditation at three different temples and believed she had been "a Buddhist in a previous life"; Glenda, a former nurse who said she was at a crucial phase in her spiritual life; Zoe, who believed in magical powers; and Lisa, who delighted in asking questions. Among the Thais were a volunteer Thai–English translator who now works for Apple; Lek, a nursing supervisor who took early retirement and devoted much of her time to practicing meditation, studying the Dharma, and making merit in the hope of achieving nirvana (breaking free from the karmic cycle of rebirth); Suze, a retired manager who had immigrated to the United States in 1965 and attended a Baptist church before she found a Buddhist temple; and Suwanna, who had been spending most of her time volunteering at Wat Thai to keep herself occupied after her Farang husband's death. Tavon, an engineer for United Airlines, showed us photo albums of his twenty-six-year-old daughter, a University of California, Berkeley, graduate, who had suffered a recurrence of leukemia. He attended to prepare himself to help his daughter battle her cancer. Achan Chaduphon, an ex-monk, came to learn more about meditation from Luang Da. All of us brought our own experiences and purposes with us as we joined the retreat.

Before the retreat, most of the women, including me, were ordained as nuns. Our white outfits symbolized that we were adhering to the Eight Precepts: eating at the proper time, refraining from wearing perfume and jewelry and all other decorative accessories, and abstaining from sitting or sleeping in luxurious places. The white clothing was a form of discipline, as it made us more aware of our body and gender; signified our shared identity at that moment; and marked the boundaries among the nuns, the monks, and lay people.

We began the day by genuflecting, chanting, and paying respect to the Buddha, the Dharma, and the Sangha. The monks chanted from memory; the rest of us read the text and followed the rhythm and melody, chanting in a low voice. After that, we practiced silent meditation and walking meditation and finally ended with a Dharma discussion. In between, we ate two meals a day—breakfast and lunch. For six consecutive days, we followed the same schedule from 6:00 A.M. to 9:00 P.M.

During the retreat, we spent the most time meditating. Luang Da, a recognized master, regarded meditation as food for the mind. He told us again and again that meditation could make our "monkey mind" calm down and help us become "mindful" (*mi sati*). "When water is still, it is clear, for the mud sinks to the bottom. When the mind is peaceful and focused, one can think clearly," he said. "Practicing" (*phuk* or *patibat*) was emphasized countless times. He urged us to love ourselves "for the purpose of doing the wholesome thing and not the wrong thing." The self is conceived of as moral.

A Dharma talk followed the meditation. One of the talks, on "loving kindness, compassion, sympathetic joy, and equanimity," reminded me of what the monks preach at the lifecycle rituals. At the birthday ritual, people are reminded to recall their parents' love and sacrifice. At the wedding ritual, the newlyweds are advised to honor, respect, and be tolerant of each other. At the funeral ritual, monks remind people to be mindful and to realize that all things are transient and impermanent. These Dharma talks touched on similar themes but with a different emphasis, in responding to the audience and the context.

After each Dharma talk, we had a question-and-answer session. During one discussion, Lisa asked Luang Da whether she had committed a "sin" by getting a cat to kill the mice in her house. Luang Da responded, "Why don't you just let the cat do his job? It's the cat's business." Everyone laughed. Luang Da acted as a therapist at that moment by advising Linda to act as though she had not intentionally brought the cat in her house to kill the mice.

Following the question-and-answer session, we had lunch. We, the nuns, ate separately from the monks. On Sunday, we joined the merit making by offering food to the monks. (We did not prepare it but used food cooked by food court volunteers.) It is generally believed that merit making facilitates meditation and that, in turn, meditation better enables one to make merit (Tambiah 1985: 90, 112).

Cultural distinctions appeared at the moment we expressed our gratitude to the monks for teaching and hosting the retreat. One group consisting mostly of Thais offered a robe; a sack of rice; and daily necessities, such as paper towels, bottled water, and aspirin, as well as an envelope with money inside. Another group, consisting mostly of Farang, offered flowers and a thank-you card (perhaps with money inside). As the time to say good-bye arrived, Luang Da urged us to continue practicing meditation rather than stopping at the end of the retreat. One can practice meditation while doing almost everything: cooking, eating, driving, talking, walking, lying down, or gardening. As Maha Winai, whom I call the Smiling Monk, put it, "Conducting meditation is through doing things."

I did not fully understand what the Smiling Monk meant until a few months later. One afternoon, I was assigned the job of spraying a row of roses with a mixture of water and fertilizer. "How long should I water them?" I asked. "Five breaths," answered Luang Pho. I had never thought that counting breaths could be used as a way to measure time. This episode helped me to see the links among meditation, breathing, and work in a different light: All things are intricately connected.

Inclusion

Wat Thai welcomes everyone, including pets, and allows people to experience the temple in their own way. Once visitors and participants intermingle with others, they may have a chance to destabilize and subvert stereotypes and bias. The common ground that many participants have here is the effort of achieving the superordinate goal of well-being and freedom from suffering. It is liberating to realize that people are more alike than different. In a society in which we still experience racism, prejudice, and inequality daily, we may find it enlightening to realize that one does not need to be a Buddhist to practice Buddhism and that one does not need to look Thai to be part of a Thai community.

When participants see that their well-being is tied to the community, they become active builders of that community. This shared struggle serves to bond participants, transcending skin-deep differences among them. Inclusion therefore becomes a communal practice. In a small but nontrivial way, Wat Thai influences the locals by dismantling this imagined wall and tells a story about interdependence and collaboration among people of different backgrounds.

The practice of inclusion, nevertheless, cannot be separated from existing social systems and norms. Even though everyone is welcomed at the temple, locating middle-class volunteers who have the time and expertise to serve is emphasized because articulating middle-class identity carries social significance in Silicon Valley. Being socially marginalized, the Thai migrants and those who are associated with them are especially eager to raise Thai American cultural visibility and exhibit their middle-class respectability. Practicing inclusion and loving kindness becomes a class practice.

Wat Thai compels us to ask, "What is Buddhism?" This is a difficult question to answer. Whatever answer one gives is deeply connected with one's position, experience, and the time at which one speaks. Thomas Tweed (2011: 23) put it well: "What we have come to call 'Buddhism' was always becoming, being made and remade over and over again in contact and exchange, as it was carried along in the flow of things." The mixed performances—Luang Pho, in his saffron-colored robe, teaching a former Catholic nun walking meditation by chanting "Jesus, Jesus, Jesus"; Tanaphon attending church on Sunday but praying to the Buddha at bedtime; Alan, together with his Thai Buddhist wife, practicing his Catholic faith by serving the Wat Thai community— highlights how spirituality is practiced.

A Buddhist community carries multiple meanings to practitioners from a variety of backgrounds. Young and old find their own niche here. Yui, a Thai Muslim, considers the temple her second home; Sabrina, who practices meditation through participating in rituals, considers ritual "a way of participating in a community"; Beth, who studies the Dharma through chanting, regards bowing to a Buddha image and to the monks as "an expression of community."

Whereas this chapter emphasizes locating people, diverse practices, and multiple belongings, the next chapter focuses on another aspect of middle-class communal practice: locating *place* and selectively reifying Thai culture in a spatial form. The construction of hybrid cultural space does not turn people away. On the contrary, it attracts more people.

3

Erecting a Chapel

Carving Out Cultural Space

> Space is a fragmentary field of action, a jurisdiction
> scattered and deranged, which appears to be negotiable
> or continuous but is actually peppered with chasms of
> economic and cultural disjunctions.
>
> —Patricia Yaeger, *The Geography of Identity*

Space is inscribed with socioeconomic, racial, and cultural boundaries, some visible and others invisible. Scholars have long argued that space is physically, materially, and culturally constructed (Gupta and Ferguson 1992: 17; Harvey 1993: 25–28; Liechty 2003: 21, 255; Somekawa 1995: 46; Yaeger 1996: 4). Doreen Massey (1993: 155) urges us to "conceptualize space as constructed out of *interrelations*, as the simultaneous coexistence of social interrelations and interactions at all spatial scales, from the most local level to the most global" (emphasis added). People migrate with their religious beliefs and often put them into a spatial form to connect with their roots and articulate who they are. By so doing, they insert their existence into space that already is laden with meanings and power. The same space that absorbs socioeconomic, racial, ethnic, religious, and class meanings is transformed and reconstructed by people over generations. Different people and practices juxtaposed in the same space communicate with one another, with the past and present, and with here and there.

Special challenges are involved in building a Buddhist temple in a predominantly Christian society. In the United States, temples often encounter enormous resistance and outright racism, whether an existing space is being converted into a temple or a temple is being built from scratch, and whether Chinese, Cambodian, Burmese, Laotian, Sri Lankan, Thai, or Vietnamese are doing the building. In Texas in the early 1980s, for example, one retired teacher who signed a petition to block building a Vietnamese temple said, "I don't want a bunch of monks under my nose. It wouldn't matter if it were a Catholic boys' school or any other kind of school."[1] In 2010, I attended a public hearing in Las Vegas because neighbors were afraid that a proposed Buddhist temple might "attract gangsters." These public hearings often are emotionally and politically charged. Zoning issues, traffic, and noise frequently are cited as reasons to oppose the construction of a temple (Cheah 2011: 92; Nguyen and Barber 1998: 139).[2] To build a temple a Buddhist community needs to obtain permission from multiple regulatory agencies and refute the notion that Buddhism is a cult. Indeed, "space is fundamental in any form of communal life; space is fundamental in any exercise of power" (Foucault 1984: 252).

Many Americans have never visited a Buddhist temple. Most, however, think that they know what a temple looks like—grandeur and a lot of wood. The reality is different. Most of the Buddhist temples scattered throughout the United States look like ordinary houses from the outside. So far, little has been written about how a temple community negotiates between American building codes and Buddhist regulations. How are sacred and mundane space reconciled? How are cultural symbols of the United States integrated with those of the country the community left behind? How are time, money, and emotion invested in cultural and communal space to articulate their belonging? We know astonishingly little about these aspects of the construction of temple space in the United States.

To address these questions, I use building a chapel at Wat Thai as an example to illustrate how temple space is constructed in Silicon Valley. In particular, I analyze how the chapel, in built form, expresses the class and cultural identities of the Wat Thai community through negotiating with different regulations and creating hybrid cultural symbols. Everyone involved—the architect, board of directors, abbot, builder, artists, and other key members—has injected multiple meanings into spatial forms, from the rooflines to the murals, the sanctified boundary stones to the depiction of the Golden Gate Bridge, and the American bald eagle to the Thai Garuda bird. Thus, how the chapel is assembled and how professional connections and expertise are used speak volumes about the characteristics of this community. Erecting a chapel becomes a *place-making and identity-making* project. Consequently, the eye-catching, million-dollar chapel not only symbolizes the planting of roots by Thai transmigrants in the United States but also becomes a distinctive outward marker of this community. It further exemplifies the interconnections between East and West, Buddhism and popular culture, this world and the cosmos.

From a Rental House to a Permanent Home

Buddhist temples in the United States often begin in a rented house. Wat Thai began this way in 1983. The neighbors quickly petitioned the city, complaining about the traffic, illegal parking, and violation of the rule of single-family use. Some residents feared having a Buddhist "cult" in the neighborhood. Audi, the vice-president of the board of directors, tried to mollify the neighbors, assuring them, "We don't do anything that a cult would."[3] His protestations were not enough. The police got involved. Noreen, who for twenty years had lived in the house next door to Wat Thai's rental property, suddenly got a parking ticket. "It seems like it was an unfair ticket because some of the other neighbors parked the way we did and they didn't get a ticket," she said "Something funny was going on there."[4] The board of directors sent a letter of apology to the neighbors and paid Noreen's fine. "We have to understand the neighbors' concerns," Luang Pho and Sombun discreetly told me many years later. However, some temple members regarded this as prejudice, plain and simple.

To solve the problem, the board of directors rented space in a nearby school and held activities there on the weekends. At the same time, the directors began looking for a new site for their temple. After examining more than a hundred properties with the help of a Vietnamese realtor who was married to a Thai woman, the board of directors purchased a 1.48 acre parcel of land that included a house and a dilapidated horse barn. The property was located in a quiet, suburban neighborhood with easy highway access. Thongchan, who was in favor of including Farang, recalled, "We [the board of directors] had a map and put the pins on each location that we knew had Thai people. And then we calculated the center. This is the engineering method, you know. So we found the population center." On April 28, 1985, Luang Pho and Achan Prem moved in.

After buying the property with a co-signed loan, the board of directors needed to have it rezoned from residential to institutional. To obtain permission, the temple had to go through public hearings. At one hearing, Thongchan recalled, he and Sombun explained to the audience, "We are not 'boat people.' We are not from Taiwan. We are from Thailand. We have two Miss Universe winners. Taiwan only has one Miss Universe [*laughs*]. We respect the neighborhood. We will not ruin your neighborhood." Jim, a Farang Catholic who studied meditation under Luang Pho, volunteered to help because he had had experience with rezoning problems when he was the assistant city manager for Long Beach. Jim represented the temple at the public hearings and made a convincing case.

As time passed, the original house on the property proved far too small to accommodate a community. The board of directors decided to build a chapel—not an ordinary one but a "Thai-style" chapel. Luang Pho reflected, "If it was in Thailand, I would like to build a small and simple temple surrounded by nature. If someone wants to see a big temple, he can just go to see the Grand Palace." But, he continued, raising his voice slightly, "Here in America, we need to build a unique Thai temple." Precisely because of the dislocation, Luang Pho saw the need to materialize the ideas of "a unique Thai temple" through the physicality of the chapel.

A striking temple often impresses viewers and arouses emotion among participants. According to the ancient texts, in northern India building a splendid temple was considered important, in part because monks were "in the business of attracting donors," as when "an individual sees what is beautiful, is deeply moved, and makes a large donation" (Schopen 2004: 33, 36). This remains true today. In Buddhist countries in Southeast Asia, a stupendous temple often is assumed to carry more power than a humble one. In the United States, too, a grand temple attracts many more visitors than do temples in ordinary houses.

In explaining the importance of building a costly chapel, Dan, the vice-chair of the board of directors, said in an interview: "If someone is affluent, he should buy the expensive model rather than the cheap one. If we build a standard building, we won't stand out. We won't be as prominent." The chapel was perceived as a site not only for displaying prominence but also for producing cultural distinction. The "we" he referred to includes Thais and non-Thais. This "we" should be understood as those who have similar interests and those who share space and goals. Temples are always being constructed and reconstructed in response to time-specific materials, technology, and ideologies. Therefore, a brief review of how temples in Thailand are created may help us gain insight into the process of constructing a chapel in Silicon Valley.

From Wandering to Wat

Historically, Thai temples, including some of the most renowned royal ones, have incorporated Hindu, Brahmin, Khmer, Chinese, and Western symbols (Ringis 1990). So have temple murals. Temple murals play an important role in depicting and teaching Buddhism in Asia. For centuries, Buddhists learned about Buddhism and the Buddha through stories, paintings, and sculptures because most people did not read texts (Lopez 2013: 2). In the late nineteenth century, Thai muralists began incorporating Western techniques into their paintings, especially with regard to perspective and shading, to create three-dimensional effects and a sense of depth (Ringis 1990: 94). Temple builders and artists tend to express what is going on locally, regionally, and globally via the temple's built form (Cate 2003). What stands out is the enduring effort to appropriate new symbols and styles into Thai temple space. Over time, many of these elements have become part of the Thai style.

Monks, in ancient times, were assumed to be "wandering ascetics" (O'Connor 1993: 330). Not having a permanent dwelling place was regarded as a way for monks to renounce the comforts of home and show detachment from the material world. Nevertheless, archeological evidence found in India indicates that magnificent Buddhist temples existed as early as the second century (Coningham et al. 2013; Schopen 1997: 258–278, 2004, 2005: 350–366). In Thailand, for the sake of control, the ruling class eventually required monks to dwell at a particular *wat* (Ishii 1986: 866). King Rama I, the founder of the current Chakri dynasty, required each monk to identify with a specific monastery and preceptor (Taylor 1993: 24).

Today, a *wat* in Thailand often has several buildings that may include a *sala, wihan, bot*, and *kuti*. Each building, usually a single-story structure, is designed for specific purposes. A *sala* is a multipurpose hall. A *wihan* is a large hall used for worship and rituals.[5] A *wihan* is considered more important than a *sala* but less important than a *bot* (chapel). Monks perform various rituals in a *wihan* but not full ordinations and monks' confessions (Kingshill 1991: 109–112). The latter can be conducted only in a chapel because it is purified and thus considered the most sacred space. No bathrooms are allowed to be built in or attached to a chapel because bathrooms are considered dirty and profane. Monks and novices live in a residence building called a *kuti*. In addition to its pragmatic function, the organization of temple space exemplifies the Thai monastic order, politics, and the boundaries between monks and laypeople.

Thai temple styles and the arrangement of space have never been static. Different materials, technology, and images have been selectively integrated with temple space in response to time-specific geopolitics and the intentions of the abbots, patrons, and artists. The creation of Wat Thai's chapel has to be understood in such a spirit.

Selecting an Architect

The board of directors searched for an architect who had the ability to create a Thai-style chapel in Silicon Valley. The directors were aware that connections were crucial for gaining the permissions necessary to build a temple in a residential area. John, a Catholic born in Berlin, Germany, was selected to design the temple. He was trained at the University of California, Berkeley, and had lived in Thailand from age thirteen to twenty-three, when his father served as the U.S. consul. As a senior architect, John knew how to get the project approved. For him, it was routine to meet the architectural, environmental, energy, and safety codes. What he found challenging was convincing the building standards commission that his design would suppress the sounds of music and the noise of rambunctious festival-goers and that he could contain the "strong pepper smells and curry smells" so they would not "waft to the neighbors." Nevertheless, he was confident that he could meet the challenge to design the first Buddhist temple of his decades-long career.

If skin color and religious beliefs had been the criteria for selecting an architect, John never would have been chosen because several ethnic Thai architects were available. John was aware of this. He bounced his ideas off the temple's construction committee, whose members, in return, supported him at the board meetings. John mediated between Thai architecture and the Silicon Valley landscape, between the construction committee and the city's building standards commission, and between the temple participants and the nervous neighbors.

Frozen Music: Structural Constraints and Resilient Agency

In May 2005, I had a chance to interview John. Although he was in his eighties, he was full of energy and occupied with ten or so ongoing projects. As we sat on a bench, in the shade of a tree, gazing up at the chapel, he said, "You know how architecture is supposed to be 'frozen music'? You have to pick out the mood and the music and the *inner peace* that you get with Buddhism." John put his understanding of Buddhism into practice. "I elevated the chapel five feet above the ground to have Buddha be above everybody else," he said. "So the chapel is actually *floating*. You see? The floating effect is like a dais. . . . Then the big terraces are typical Thai additions, which are like a big balcony going all around, so people can mingle, chat, and talk to each other and still the sanctuary inside is inviolate." John designed the chapel space to serve particular functions. Unlike at Catholic churches, which usually have a set schedule of masses and sermons, visitors drop in at Buddhist temples at all times of day. Therefore, providing open and interactive space is crucial so people can easily move in and out. While paying attention to the special needs of Wat Thai, John drew inspiration from the architecture of churches and designed the roofline to represent "a prayerful hand." For him, such a roof conveys "peace and softens everything. Otherwise, the building looks too stoic. It hits you," he said. The floating space and angle of the roofline were imbued with Buddhist meanings mixed with Catholic elements. Thus, certain features of the chapel reflect how the architect imagined a Buddhist temple.

John was pleased with the roof, but some Thai participants were disappointed because it did not correspond with their memory of chapels in Thailand. Wutilat, an engineer, said, "A chapel roof should be very tall. This one looks sloped. It is not really Thai." He did not know that the city had imposed a height limit of thirty-five feet in a residential area to prevent any building from overpowering its surroundings. To create enough height, John had to take a more costly approach by digging down and tucking a multipurpose hall underneath the chapel, because he lacked the space to accommodate a separate chapel and multipurpose hall, as would have been built in Thailand.

Indeed, the roof serves as a reminder of how the architect and builder negotiated structural constraints from the inside out and from top to bottom to address the conflicts generated by American building codes and Thai cultural expectations. Knowing the codes helped the construction committee figure out how to circumvent certain regulations to meet the temple's needs. For example, Wat Thai was required to build a covered parking garage for the residents, even though there were forty-seven uncovered parking places on the temple grounds. So a structure that looks like a garage from the outside was built whose inside is designed with large mirrors along the interior walls to serve as a dance studio for the temple school.

Creating temple space in the United States often meant solving unexpected problems. Sometimes the arrangement of a building's features collided with Thai Buddhist cultural logic with regard to sacred space. One day when a steel beam was going up to support the ceiling, Luang Pho asked Mani, an ethnic Chinese Thai builder, "Is that beam going to be there?"

"Yes," she replied.

"Oh, no," Luang Pho fretted. "If that beam goes there, then where is the Buddha statue going to sit?"

The location of the beam violated Thai cultural logic and a monastic decree that the principal Buddha statue should be at the highest point of a chapel, with nothing hanging over the Buddha's head. In Thai society, the sacredness of the Buddha has been represented spatially through elevation. Although Luang Pho had said that Buddhism is just a brand name, at this moment the statue represented the Buddha. He would not compromise. Finally, the beam was relocated.

Not all clashes could be avoided or fixed. The temple had to comply with the requirements of the public accommodations portion of the Americans with Disabilities Act. An elevator and wheelchair ramps were required. An elevator was installed, but it is almost never used. Bathrooms were built downstairs, below the chapel.

U.S. building codes and Thai monastic regulations have different reference points. The placement of the steel beams, the arrangement of the Buddha statute, and the integration of the bathrooms tell us stories, silently but powerfully, about the community's imagination, creativity, flexibility, and ability to overcome certain constraints.

Reconfiguring Buddhist Space

In the process of carving out cultural space, the monks sometimes had to reinterpret certain Buddhist beliefs to fit the way they reconfigured the space. In Thailand, the direction east, where the sun rises, is considered more auspicious than west, where the sun sets. South, I was told, is undesirable because the Thai word for "south," *tai*, puns with the word "underneath" or "below."[6] In the United States, however, the direction a building or a house faces often is decided by local building codes and the scenery. When the question of which direction the chapel should face was raised, Luang Pho suggested that it face south. He reasoned that facing south would represent the Buddha's teachings by embracing, rather than turning its back on, the community. However, south is not the only direction that could be interpreted as facing the community. To the east and the west of the chapel are single-family homes. To the north are foothills; to the south lies the main road and entrance to the temple complex. With this picture in mind, it could be argued that facing east—the direction chapels in Thailand usually face—could just as easily be interpreted as embracing the community. However, if the chapel faced east, the queen's insignia and other symbols inscribed on the front of the chapel would not be visible from the road. In addition, the open area in front of the central entryway would be too cramped. In other words, facing south was the best choice in terms of visibility and the efficient use of space. By emphasizing embracing the community instead of voicing practical reasons, Luang Pho shrewdly created spiritual meaning to offset the negative Thai cultural meaning embedded in facing south. Through such reinterpretation, Wat Thai transcended the boundaries between auspicious and unlucky directions.

As mentioned in Chapter 1, in June 1997, the chapel space was purified by a delegation of Thai monks led by Somdet Phramaharajamangalacarya. The physical presence of 151 Thai Buddhist monks standing side by side no more than six inches apart, ritualistically removing "preexisting boundaries" or "bad spirits" via their bodies and yellow robes, was striking (Figure 3.1). Without this demarcation ritual, the chapel would not be accepted as legitimate by Thailand's monastic authorities, even if it met all U.S. building codes and standards.

Nine sacred boundary stones were a gift from Wat Paknam, where Somdet Phramaharajamangalacarya served as the abbot. Boundary stones delineate sacred from mundane space. In Thailand, eight boundary stones are placed around the chapel, each stone pointing toward a different direction—north, south, east, west, northwest, southeast, northeast, and southwest. The principal demarcation stone, the ninth stone, is buried underground at the center of the chapel. At Wat Thai,

Figure 3.1. Monks performing a demarcation ceremony at Wat Thai of Silicon Valley, 1997. (Reprinted with permission from Wat Thai's Temple Archive.)

however, placing the principal boundary stone in that position would have been regarded as improper because the multipurpose hall is underneath, sharing the same territory.

An ingenious solution was proposed: to place the principal boundary stone underneath the Buddha statue, below the surface of the chapel but above the multipurpose hall. In this way, the principal boundary stone symbolically separates the mundane space of the multipurpose hall from the sacred space of the chapel. The bathrooms and the multipurpose hall would be closed when certain religious activities were taking place in the chapel—an innovative spatial maneuver and cultural performance.

Carving Out Class-Based Cultural Space

The ties of affinity with monastic and royal figures are present in the chapel space, if one knows where to look. The gables are a good place to start. The four gold-colored gables are inscribed with exotic images and display Wat Thai's connections with the Supreme Sangha Council of Thailand, the Thai monarchy, and the United States (Figure 3.2). The

Figure 3.2. *Clockwise from top left:* The four gables, facing south, west, north, and east, 2005. (Photograph by the author.)

gable that faces south bears the queen's insignia. Wat Thai has capitalized on Queen Sirikit's patronage since she first visited the temple during her tour of the United States in 1993. Her patronage is amplified in spatial form through her logo. Identifying with the queen is not just a form of empowerment but also a prestigious asset. This gable, at least in the minds of Thai Americans, communicates their cultural and class identity to viewers.

The gable facing west is decorated with a hybrid bird: a combination of the American bald eagle and the mythical Garuda bird, the emblem of the Thai nation and the symbol of Thailand's monarchy.[7] (In Hindu mythology, the Garuda is known as the king of birds.) According to a pamphlet printed by the temple, this bird aims at conveying "the harmony between Thainess and Americanness" (*khuam glomglun rawang khuam ben thai kap khum ben amerikan*), and the fact that Thai Buddhism "has taken root" (*pratitsathan*) in the United States.[8] The bird, created by combining the most recognizable symbols from both nations, represents the ways in which Wat Thai constructs Thainess and Americanness and reaffirms power structures in Thailand and the United States.

The gable facing north contains a composite of hybrid Buddhist symbols, including *om,* a sacred mantra that originated in India, and the numeral nine written in Thai script. *Om* and the numeral nine are fashioned to represent the shape of a pagoda. Inscribed below the pagoda is the word *Phutthawaro* (the Great Buddha). Underneath that word are four letters written in *khom*, a sacred ancient Khmer language, a reference to Buddha's teachings. Combined, they form a unique icon. This particular spatial arrangement of symbols is designed to express the route of Buddhism from east to west, beginning in India, then traveling to Cambodia, Thailand, and now the United States. This expressive image with its potent meanings was designed by Luang Pho's mentor, Somdet Phramahadhiracarya.

The gable facing east is decorated with the emblem of Wat Paknam, a royal temple in Bangkok. Of the $120,000 Wat Paknam donated to Wat Thai, $15,000 was designated to pay for this gable. Wat Paknam exchanged economic capital accumulated in Thai society for symbolic capital in the United States. The impact that Thai history, the monarchy, and monastic leaders have had on Wat Thai can be seen and felt on these gables.

The chapel endorses national symbols and expresses class status. One board member suggested using blue, the queen's birthday color and the color of the monarchy, for the chapel roof, to signify the dignity of the monarchy. Thongchan, however, argued against it, saying, "It's too royal. It's too close to the royal family." Even royal temples in Thailand that receive patronage from the monarchy have gold-colored roofs, not blue. As a compromise, John, the architect, suggested glazed green-and-yellow terra cotta tiles to echo the trees that border the chapel and the gold-colored hills behind it. Thus, the choice of color is not just an aesthetic preference. It is informed by an understanding of the meanings, power, and taste inscribed in the color.

Wat Thai's ties with the monarchy have been continuously fostered and expressed literally, figuratively, and materially via spatial forms. Two white marble plaques framed in gold commemorating the queen's visit—one in Thai and the other in English—are mounted beside the main entrance to the chapel. The objects that the queen used during her visit, such as the chair she sat in, are preserved in the multipurpose hall. In 1996, Princess Soamsawali, the crown prince's ex-wife, was invited to add a *chofa*, or sky hook, to the chapel's curling roof finials. Earlier, she, Princess Bajrakitiyabha (her daughter), and Princess Bhansawali Kitiyakara (her mother) had each planted a tree in the courtyard not far from the magnolia tree that Queen Sirikit planted. Each tree has a sign explaining who planted it and when, again highlighting the prestigious patronage that the temple embraces. As of 2012, eight trees had been planted by royal family members, monastic leaders, and a former prime minister and two trees had been planted by local patrons.

Decorating the chapel remains an ongoing place-making project. The north-facing mural, "The Defeat of Mara and the Enlightenment," was completed in 2005. However, it remained covered by a piece of transparent white cloth for eight years. Finally, on November 17, 2013, Princess Soamsawali, in her role as the daughter of the mural's main sponsor, Princess Bhansawali Kitiyakara, presided over a dedication ceremony as part of Wat Thai's thirtieth anniversary celebration. What to display, what to conceal, and what to include or exclude communicate the values, connections, and identities of those who create and use the space.

A Temple Mural: The Conflation of the Cosmological World and the Social World

The hand-painted, twenty-four-by-fourteen-foot "Three Worlds" mural adorns the center of the chapel wall. It is the largest mural in the chapel. As one climbs up the stairs and enters the chapel, one immediately sees it behind the principal Buddha statue.[9] This mural provides a vision of a Buddhist moral universe. The artist who painted the mural, Achan Arun, told me, "This is a dreamland, neither Thailand nor America." The mural symbolizes an imagined community—or, indeed, "a community of sentiment" (Appadurai 1996: 8).

Achan Arun was a professor of art at Silpakorn University, Thailand's premier fine arts college, until 1982 when he, his Farang wife, and their two children immigrated to the United States. He loved teaching. His degree and teaching experience, nevertheless, were not recognized in the United States, and he has had to work as a freelance artist. Initially, he traveled from state to state, putting more than 100,000 miles a year on his car, selling his paintings at flea markets. "Americans don't like to buy pictures of tropical birds, or bright colors," he said. "I had to figure out what people wanted. I did everything: sculpture, painting, and graphics." With the help of his sister-in-law, a decorator in New York, he began receiving commissions to do decorative paintings for homes.

In our interview in 1997, he said he felt honored to paint the mural: "No one [in Thailand] would give me a job like this, because I have never painted a big mural before or won any national competitions." In fact, except for sightseeing, he had rarely visited temples when he was in Thailand. He believed that painting Wat Thai's mural was his destiny, because he was asked to do it just as his wife was diagnosed with cancer. Painting the mural became his way to make merit for his wife.

Achan Arun charged the temple a minimum amount of money but was committed to giving his maximum effort. He explained the difference between executing a painting for his rich clients and for Wat Thai: "I sell my imagination, my creativity, to make the client's idea become real," he said, "but I don't give them 100 percent." When a client was satisfied with his work, he stopped. However, when he painted Wat Thai's mural, he tried his best. "It gives pleasure to many people," he said about the mural. "I did not get much in return in terms of money, but I learned about the Dharma and I learned about meditation. When you do not expect anything, you get something. When you expect something, it becomes commercial." Drawing on many hours of research and discussion with the monks, especially Luang Pho, about Buddhism, Achan Arun invented and modified various images to express the relationship between heavenly angels and the human realm, and between here (the United States) and there (Thailand).

The "Three Worlds" mural consists of three parts: heaven, the human world, and hell. The heavenly realm is located at the top, vertically reinforcing the hierarchies. The Buddha is sitting in the middle at the very top; four enlightened monks—the acting supreme patriarch and three Somdets with whom Luang Pho has had close relationships—sit next to the Buddha. The Buddhist belief in rebirth is represented not only by a transformation of Buddha into a Buddha-human returned to earth but also by a standing Buddha surrounded by flying international angels. Among dozens of Thai angels, there is one Farang angel with white skin and brown hair, one African American angel in a green outfit, and a pigtailed Chinese angel in a red outfit. The racialized angels were designed to convey the idea that the temple is open to everyone.

The human world is represented in the middle of the mural. Wat Thai appears in the painting next to two California landmarks: the Golden Gate Bridge and the Lone Cypress in Monterey (Figure 3.3). San Francisco Victorian houses are juxtaposed with a traditional

Figure 3.3. Wat Thai in an imaginary landscape, 2005. (Photograph by the author.)

Thai stilt house. Upstairs in the stilt house, a well-dressed man and woman are chatting and holding hands. A boy nearby is smiling, perhaps eavesdropping on the couple's conversation. Below the Thai stilt house is the space for raising chickens and domestic animals and storing tools. In front of the house, a muscular woman and man, in comfortable gender-neutral draped pants—perhaps servants of the couple upstairs—are threshing rice with a mortar and pestle. Such a human world exemplifies the links between Wat Thai in California and an idealized, hierarchical, but peaceful village life in preindustrial Thailand.

The human realm also includes portraits of several Thai monks with special ties to Wat Thai. One is the abbot of Wat Daowadueng, a royal temple in Bangkok, who for years sent his most promising monks to serve at Wat Thai. Next to him is Luang Dae, the abbot of Wat Thai of Los Angeles. Below these two is the abbot of a forest temple in central Thailand who donated $24,000 to Wat Thai's construction fund. Again, the mural space becomes a memorial, honoring the monks who supported Wat Thai spiritually and materially.

Hell is depicted at the bottom. It shows that humans who did not do enough good or who were too greedy suffer in the afterlife by being drowned or burned in a monstrous underworld. The mural serves as a mirror for individuals to look into and locate themselves within the Buddhist cosmos on the basis of their conduct. Not only do the system of meanings and the order of the cosmological world become revitalized via this mural; an imagined transnational community also comes into being. The mural space, like the chapel space, is never given ontologically.

Transforming the Silicon Valley Landscape

The chapel—an expensive product of this place-making project—connects Thailand and the United States in a particular way. It is hard to tell where Thai culture starts, where American culture ends, and which influences are Indian or Cambodian. Something new emerges in-between. The chapel symbolizes Theravada Buddhism being reimagined and reterritorialized in Silicon Valley, disrupting a homogeneous landscape.

Wat Thai neither caused property values to fall nor was driven away by its neighbors. On the contrary, Wat Thai has been designated a city landmark, for it has captured the imagination of many onlookers. Landmark status marks public recognition and testifies to the power of the community. "If somebody wants to tear down this Buddhist temple, they are not going to get away with it. They can't. It's protected by law," said Thongchan. One engineer told me that, had he stayed in Thailand, he could not have imagined achieving anything of this magnitude. No one at Wat Thai had any previous experience in building a temple.

Mani, the builder of the chapel, stood about five feet tall and weighed less than ninety pounds but was a tough, sharp, no-nonsense entrepreneur. As we talked about the chapel at her spacious, elegant Thai bistro in downtown San Francisco, her voice rang with pride: "I really feel good that I had the power to make it happen. Some people donated lots of money to help us build. Some donated a small amount of money. We all feel that the temple is part of us. The more members the *wat* has, the better. But we always feel that we are the founders of the temple. We are the heart of the temple. We put this temple together. We are not boat people." Mani sees the chapel as a symbol of a middle-class community, which is one of the reasons the members, Thais and non-Thais, have invested so much in the building. The chapel has become a public space transmitting their class, cultural, and Buddhist identities.

Through endless contrasts and mixtures and through the display of translocal connections and resources, Wat Thai enhances its members' multiple belonging. The physicality of the building has turned their communal dream into reality. Building the chapel is more than a negotiation between sacred and secular space and between U.S. building codes and regulations imposed by the Supreme Sangha Council of Thailand. The more the community explores national cultural symbols, the more it aligns with influential local and transnational figures to work against racializing Asian immigrants as working class. It is not an overstatement to say that carving out Wat Thai's cultural space is a joint transnational enterprise. The process of building the chapel can be seen as integral part of the larger process of making a middle-class community in a spatial form.

4
Monks in the Making

Buddhist monks and Buddhist temples are ubiquitous in Thailand and constitute a significant part of the social fabric of Thai society. About 290,000 Bhikkhus (male monks) reside at approximately 30,000 Buddhist temples in a country with a population of 67,741,401.[1] There are also a small number of Bhikkhunis (female monks), who are not recognized as legitimate by the Supreme Sangha Council of Thailand and the Thai government.[2]

In the United States where a majority of the population is Christian, Buddhist monks, however, remain largely mysterious figures. Thai Theravada monks are often asked, "Why do you shave your head?" "Why do you wear a yellow robe?" "Can you have a girlfriend?" "Can you eat meat?" "Can you watch television?" "Are you enlightened?" People ask because they do not know that Thai monks follow the Pali Vinaya, the monastic disciplinary code that governs conduct, appearance, manners, and morality. Monks shave their heads to show their commitment to monastic life; their saffron-colored robes represent renunciation of the secular world. They are celibate and are regulated to avoid any physical contact with the opposite sex. They eat two meals a day, whatever people have offered them, including meat.[3] They are disciplined not to harm or take the life of living beings, not even a pesky mosquito. They live and work at a temple. They may watch television, but not for entertainment.

In the United States, church and state are separate, at least in theory. In contrast, Thailand's constitution stipulates that the king must be a Buddhist. The Thai nation, Buddhism, and the monarchy are intertwined (Tambiah 1976). It is against the law to criticize Buddhism or the monarchy. Such structural differences significantly shape the monks' transnational experiences. In Thailand, Buddha images are revered as sacred. In the United States, Buddha images are sometimes exploited to promote consumer goods. There, monks are provided with free medical care and local transportation. Here, monks pay like everyone else. There, monks are prohibited from driving a car out of concern over accidently taking another person's life. Here, without a car, monks' mobility would be greatly limited. There, monks are addressed as "Venerable" and considered more trustworthy than government officials (Darlington 2009: 201; Van Esterik 2000: 82). Here, they are called "Mr." There, the saffron-colored robe commands great respect (Kirsch 1985: 304). Here, the distinctive robes can sometimes arouse misunderstanding and misrecognition. Maha Pattana, a monk in Las Vegas, was mistaken for a woman in the men's bathroom at an airport because of his robe. For the same reason, someone once asked Luang Pho if he would give him some *ganja* (marijuana). A stranger asked Achan Prem to teach him kung fu. Some people make jokes, saying that the robes make the monks look like oranges or bananas. Many Buddhist monks throughout the United States have shared similar experiences.

Western television, films, and commercials tend to represent monks as mysterious masters of martial arts and meditation. Many people, including my students, expressed disappointment when they saw monks involved in fundraising or using a smartphone, a computer, or a digital camera. As Jane Iwamura (2010: 6) points out, Buddhist monks have been constructed as "the icon of the Oriental monk," upon which "we project our assumptions." A Buddhist monk in real life, however, is different from the monk "who lives in the Western imagination—the ascetic monk who wanders alone 'like a rhinoceros' in the forest, sits at the root of a tree in deep meditation, and has cut all ties with the world" (Schopen 2004: 25–26).

Buddhist monks everywhere have been involved in economic activities, although exactly what they do varies according to time-specific socioeconomic conditions. Ancient Indian monks had to "transport taxable goods . . . sell the property of deceased monks, hire and oversee laborers, and buy food" (Schopen 2004: 15). Ancient Chinese monks grew and traded tea, manufactured salt, and produced and sold for profit silver, silk, paper, ink, and other goods for the benefit of the monasteries (Kieschnick 2003: 5, 23; Walsh 2007: 474). At present, in rural southwestern China, monks "collect sap from rubber trees" to pay the temple's expenses (Borchert 2011: 163). In rural Thailand, some monks ordain trees to protect them from loggers (Darlington 2009: 191–195; Sanitsuda 2001: 128). At Wat Thai, monks raise funds by conducting various rituals, including blessing the grand opening of new businesses.

Everyday socioeconomic activities are, in fact, an important part of the monks' spiritual quest. The key is to be diligent. "Work out your own realization with diligence!" is an admonition the Buddha uttered shortly before his death (Lafleur 1988: 38, citing Davids and Davids 1951). Realization covers a wide range of subjects, such as recognizing that the world is impermanent, that desire contributes to suffering, and that laziness is an obstacle to practice. Monks are urged to meditate on these realizations. However, up to now, Theravada Buddhist monks in North America most often have been studied in relation to their adaptation to American society, meditation, and rituals (Cadge 2005: 89–91; Numrich 1996: 61–62, 81–84, 1998: 147–162; Van Esterik 1992: 62–66, 1999: 57–68). Unlike in Asia, scant attention has been paid to the monks' physical labor and their role in transferring economic capital into religious and social capital for merit makers. The interconnections among physical labor, economic engagement, and spiritual pursuits have been largely overlooked.

Conducting minute, unglamorous, and monotonous work is one of the greatest challenges that Thai monks face in the United States. A good monk at Wat Thai is expected to be able to explain the Dharma, teach meditation, lead the chanting, conduct rituals, raise money, and perform physical labor. He is expected to be productive; he is evaluated by what he does for the community, which is like a good monk in ancient India who was not an "ascetic monk" or a "meditating monk" but the one who "took care of the sick and dying" (Schopen 2004: 8, 15).

Going beyond our imagination of what monks do, this chapter focuses on the monks' daily activities, their agency, and the structural constraints they confront. I scrutinize the kinds of work they routinely perform, how they reinterpret the Vinaya to meet new social challenges and how they negotiate cultural differences and gender rules in Silicon Valley. The narrative is interspersed with the rhythm of the tedious and repetitive manual labor that a handful of Thai and Farang monks must perform to maintain the temple and sustain the community. Their physical labor constitutes an important dimension of their spiritual practice, their integration into the community and into larger society. I suggest that both Thai and Farang monks experience displacement but in different cultural contexts: Thai monks in the context of the United States and Farang monks in the context of a Thai Theravada Buddhist temple. Although both groups are governed by the Vinaya, each encounters culture-specific shocks and undergoes a distinctive transformation. Together, they act as community builders, laborers, ritual performers, meditation teachers, and social workers. Their daily lives are constructed by monastic regulations, cultural differences, and gender regulations. With an awareness that monks engage in a wide range of socioeconomic and Buddhist activities as part of their spiritual practice, we will not be surprised or disappointed when we see monks using iPads or pumping gas.

A Brief Introduction to the Sangha at Wat Thai

Typically, Thai monks remain affiliated with their home temples in Thailand while serving at overseas temples.[4] The length of service is one to two terms, each term lasting for three to five years.[5] The number of resident monks at Wat Thai has fluctuated from five to seven; occasionally, only two or three have been in residence. Luang Pho is the only monk who has been there since it was founded in 1983. As of 2008, all of the Thai monks had been fully ordained for fifteen to more than forty years. Of the two Farang monks, Than Gabriel—the first Farang to have full ordination at Wat Thai—served at Wat Thai from 2000 to 2008. Sutama Bhikkhuni, a female Farang monk, lived and traveled in India, South Korea, and Thailand for ten years or so before she was fully ordained in 1997 by a Sri Lankan monk in Los Angeles. She served at Wat Thai for about seven years.

Although Buddhist monks often are portrayed as upholders of "tradition," Thai monks who serve overseas have earned at least a bachelor's degree. Of the seven Thai monks at Wat Thai in 2008, four had master's degrees and three had bachelor's degrees.[6] They, in general, are better educated than the average monk in Thailand. Each of them has a specialty, such as teaching meditation or interpreting the Dharma. Most Thai monks are from Isan, where becoming a monk is an opportunity to make merit for one's parents and to receive an education and acquire social mobility (Bowie 1998: 473; Keyes 1987: 139; Kingshill 1976: 164; Saeng 2002: 13). It is no coincidence that all of the Thai monks at Wat Thai in 2008 were from Isan.

When a monk from a rural area earns the title "Maha," his family gains respect from the villagers. Maha Winai, the Smiling Monk, is a good example. At six, he was steaming sticky rice for the family and performing simple household chores to help out. He became a novice at thirteen and was fully ordained at twenty. He became a Maha with level-five Pali expertise and earned a bachelor's degree in economics. Now in the United States, the Smiling Monk has made his family proud.

Working with and around Monastic Codes

According to the Vinaya, monks should not prepare their own food. Going forth at dawn to the street to receive alms food from laypeople is a hallmark of Theravada Buddhism in Southeast Asia. However, in the United States, most Americans are unfamiliar with alms giving. In response, many women and restaurant owners take turns taking food to Wat Thai and offering it to the monks. (This modified Buddhist practice prevails at Theravada Buddhist temples throughout the United States.) Not only monks work around the monastic codes; the laypeople do, too.

To better blend into the new landscape, some Thai monks began wearing less conspicuous robes outside the temple, especially in the 1980s and early 1990s. When he attended classes at the University of California, Berkeley, Achan Prem purposely wore a less eye-catching, dull maroon-brown robe. Sutama Bhikkhuni explained that "Americans are not familiar with Theravada Buddhist robes. The dark orange robes look more like the Catholic one, so it is more familiar." Whether the robes are less eye-catching or more familiar, the bottom line is not their color but that they signify otherness.

A Theravada monk is prohibited from handling money because money and material goods embody attachment to worldly things. A layperson usually handles money on the monks' behalf (Tambiah 1970: 143, 149).[7] However, these days currency is no longer a symbol of luxury.[8] Without money, monks are immobilized. Luang Pho once explained to me, half-jokingly and half-seriously, that using a credit card is different from directly touching money because "it is a piece of plastic."

Like Luang Pho, Thai monks often innovatively redefine their new conduct. In Thailand, to avoid temptation, monks are prohibited from shopping at malls. However, in the United States, especially when a temple is first forming, monks may have no choice but to purchase supplies themselves. They tend to emphasize that they do not shop for pleasure but to get work done. Monks who drive cars often state that they drive not for sightseeing but to get from one place to another. Similarly, monks emphasize that smartphones are used for communication, not to play music or games. Thus, while they do not hesitate to cross boundaries and to use new technology, they redraw the boundaries between work and pleasure.

Certain rules persist. Sitting or walking alone with a woman in a private place is still considered taboo.[9] To eliminate a monk's sexual desire, physical contact with the opposite sex is strictly regulated. I witnessed a layman criticize a male monk and Sutama Bhikkhuni for having a conversation in a small computer room without a third person present. (I had caused the trouble by stepping outside for a few minutes.) The monks are under constant public scrutiny.

Monks have to perform in public responding to American cultural expectations. Maha Song told me that a female English-language teacher had placed her hands on his shoulders while dividing the class into different groups. "I did not want to embarrass her," he said. "I explained to her later." Maha Pattana told me that he had had to shake hands with a woman for the sake of politeness because the woman had already stretched her hand toward him. After shaking hands, he told her that it was against the rules for him to have physical contact with a woman and asked her to respect his discipline in the future. On these occasions, the monks renewed their vows after returning to the temple.

Monks also have to switch back to their previous practices when they return to Thailand. There, they do not drive cars, shop at malls, or wear socks or hats. Maha Aphai, who is now the abbot at a temple in Bangkok, said, "We have to go along with the world and along with the society." Flexibility, performing, and reinterpreting have become the key to becoming a transnational monk. Their reworking of the codes and their changed behavior may reflect how they neither rigidly adhere to nor compromise the Vinaya.

Noble Heart, Servant's Body: The Merging of Physical and Spiritual Work

"Monks are laborers," Luang Pho told me in 1997. "They have no salary. When people see the monks working for the community and for a prosperous temple, then they are *happy* to give." In 2012, he said in an interview, "I remind the monks that, if you do not help [work], go somewhere else. Do not stand and chat with laypeople when other monks are working. The community judges the monks." "Noble heart, servant's body" (*chai pen nai, kai pen bao*) is a Thai phrase the monks quote to convey the image of an ideal monk. Maha Ampon, who was given the nickname "Happy Man" by his classmates at an adult school, once said to me, "The most important thing a monk needs is endurance. Without endurance, he really cannot last very long." His comments reveal the self-discipline required to succeed as a monk. As a result, the three "*Sas*"—*saat*, *sawang*, and *sangob* (clean, clear, and peaceful)—have been implemented vigorously. "The external cleanliness of the temple reflects the internal clarity of the monks. Whatever we do is related to Buddhism," the Smiling Monk said.

Wat Thai is open seven days a week, 365 days a year. In the United States, participants tend to linger at the temple and ask a lot more questions than participants do in Thailand. The demands on the monks' attention and time are unceasing. Each morning at 6:00 A.M., the monks gather in front of the Buddha image. Luang Pho lights the candles and burns incense, which signals the beginning of thirty to forty-five minutes of chanting, followed by fifteen minutes of silent meditation. A few lay practitioners may join in and sit behind the monks. If a festival or religious event is scheduled for that day, Luang Pho announces, "No meditation today. There is a lot of work that needs to be done."

At 7:00 A.M., the monks scour the areas they are charge of cleaning. Monk A might vacuum the chapel, then sweep and mop the balcony. Monk B might sweep and mop the stairs and scrub the toilet. Monk C might appear to be absent but actually is cleaning the monks' living quarters. Monk D might weed the lawn and water the roses, trees, plants, and shrubs. The rhythm of the work and sounds of the sweeping are the morning symphony of Wat Thai. Luang Pho does not have any assigned tasks. Instead, he monitors everyone. Sometimes he does the laundry in between answering phone calls, making arrangements for the day's activities, and reading the headlines of the local newspaper. The other residents—volunteer teachers from Thailand, temporary nuns and novices, and visitors like me—join in the cleaning, sweeping the courtyard, preparing breakfast for the monks, changing the water in the flower vases, rearranging the flowers, and polishing ritual vessels.

During the day, if no rituals or events are scheduled, Luang Pho usually receives visitors; the other monks work according to their specialties or the project assigned to them. Monk A is in charge of the monthly newsletter and administrative work; Monk B purchases supplies for the temple; Monk C manages the temple school, the Dharma lecture, and the food court; Monk D takes care of the landscape and grounds and repairs the facility as needed; Monk E specializes in website maintenance and financial management. Each monk has his or her focus and priority, but all pitch in when needed. In addition, they have to train temporary monks and novices, comfort the sick and dying, teach meditation, and so on. Once an elderly man asked whether the monks would prune the shrubs in his yard. Later, the monks loaded up a truck with equipment and drove off to help.

This continuous demand for manual labor includes weekly preparations for the Sunday food court. Although lay volunteers come to cook and sell the food, the monks are responsible for setting up awnings and tables, scrubbing the cooking stalls, and chilling tubs for bottled water and soft drinks. On a typical Sunday, the food court serves more than two hundred customers. For Thai New Year, it feeds more than one thousand. After everyone leaves, the monks pour the used cooking oil into a container and dispose of it; they also clean the entire area, which includes hosing down the tables and washing the bottoms of the trash containers.

Monks occasionally have to pick up work that was assigned to laypeople. On April 10, 2009, the day before Thai New Year, I saw that the Smiling Monk was steaming a huge mound of sticky rice. Five more monks were slicing papaya, a key ingredient of green papaya salad. I was struck by the scene and took out my camera. Maha Amnui stopped me. "Please don't," he said. "Thai people will not accept it."[10] I realized that Maha Amnui did not mind slicing papaya but was concerned that a picture of the monks preparing food would be perceived as breaking a Vinaya rule.

In addition to getting ready for the food court each week, the monks have to prepare for monthly events. A monk may feed the temple cats at

Figure 4.1. Getting ready for the Thai New Year celebration, 2009. (Photograph by the author.)

one moment and drive nails like a carpenter the next; then he may join the other monks to carry a long table from the multipurpose hall to the courtyard (Figure 4.1). Before the day of the event arrives, the monks make sure that the chapel's ceiling is dusted; the carpet is cleaned; the religious utensils are polished; the grass is cut; the roses and trees are trimmed; the water in the fountain is clear; signs are posted; and every nook and cranny of the temple has been thoroughly cleaned.

It is a challenge to handle such a large volume of work and still find time to study. Than Gabriel, the Farang monk, told me, "If I can do all these things as a first step, then I can learn to find time to read and study, like Achan Singtong does. You see how he does so many things cheerfully. If this meets the needs of the community, I do *not* need to attain enlightenment." Achan Singtong was known for his Dharma talks and for cleaning the dirtiest and least visible spots at the temple. In emulating Achan Singtong, Than Gabriel sometimes labored to the point of exhaustion. "I just lie down and say, 'This is nothing. This is nothing,'" he said. "I just lie there ten to fifteen minutes. Then I move on."

Like the Thai monks, Than Gabriel was always busy. I interviewed him three times, and each time he was working on something—for example, polishing ritual vessels—as we talked. For a few years, Than

Gabriel was the designated driver for the temple because he was the only monk with a driver's license. Sometimes a layperson would ask him for a ride to the airport or the Department of Motor Vehicles. Occasionally, people who lived near Wat Thai asked him to feed their pets and collect their mail while they were away. Than Gabriel was also in charge of signing the checks, using the temple's credit card, and buying supplies. He was amazed at how much the monks were involved with "sort of *non-religious* activities," he once admitted, "yet it is a *big* part of a monk's work."

For some monks, this unremitting drudgery is too difficult to sustain. Once I overheard a monk complaining to an acquaintance about the boring work. A few months later, he disrobed. The long hours, to a certain extent, deprive monks of the time they need to rest or study. The Smiling Monk once fell asleep in his adult school English class, exhausted after working ten or twelve hours at the temple that day. Embarrassed at not doing well, he stopped attending class but practiced speaking English with Than Gabriel, picking up phrases here and there.

The monks' productivity make some participants feel that the temple is worthy of their support. Some people became volunteers because they were inspired by these monks. Wuwanna, the owner of a bridal shop, said, "The most dedicated people at this temple are the monks. They work all the time, work hard. But no salary, no privacy. They have to live following certain rules." Harvey characterized the difference between the Thai monks in Thailand and in America by saying, "Monks have an easy life in Thailand. Laypeople take care of them. Here monks are laborers." The Smiling Monk once used the phrase *sabai sabai* (easy) to describe being a monk in Thailand in contrast with the challenges monks in the United States must meet.

A Monk in the Making: Than Gabriel

When Than Gabriel donned the robe, he, like all monks, immediately became subject to monastic regulations. He lived, ate, and worked together with Thai monks; he relinquished his own space, his time, and his food preferences. He learned to speak in a low voice and not laugh loudly. He observed how the monks tend to remain silent when Luang Pho is present, speaking only when spoken to. As time passed, he learned with whom he could joke and with whom he could not, when he could speak up and when he needed to keep quiet. Little by little, step by step, Than Gabriel slowly changed his habits.

In our interview, Than Gabriel recalled that he was baptized a Christian in the Lutheran church to honor his grandmother. His father had had a bad experience in being forced to attend church as a child, so he did not impose the same discipline on his children. Than Gabriel first became interested in Buddhism in high school. "I appreciate Christianity, but one of the things I sort of loved about Buddhism was that idea about not forcing anyone to be anything out of fear or guilt," he said. "I love that openness. Buddhism is for anyone. Anyone can meditate."

In 1990, Than Gabriel found Wat Thai in the phone book. He met Luang Pho and said, "I want to be a monk." Luang Pho just laughed and said, "Don't be a Buddhist. Be yourself. No label. And if you have a girlfriend, be the best boyfriend that you can be. If you are a son, be the best son that you can be. And if you are a friend, be the best friend that you can be. If you are a brother, be the best brother that you can be." Than Gabriel recalled, "He went on and on and on. But he never once said, 'Oh, please come. Here's a book, and now I want to tell you about the Lord Buddha and what he can do for your life.' No. He never said it." Than Gabriel was attracted more by Luang Pho's rebuff than he would have been if Luang Pho had tried to press beliefs on him.

For several years, Than Gabriel visited Luang Pho intermittently to learn meditation and to discuss the Dharma. Nine years after his first visit to Wat Thai, following Luang Pho's suggestion, he volunteered to teach English in Thailand, first at a monastic school, and then at an elementary school in Luang Pho's home village. He could not emphasize enough the influence that living in Thailand had had on him. "I think it was very important for me to have been in Thailand for the ten months," he said. "I lived with a family in Bangkok. I lived with a family from Isan. I saw funerals with the family. I saw weddings with the family. I saw many, many things. I was the only American with the Thai people, and I think that really helped me. I soaked in a lot about behavior and, you know, just the little subtleties of the culture."

In August 2000, at twenty-nine, Than Gabriel was ordained as a novice at Wat Thai. Usually, a man twenty or older is ordained as a monk; in Than Gabriel's case, serving as a novice was a kind of probationary period to see whether he was ready for full ordination. He received full ordination on June 30, 2002.

Than Gabriel had a lot to learn, although he had a bit of a head start from having lived in Thailand. He gave me one example: "One morning after I finished my cereal, I drank the milk out of my bowl, right? Luang Pho said, 'Please don't ever do that again.'" According to the Vinaya, a monk should "eat alms food methodically," never "eat sticking out the tongue," and not make "a slurping noise."[11] Than Gabriel also learned that he should not walk and drink at the same time. If he drinks, he has to take a seat, drink, finish, and then get up and continue. He also changed how he walked. "When I came here, I walked on my heels, boom, boom, boom, and Achan Singtong told me, 'Please walk on your toes. Walk softly,'" he said. "Since that day, I don't make a racket when I walk through the house." Over time, he gradually internalized these regulations.

Being "a decent person" and doing things in the proper manner according to the Vinaya mattered to him. He has learned from his mistakes:

> Every time I've been reprimanded, it sticks in my mind, because you feel kind of embarrassed. One time I visited [the Thai temple in] Houston [with Luang Pho]. The abbot of the temple was talking with Luang Pho, and they were kind of lying on the floor. I was walking, and I thought, 'What do I do here? If I walk between their conversation that is rude. But can I walk behind them?' So I walked behind them. Luang Pho quickly said why did I walk so close to his head? I sort of cut across his pillow area, so that wasn't right at all. A Thai would just have never done that. I just made the *wrong* choice. But just that one little thing made me understand the importance that the Thai people place on the head, and on the feet, and about the abbot of the temple.

For Thais, the head is the highest part of the body and the most respected, while the feet are the lowest and least respected. Placing one's foot close to someone's head is an insult. This incident taught Than Gabriel that, among Thais, the individual body is not a given physical entity but, instead, imbued with a hierarchical order and meanings.

Than Gabriel had to learn every detail about becoming a monk, including where to sit according to the hierarchies. He would never sit in Luang Pho's chair at the head of the table, even when Luang Pho was away. The same was true for seating at the chapel. Luang Pho sits in the first seat closest to the Buddha statue, and the other monks sit in hier-archical order based on the year of their ordination—the way of reck-oning seniority among monks. Every monk appears keenly aware of his standing. Even when Than Gabriel was the only monk at the chapel to receive offerings, he sat in the third seat: "No one told me to do this, but you just feel it wouldn't be appropriate. And I've seen other monks do the same thing." He performed accordingly. The socially constructed space and order of the seating disciplines the monks and makes each monk aware of his position in the monastic order; at the same time, the monks' seating arrangement becomes a form of expressing respect.

The most difficult thing for Than Gabriel to get used to was the lack of scheduling, of not knowing what was coming next. Citing an example, he said,

> Today, going to San Jose. I didn't know I was going until the last minute, and it was like, 'You're going to San Jose.' When I first came here, the first year, that used to really get me frustrated. I was getting ready to go to sleep, and now I'm driving to San Francisco at midnight [to pick up monks at the airport]. You just get used to it. It is funny and in a *strange* way, it might be a kind of *training*. I think there is training involved with feeling that sort of frustration or whatever and then letting it go. Just do it. So it was really helpful in breaking that down [*laughs*].

By taking the lack of a schedule as training and learning to let it go, he reworked his emotions and habits, trying to live in the present as part of his spiritual practice. Although he was good at taking advice and criticism, occasionally he felt irritated. "Why can't you just leave me alone?" he sometimes thought. But he then reminded himself that this is "the culture, . . . the way of behaving for the Thai monks."

Than Gabriel was welcomed and loved by young and old at the temple. Most food offerings to monks are Thai, Lao, or Chinese dishes, but some members occasionally brought Than Gabriel pizza, ham-burgers, and French fries. Some gave him advice on how to eat certain foods, such as "Chinese donuts go well with coffee." Many thought the temple was fortunate to have him there. At least three people discreetly mentioned to me that having a Farang monk as Luang Pho's disciple raised the temple's visibility. Than Gabriel said, "I really haven't had to think too much about 'I'm a Caucasian in an Asian temple.'" He felt personally appreciated and respected. However, he attributed much of this to "Thai really respecting the robe."

Over time, Than Gabriel picked up the Thai language through daily interactions. By 2006, he could speak and understand Thai well enough to communicate about simple matters. Young Thai Americans often treated him like an older brother. Muay, who had attended a Catholic school during the week and the temple school on weekends, recalled, "Whenever we had a Buddhist question or we wanted to know more about Buddhism, Than Gabriel was the go-to guy." Meditation practitioners also sought his advice. Once Jennifer, a devout Catholic, told Than Gabriel that she did not feel comfortable bowing and chanting about seeking refuge in the Buddha, the Dharma, and the Sangha. He explained, "The Buddha is just compassion; the Dharma is wisdom; and the Sangha is morality. So we don't have to think about anything other than that. Don't make it a different religion, you know." He also helped train newly ordained English-speaking novices and monks by showing them how to wear the robe, how to sit, and how to eat according to the Vinaya. Than Gabriel served as an intermediary between Thai and Farang and between monks and laypeople.

Than Gabriel often represented Wat Thai when the temple received invitations from local schools and other institutions to talk about Buddhism. He explained that the Buddha sent monks out to "teach the Dharma for the happiness and welfare of all beings. But the Buddha did not ask monks to make people become his students." For Than Gabriel, it was important not to thrust Buddhism on people. He often said to those who are interested in Buddhism, "If you're Jewish or Christian or Muslim, Buddhism teaches that what I should wish for you is to be happy, successful, and peaceful in your mind. Not to change your beliefs. Not to become Buddhist."

After a while, I noticed that Than Gabriel was absent from the 6:00 A.M. chanting and meditation session. He explained to me that he was a night person and that Luang Pho was unperturbed by this. "The abbots of temples know what issues they really need to push and which ones to let go." He continued:

At certain times, it's almost like I never left home, because Luang Pho will walk into my room and open the curtains like my Mom used to do [laughs]. I don't know if you ever had that experience with your parents, but in America when you sleep too late on the weekend or something, and your parents want you to get up, they come in and pull open the drapes, pull open the shutters so the light comes in. That's the technique a lot of parents use. He walks in. He'll tell me what time it is and open my curtains. I don't know if this is relevant to anything you're writing, but for me, nothing should make a *real* monk angry. He's showing me that his practice is really pretty true, because it is just that. He's not going to let it upset him.

Discipline did not exclude compassion. Luang Pho gave him some space but did not let him overdo it. Than Gabriel's comparison of Luang Pho to his mother reflected the close relationship between the two. For him, Luang Pho's ability to control his emotions was the sign of a good monk. Than Gabriel was caught between his lifelong sleeping habits and the monks' early morning schedule. Not long after our conversation, Than Gabriel joined in the 6:00 A.M. chanting and meditation. He was not just being made into a monk but was an active agent of his own making.

Trailblazer: Sutama Bhikkhuni

Sutama Bhikkhuni and Than Gabriel have many similarities. Born in Washington, DC, in the 1960s, she rarely went to church as a child. "My mother considers herself a naturalist and got her Ph.D. in phenomenology," she said. "My dad is a physicist and a Daoist." Like Than Gabriel, she lived in Asia before she was ordained as a monk in the United States. She left her university at nineteen, after a close friend's sudden death, and lived in India for a while. She then went to South Korea, where she joined a women's monastery. She learned about Buddhism from senior Korean Bhikkhunis for several years. When she came to Wat Thai, she performed all kinds of work, although she did not go shopping or conduct rituals, as Than Gabriel did. She also obeyed the Vinaya. Despite these similarities, however, Sutama Bhikkhuni experienced something Than Gabriel never encountered: gender prejudice.

Her experience has to be understood in the context of Theravada Bhikkhuni history and the gender politics of Thai Buddhism. Today in Southeast Asia, full Theravada ordination for women is available only in Sri Lanka. Recently, Chatsumarn Kabilsingh, a prominent Thai female Buddhist scholar, received full ordination in Sri Lanka and became the first Theravada Bhikkhuni in contemporary Thailand. A few other women have followed in her footsteps, joining the world-wide Buddhist women's movement in seeking equal access to becoming monks. However, many Thai women, the backbone of Thai Buddhism, find the idea of female monks offensive.[12]

Sutama Bhikkhuni was the first female monk I met at a Theravada Buddhist temple. Luang Pho introduced her to me. As she led me to the women's dormitory, I addressed her by her first name, just as Luang Pho had. She stopped and said in a startled tone, "You call me by my name." I was embarrassed by my blunder. "I'm sorry," I said. "What do you prefer me to call you?" She asked me to add "Bhikkhuni" to her name. At the time, I had no idea how much the title meant to her or how to interact with a female monk.

In a similar way, Southeast Asian migrants who grew up in socie-ties where there were no Bhikkhunis have no idea how to act toward a female monk because there are no precedents to follow. Some were confused, unsure whether they should treat a Bhikkhuni as they would a male monk or a nun. Some respected Bhikkhunis for fighting for the right to be monks. Some believed that it was impossible for a Farang woman to obey 311 rules. Some were "disgusted" about having a Bhik-khuni at all, fearing that she might undermine a male monk's vow of celibacy. In contrast, many young Thai Americans and local non-Bud-dhists treated her no differently from Than Gabriel.

Sutama Bhikkhuni noted that more women than men, and espe-cially women who were big donors, resented her for being a monk. She believed that she offended them by transcending gender boundaries. In our interviews Sutama Bhikkhuni recalled that one woman acted as a gatekeeper, berating her: "You can't wear this robe. You should not do this here." Another Thai woman explained to Sutama Bhikkhuni that having been born female meant that she needed to improve her karma by performing meritorious deeds so that she could be reborn as a man and then become a monk. Sutama Bhikkhuni, however, responded, "The Buddha never asked people to postpone their merit making [by becoming a monk]."

Some monks also rejected her. The abbot of a Burmese temple characterized Bhikkhuni as "the most dangerous thing in the world." For him, women were polluting agents because of menstruation and sexuality. Sutama Bhikkhuni described her experience of visiting that temple as "very scary." It was "very clear, though," she said. "No ambi-guity. Going there one time, not to go there again! [*laughs*]"

Unlike the Burmese abbot, Luang Pho and the board of directors accepted Sutama Bhikkhuni as a visitor. Luang Pho and other senior monks provided her with a "tremendous opportunity for learning through observation, seeing, and listening," she said. However, her role as a monk at Wat Thai was circumscribed. She was welcome to meditate, do physical work, and teach Buddhist ethics. She was, however, excluded from conducting rituals. She conceived of conducting rituals as a way to legitimize her status as a monk in this community. In November 2004, the day before Kathin, the robes-giving ritual, Sutama Bhikkhuni asked Luang Pho whether she could join in the rituals with the other monks.

"No," Luang Pho said.

"Would you mind if I did research on this subject?" she replied.

"Yes [do the research]," Luang Pho said. "But you will not be able to attend it this year. Maybe next year."

Their conversation ended. The next day, while the monks and lay participants were chanting in the chapel, I ran into Sutama Bhikkhuni, who was standing alone about a hundred feet away from the chapel. She asked me whether we could talk. It appeared to me that she did not want to be by herself. As we talked, I asked about the results of her research. She was taken aback that I had overheard their conversation. Her answer surprised me: "Actually, neither the abbot nor I know what research I should do." This response made me realize that both of them were performing. Her tactic was to engage Luang Pho in seeking the opportunity to participate in rituals. Luang Pho, in return, played his part in this game.

As our conversation continued, Sutama Bhikkhuni pointed out, "Those of us who join the monastery are very idealistic. But within the monastery, you also find problems similar to what you find outside the monastery. It is very painful." Talking about the constraints and gender inequality that she experienced both within and outside the monastic community, she said, "If I had never lived with senior Bhikkhunis [in Korea], I don't know if I could make it. But now, even though they are not with me, I can see them. I have them *imprinted* on my heart. I can feel it. This makes me stronger. It might be Buddha's intention."

Sutama Bhikkhuni was resilient. One incident in particular gave me insight into her determination. On May 21, 2005, she and I worked together separating paper boxes from waxed cardboard boxes and emptying plastic bottles and aluminum cans to make sure that no liquid was left inside before selling them at a recycling center.[13] I had trouble fitting a small plastic bag on the rim of a trash container. Sutama Bhikkhuni took over and made it fit. "My life as a female monk is just like this," she said. "You need good judgment to see how much you can stretch but not stretch too much and break it." What a powerful metaphor, I thought.

Because we both got very dirty sorting the piles, she mentioned in passing that she had to wash her robe that night and hoped it would be dry the next morning. This statement made me realize that partial exclusion had emotional and material effects. Since she was not allowed to conduct rituals, she did not receive any envelopes with money inside that laypeople customarily offer the monks, although Luang Pho quietly provided her with pocket money, especially when she had to travel.

Sutama Bhikkhuni regarded Luang Pho as her mentor. She nevertheless was frustrated about the ambiguity she encountered daily. "Luang Pho is very flexible," she said. "He has respect for lots of different opinions and tries to accommodate everyone. I don't know if he ever finally actually makes a decision about anything. I feel like his mind is always open about things and can change at any time." Sutama Bhikkhuni yearned for unambiguous acceptance. In contrast, Luang Pho felt constrained by the rules of the Sangha Supreme Council of Thailand. Once I asked Luang Pho point blank what his opinion was of women's ordination. He said that the Sangha "should embrace Bhikkhunis in the United States" but that he had to be concerned about the "community's feelings." From my observations, he made his decision about whether to include Sutama Bhikkhuni according to his audience. For example, he took both Than Gabriel and Sutama Bhikkhuni to an interfaith Thanksgiving celebration. However, when he went out to conduct a Buddhist ritual at an individual's home or business, he included Than Gabriel but never Sutama Bhikkhuni.

Luang Pho supported Sutama Bhikkhuni's idea to found a monastic retreat for women. After many discussions, Sutama Bhikkhuni established a women's monastic residence. On August 20, 2005, Thai and Farang monks, headed by Luang Pho, conducted a ritual to bless the residence. Luang Pho also gave Sutama Bhikkhuni a Buddha statue and a Bodhi tree, the symbol of the Buddha achieving enlightenment.

After almost seven years of participating at Wat Thai, Sutama Bhikkhuni was looking forward to starting a different journey. "I am no longer living underneath a male abbot in a male monastic community," she said. Nevertheless, she saw a disadvantage in being away: losing the "opportunity to learn from senior monks." Therefore, she decided to rent a house nearby. Being close made it convenient to participate in activities held at Wat Thai, such as the midweek middle-way Dharma gathering and the full-moon, all-night meditation. In this way, she associated with but did not formally affiliate with Wat Thai.

At her new home, Sutama Bhikkhuni, similar to the monks at Wat Thai, emphasized the practice of mindfulness while sweeping and cleaning the retreat. She led both the morning and the evening chanting, conducted rituals such as the dedication for the deceased, and blessed participants with holy water. Like Luang Pho, she sat in the seat closest to the Buddha statue; the others sat in order of seniority. Just as male monks do not share a table with nuns, neither did Sutama Bhikkhuni. What distinguished her from a nun was not race but the hierarchical order that she conformed to and respected. She chose to follow the monastic hierarchical order rather than the American ideals of equality and informality. How she operates the retreat and the ways in which she practices Buddhism reveal both her agency and the powerful impact the monastic community had on her.

Besides continuing some practices that she learned from serving at Wat Thai, Sutama Bhikkhuni did something innovative: She received food offerings by walking around her neighborhood. According to the Vinaya, monks should walk silently, with eyes downcast as they receive alms on the street.[14] Sutama Bhikkhuni followed American cultural principles instead. She told the neighbors what she and her associates were doing and answered questions while looking straight into their eyes. She also started some new practices that included not driving a car and handling money, which she referred to as "pure Buddhism." Such reworking reveals the ways in which she contemplated what to follow and what to modify.

Her choices often were made in response to the circumstances. For example, her first name, the name I called her by when I first met her, I later found out, was a Korean name that she had adopted. Using a Korean name instead of her American name became her way to identify with the Mahayana Korean female monks who trained her. As time passed and she interacted more frequently with Theravada Buddhists, she used her Korean name less and a lengthy Dharma name more. By the time she had established her retreat, she used only her Dharma name. Her choice of using or not using American, Korean, or Dharma names embodied her multidimensional identities and the ways in which she flexibly positioned herself.

All of these practices and choices illustrate how Sutama Bhikkhuni, a pioneer female monk, lives with constant ambiguity and tension. Her conformity to the existing hierarchical order, her nonconformity, and fighting for the right to be a monk, exist side by side. Her very existence challenges the exclusion of women from the monastic community.

Interconnectedness

Thai and Farang monks appear to cross boundaries in opposite directions: Thai monks move from "traditional" to "modern" by driving a car, shopping at the mall, and using the latest technology. Farang monks move from a "modern" society to a more "traditional" community by learning how to walk, sit, and eat properly according to the monastic rules. Sutama Bhikkhuni even stopped driving a car and handling money. Yet each crosses boundaries between religious and nonreligious by meeting the needs of the community. Various dichotomies—modern–traditional, sacred–mundane, East–West—may provide a familiar framework for grasping this ongoing dynamic. Yet such dichotomies erase the ambiguity and fluidity of everyday practices.

Ambiguity and tension generated from these juxtapositions characterize the monks' routine practices. In principle, by becoming a monk one renounces a worldly life. In practice, he or she still must engage with the mundane world. While detachment from the material world and compassion are emphasized, the monks continue to conform to the hierarchical order within the monastic community. When one works diligently, one may still struggle between a preference for doing physical labor and practicing meditation. While one monk made no distinction between conducting religious and nonreligious work, he did attempt to keep certain transgressions—for example, slicing papaya—invisible to the public. In the same manner, Luang Pho included Sutama Bhikkhuni, but only partially. His ambivalence kept him from directly confronting the Supreme Sangha Council of Thailand and those in the community who resisted Bhikkhunis. Sutama Bhikkhuni, on the one hand, sought to learn from senior male monks; on the other hand, she chose not to affiliate with them structurally. Her agency was demonstrated through both emancipation and conforming to a hierarchical monastic order. Surely, the Sangha is no less dynamic than the lay community.

Thai and Farang monks have experienced a different process of self-making and being made. Working overseas makes the Thai monks aware of privileges that they took for granted in Thai society. As they participate in transplanting and rearticulating Buddhism in the United States, they become transnational monks and have experiences that are different from those of the monks in Thailand. In comparison, Farang monks have to remake themselves by changing their lifelong habits and values. Each has to meet different challenges and do different kinds of emotional work according to particular circumstances in the process of achieving self-realization. At the same time, Thai and Farang monks influence one another, teach Thai and English to one another, and work together. Whereas the Thai monks teach the Farang monks how to act according to the Vinaya, the Farang monks use their English and cultural capital to serve the community. Doing whatever the temple needs is an important part of a monk's spiritual quest: to be mindful, live moment to moment, and be aware that nothing is permanent. While the monks serve the community, the community provides them with necessities. Giving and receiving are further developed in the context of making merit, the focus of the next chapter.

5
Merit Making

Transnational Circuits

The Smiling Monk was surprised when his English language teacher asked him, "Why do monks live off of *charity* by accepting food from the public?" It had never occurred to him that receiving alms could be interpreted as "living off of charity." For him, accepting food is a big part of living a monastic life. Eating whatever people give helps him cultivate detachment from desiring certain foods. Also, it enables laypeople to make merit, as food is believed to be transformed into merit for the almsgiver.

Thambun (making merit) is the primary means to accumulate positive karma by giving and doing good things. The money and alms offered to monks and nuns are exchanged "for spiritual merit to provide for the well-being" of merit makers "in this lifetime and the next" (Lopez 2001: 10). *Thambun* entails a reciprocal relationship. No English term can fully convey the meaning of *thambun*, just as there is no equivalent word in Thai for "donation." Although merit making and making donations have different connotations, Thai Americans do use the word "donation" for *thambun* when they speak English.

Suree, a Chinese Thai writer and volunteer teacher at Wat Thai, gave a personal spin: "For a donation, you give because you want to give. But for merit making, you give because you owe it." From her perspective, one may donate by giving something no longer needed, such as used clothing or old furniture. For merit making, one gives the best he or she has to repay debts owed to one's parents, ancestors, teachers, and community. Whereas Suree made a clear distinction, others were more relaxed about it. The key, they told me, is one's intention (*chetana*), regardless of the choice of words. To make the situation even more complicated, *thambun* often is intertwined with other interpretations, interests, and purposes. Therefore, the use of the terms "giving," "donation," and "fundraising" depends on context. None of these terms, however, is divorced from the principles of merit making, and all remind us that spiritual pursuits take place in a material world.

Theravada monks are considered a "field of merit"—"a rich soil in which to 'plant' one's good deed" (Ohnuma 2005: 107). Monks are perceived as a conduit between the material and the spiritual world and are located in a position superior to that of the merit maker, the almsgiver (Bowie 1998: 469; Tambiah 1976: 457–458). Therefore, a merit maker would say "thank you" and show respect to the monk via body language, but a monk does not need to say "thank you" in return.

Monks have no choice but to engage with the existing system. Gregory Schopen (1997, 2004, 2005, 2009) provides convincing evidence that the Sangha in ancient India was organized into something akin to a corporation. Although Thai monks in the United States do not carry personal seals or own property, as ancient Indian monks did, they do run the temple as a nonprofit corporation and conduct merit making to meet the needs of the merit makers and the temple. Otherwise, a temple would not be able to pay the rent or the mortgage, or the water and electric bill, basic items needed for survival. No wall exists between a dedicated abbot and a shrewd chief executive officer or between a pious monk and a wise businessman in the process of building and maintaining a Buddhist temple. The "orientalist model of the monk who rejects money" exists in the Western imagination but not elsewhere (Anderson 2013: 139).

Alan Klima (2004: 450–451) tells a story about how merit-making rituals were organized by a prominent Thai monk for the purpose of transferring individual merit to the nation-state. Merit making, Klima argues, is at once an economic affair—collecting cash and gold to raise the national reserves—*and* an affair of the heart. As he put it, merit making is one of the most performative of all Buddhist activities because it involves loving kindness, compassion, and generosity, on the one hand, and a public display of one's wealth, on the other (Klima 2004: 460).

In contrast to merit making as a national project, as presented by Klima, I examine how merit making—a performance entangled with the systematic accumulation, conversion, and transfer of merit—is conducted via local and transnational pathways. Not only do Thai Americans extend their merit making to Thailand by contributing to the renovation of Buddhist temples and sponsoring youth education there; elites in Thailand also make merit at temples abroad by giving Buddha statues, royal robes, money, and so forth. This circulation can be seen as the transnational movement of beliefs, money, symbols, practices, and materials. Local and transnational merit making provides a public forum for constructing and articulating class and religious identities. I agree with Mark Liechty (2003: 253) that "much of middle-class practice is about the *transformation* of class into social currency, the *translation* of market privilege into cultural privilege, and the *deployment* of a limited resource to create a limiting form of cultural life." Merit making enables participants to transform and display their religious, economic, and cultural capital. It also illustrates the interconnections and interpenetration of the spiritual and the material in everyday practices.

Therefore, I probe how laypeople and monks conflate Theravada Buddhist spiritual pursuits with capitalist activities through giving and accepting gifts. Michael Blim (2000: 28) declares, "Capitalist activities are—and should be—related to the *fulfillment of our fundamental needs*" (emphasis added) and often bear local characteristics.[1] Indeed, merit making fulfills vital needs of Theravada practitioners. Providing day-to-day support to temples, monks, and nuns is practiced by Burmese, Cambodian, Laotian, Thai, and Sri Lankan Buddhists, as well as by other Theravada practitioners around the world, because it is believed to underpin the welfare of the individual, the community, and the nation-state. Thai Buddhists, in particular, are well known for a preoccupation with merit making informed by beliefs in karma and rebirth (Fuengfusakul 1993: 166; Kirsch 1977: 248; Mulder 1969: 110; Taylor 1993: 291). It is crucial for us to unpack the complex reciprocal relationships between and among individuals and the community in relation to the past, present, and future. Merit making is more than just a spiritual practice and an exchange of money for merit between laypeople and monks. It combines morality and emotions and translates economic capital into social and religious capital beyond national borders. Merit making is the most effective fundraising mechanism for

Theravada Buddhist temples in the United States, where members are able not only to display individual economic capital and moral worth but also to collectively project the image of a respectable community.

The Construction of Giving

According to the Four Noble Truths, the first Dharma talk given by the historical Buddha more than 2,500 years ago, suffering is caused by endless craving and clinging—or, succinctly put, attachment—to transient things. On the basis of this logic, everyone experiences pain and suffering. The principal method to eliminate greed, hatred, and suffering is to observe the Five Precepts and follow the Noble Eightfold Path through "right" actions and mindfulness. Giving is considered a fundamental moral act that leads to detachment and compassion, and, eventually, the end of suffering. The Dana Sutta, a Buddhist text about generosity, highlights this aspect of giving:

> Giving is good, dear sir!
> Even when there's next to nothing,
> Giving is good.
> Giving with conviction is good!
> The giving of what's righteously gained is good!

And further:

> Giving with discretion is good![2]

At Wat Thai, the meaning of giving is often discussed in Dharma talks during rituals. At a birthday ceremony for the owner of a Thai restaurant in San Francisco, Than Gabriel expounded on the connection between giving and nirvana: "If we have a heart that is generous, then the mind will be peaceful. From there we can develop meditation skills and go on toward higher wisdom and the ultimate goal, which is nirvana: no more suffering." What Than Gabriel said reminded me of what John Kieschnick wrote in *Impact of Buddhism on Chinese Material Culture*: "Indeed, it was the sacred duty of the laity to support the monastic community with material donations, an act for which they were compensated by happiness in this world and a better rebirth in the next" (Kieschnick 2003: 6).

What Than Gabriel did not touch on is the notion of rebirth and karma in relation to giving. Merit makers, however, often are well aware of rebirth and karmic rewards because "Buddhist texts do not shy away from describing these rewards in enormous detail and using them to motivate the giver" (Ohnuma 2005: 110). Buddhist doctrine states that a person is born into one of six realms of existence—heaven, hell, humanity, Titans, hungry ghosts, or animals—according to accumulated karma. Karma often is conceived of as the sum of the merits and demerits one has accumulated in this and all previous lives (Keyes 1987: 224; Smith-Hefner 1999: 13; Spiro 1966: 1167; Tambiah 1970: 53). With positive karma, one is believed to be reborn into a higher realm and ultimately to escape *samsara*—the cycle of birth, death, and rebirth (Saeng 2002: 7–8; Swearer 1995: 400). Shaped by this worldview, people are motivated to give as a way to direct their destinies.

Giving is a practice one can witness daily at Wat Thai. Some elderly Thai women do not talk to anyone about their problems and just come to give alms. They believe that performing good deeds will help take care of their troubles. Tavon, the engineer who prepared to help his daughter battle leukemia, admitted that he practiced Buddhism "simply by giving." Chayan, a retired blue-collar worker, told me he was not rich but that he donated $20 every month. "I cannot donate $10,000," he said. "My donation is like this." As he spoke, he poured out the water from his water bottle, a small but steady stream. Through gifts and offerings, these people invest in well-being for themselves and their families. For others, giving was easy to talk about but hard to do. Wuwanna, the owner of a bridal shop, was aware of the challenge to be generous. "Being stingy is defilement," Wuwanna said. "If one gives more often, one will reduce stinginess. So reduce it little by little."

Giving is regarded as a spiritual practice, regardless of what and how much is given. In theory, no strings should be attached to a gift. In practice, however, what and how much one gives does matter, because laypeople, monks, and the board members are not insulated from socioeconomic systems. A gulf between belief and practice does exist. According to Stanley Tambiah's research at a village in Thailand, building and financing a Buddhist temple are considered the most virtuous forms of merit making. The next most virtuous acts, in descending order, are to become a monk or to have one's son become a monk, to give money for the repair of a temple, to offer food to monks, to participate in the Buddhist Sabbath four times each lunar month, and to follow the Five Precepts (Tambiah 1970: 146–147).

Different kinds of giving are believed to accumulate certain amounts of merit. Some people believe that one acquires more merit by feeding many monks than by feeding just one monk (Spiro 1966: 1168). Some travel long distances to study with and make merit through specific monks whom they respect (Taylor 1993: 292). Well-known temples and high-ranking monks, therefore, tend to receive more offerings. Melford Spiro (1966: 1163) observed that poor farmers in Burma invested a staggering proportion of earned income in merit making, in part because "religious spending is a much sounder and much more profitable investment than economic saving." Economic behavior is profoundly shaped by a belief in rebirth.

Pure gifts are rare (Mauss 1979). It has been reported that donors in the United States prefer to give money to, say, build a pedestrian bridge rather than to renovate a decrepit sewer system, even if the sewer system is much more urgently needed. At a university, philanthropists rarely donate money for a parking garage but for buildings with their names prominently attached. Despite the strings, giving is regarded as a positive act.

Many Thais believe that generosity can erase one's disreputable past and transform a "bad" person into a "decent" one. Suree claimed that she could tell which Isan women at Wat Thai had once been bar girls or prostitutes by how they dressed and talked. Then she added, "A lot of them came from poor families and did not have any choice. They had to do it. But they no longer do that here. They *thambun*, and it redeems them." Merit making can be about atonement.

Giving is especially significant for working-class men and women because it enables them to move up into a higher realm according to the logic of *thambun*. However, such a moral discourse can be a vicious cycle, because having money is conceived of as an outward sign of inward good and being poor is seen as a sign of demerit or a lack of merit (Hanks 1962: 1248). It puts pressure on the poor who do not have much to give. Ludda, a Thai female engineer, told me that one member had donated $250 but his check bounced. "I returned his check because the temple did not need his money," she said. Then she lowered her voice and said, "I wish the monks would teach people to give according to their ability to pay."

Monks occasionally practice merit making by not taking gifts that are offered. For example, a group of Thai college students made an offering to show their gratitude for having stayed several nights at Wat Thai on their way back to Thailand after internships at Disney World in Florida. Luang Pho gave the money back and told them he appreciated their good heart.

Merit making is connected not only with morality and money but also with emotions. Madison, a college student, used the Thai term *chidchai sangob* (heartfelt peacefulness) to describe her emotions after making merit for her boyfriend in Thailand on his birthday. She said no English phrase could perfectly capture such a feeling. Others used the phrase *dichai makmak* (very happy) or *sabai chai* (satisfied heart) to describe how merit making made them feel.

When Kamala first came to the United States, she just wanted to make money. Having money meant she could improve the lives of her impoverished natal family, which made her feel good. However, since she became a millionaire, money alone does not make her happy. She described her emotions in relation to giving: "When people get stressed, some people have to go to the movies. Some have to buy things or go to a bar. Not me. I have to donate. I have to help. Then I feel better. When I had a problem with my husband, the first thing that came into my mind is that I have to do something good." Kamala internalized the value of merit making so that her act of giving, which included donating money, time, and labor and providing the temple with a large no-interest loan, reduced her stress and made her happy. In a similar manner, Sombun said in 1996, "Satisfaction does not come from making money but from what we have done with the temple for the community and for the younger generation."

Like these participants, Luang Pho was keenly aware of the connection between giving and satisfaction. Indeed, he referred to merit making as a "happy business." When I asked him what he meant, he answered, "This [merit making] is a religious business. It's different from pure business, because it makes people *happy*. The people donate money and goods to the temple because they need to be happy." On another occasion, he elaborated: "People do not just want to be happy in this life but also in the next life. They invest in hope. One, they want to help themselves; two, they want to support the community." From his perspective, giving provides both present and future happiness and connects individuals to the temple.

At Wat Thai, ethnic Thai, Chinese, and Lao make up the majority of attendees at merit-making rituals, but Farang are also visible. Sometimes Farang attend the ritual with their wives. Some bring their children or grandchildren. They line up with the others and give alms to the monks or release doves as a way to teach the youngsters about their "cultural heritage." Occasionally, a Farang comes to make merit for a good friend or co-worker who has passed away. Sabrina, the Farang who practiced meditation and joined in rituals, viewed merit making as a reciprocal relationship: "The laypeople, through their generosity, support the monastics materially, and the monastics support the laypeople spiritually."

The notions of reciprocity and karma are reproduced and reinforced in everyday discourse. Luang Pho often uses examples to show that "once you are good, good things will come to you." One day Wat Thai received a phone call asking whether monks could conduct a funeral ritual at a home about three hours by car away from the temple. Despite the short notice and the long distance, Luang Pho responded warmly and led a contingent of monks there. It turned out that the funeral was being held for the mother of two physicians. The brothers were very pleased with the ritual, and they mentioned this to a good friend, the owner of Thailand's largest brewery, Chang Beer. Later, the beer mogul donated $100,000 to Wat Thai because compassionate monks are believed to be more potent at converting economic capital into religious capital. Another time, Luang Pho was invited to the office of the Hong Kong Chinese chief executive officer of a computer firm who was suffering from emotional distress. The two hit it off instantly. The executive donated $20,000 to Wat Thai after he sold his company for a big profit. The consistent themes are that merit makers are rewarded for their generosity and that the monks' compassion has positive economic consequences.

The Organization of Merit Making

Theravada Buddhist temples in the United States tend to follow the custom of not charging fees for participating in activities, including learning meditation. Even though Wat Thai's bylaws state that regular members have to pay a membership fee, this never was put into practice. Nevertheless, building a temple, maintaining a community, and supporting the monks require money. The boards and the monks were under great pressure to raise money from 1983, when the temple was founded, to 1996, when the chapel was completed. Reminiscing about those days, Kamala said, "Each time we had a [board] meeting, we talked about the same thing: 'no money, no money.'" Coming up with creative ways to raise money through tapping into the notion of *thambun* is crucial for Wat Thai's survival. To encourage participants to *thambun* to build a wall around the temple property, metal recognition plaques inscribed with the names of contributors—some in Thai and others in English—were designed and later placed along the finished wall. Although the plaques have rusted, they serve to acknowledge and honor the merit makers.[3]

A few previous forms of fundraising, such as beauty pageants, were abandoned because some thought they did not reflect well on the temple. Other forms have emerged and gradually developed. One example is the creation of the Sunday food court. In 1988, a temple member lost her job. To help her out, she was permitted to sell snacks at the temple. This activity mushroomed into a group of women selling homemade food on Sundays. While selling food, these women also offered alms to the monks. At that time, the board required only that sellers pay $25 a month for access to the facilities and donate the money they made at big events. The food court continued to grow. In 2002 the board changed the rules: Only volunteers who donate all profits may sell at the food court. Expenses can be reimbursed. The new regulations have provided the temple with a fairly predictable income stream. According to one board member, in the old days the food court raised only $5,000–$6,000 annually for the temple. After the new rules were implemented, however, the food court began netting $1,000–$2,000 every Sunday. Gradually, this amount increased to about $3,000. In 2010, Alan, the Farang Hispanic board member, told me that the food court often made about $5,000 each Sunday. "The economy is bad, but people still need to eat," he said. "People like the atmosphere and the food here." Over time, informal selling and merit making has transformed into institutionalized merit making and fundraising.

Major temple activities are organized around annual events such as International New Year, Magha Puja Day, Thai New Year, Visakh Puja Day, Buddhist Lent, memorial services for the departed, birthday celebrations for Thailand's king and queen, the folk festival Loi Krathong, and so on.[4] One such event takes place every month. Sometimes several functions are celebrated in a single day.[5] No matter how varied in content, all events include merit making.

In dealing with money, Wat Thai follows the principles of non-profit organizations. "Transparency is the main ideology that we have," Sombun said. The board publicizes expenditures—the purchase price of property and its monthly mortgage payment, for example—and income such as donation totals and the amount of money made at the food court. Merit makers are issued a receipt with the temple's non-profit tax identification number and a statement that the donation is tax-deductible. To honor those who give, the names of the merit makers and the amounts are published in the temple's monthly newsletter. In referring to the temple being run in a quasi-corporate manner, Luang Pho once said, "Americanness is working here."

The board carefully decides how and when to spend the temple's resources. The board members sometimes have heated discussions—for example, when they debated the right time to begin constructing the chapel. In 1994, after nine years of fundraising, Luang Pho suggested starting construction. He predicted that "more money would come" when people saw the ground broken for the chapel. "People like to *thambun*; the key is how you can match their expectations," he said. However, some board members, especially Farang, wanted to have all of the needed money in hand because they deemed it unwise to start building without guarantees that funds would be available to complete the project. Finally, Mani, who had won the bid to construct the chapel, convinced the board to commence. "If the money runs out, I'll stop," she promised. "If I can advance, I will keep working. If it takes two or three years, it'll be fine with me." Her willingness to take this risk helped the board make its final decision to begin.

Sure enough, just as Luang Pho predicted, donations increased once construction began. For many practitioners, it was very gratifying to see the chapel actually being built. Indeed, some were so proud that they gave as much as they possibly could. Sami, a hairdresser, told me that she saved all her tips to contribute to the building of the chapel. Consequently, Wat Thai's two-story chapel was completed in just twenty-one months (February 14, 1995–November 24, 1996). It cost about $1.2 million dollars to build, paint, decorate, and furnish the chapel.

By the end of 1999, Wat Thai was debt-free. In 2004, the board of directors, with the permission of the board of trustees, bought an adjacent parcel of land (about an acre) for $1.6 million. Some temple participants were unhappy about taking on the debt. One person told me that the land was purchased because the board of directors "thinks like an entrepreneur" (*khit baeb turakit*). Alan believed that the temple "already had enough space" and voted against the purchase but he was outvoted.

When the pressure to raise money increases, monks work more vigorously to boost merit making. Some monks, especially abbots, are skillful in knowing whom to approach for donations. I witnessed a fund-raising solicitation. On July 1, 2007, five women and I were celebrating with Yok, an Isan woman, at her home on her birthday. Luang Pho and Maha Singtong knocked on the door to wish Yok a happy birthday; Yok invited them in. The monks sat on the sofa; we sat on the floor. The monks chanted and tied white strings, in typical Isan style, on Yok's wrist. The string symbolizes being blessed and provides protection. Luang Pho mentioned in passing, with a smile, that the monks would be happy to perform a ritual to bless the new roof that Yok had just put on her house. Then he asked Yok whether she would consider making merit by giving $1,000 to commission the painting of a small mural for the chapel, commemorating the death of the Buddha and his entry into nirvana. How could Yok possibly turn down this chance to make merit on her birthday? Luang Pho asked for $1,000; she offered $1,500. Later, Luang Pho told me that he knew she would. Not long before, Yok and her husband, Phillip, had donated a $26,000 van to the temple.

Luang Pho knows how and when to approach someone who has money. He is not alone. Luang Dae, the late abbot of Wat Thai of Los Angeles, helped raise money for Wat Thai when it was needed most. Thongchan, the engineer with a doctorate, shared his experience with me. "Luang Dae was a very, very good salesman. He could sell any-thing," Thongchan said. "Once he talked to me while holding a basket of eggs [that someone had offered to the monks]. Nobody can persuade me to do anything I don't want to do, but he did. I don't like eggs. He convinced me to buy the eggs [for $20]. I don't know how he did it." Indeed, head monks such as Luang Pho and Luang Dae are shrewd businessmen. Below are the five key strategies the board of directors uses to tap into notions of merit making, marketing, Thai popular cul-ture, and American middle-class taste.

Institutional Merit-Making Strategies

First, the board of directors publicizes the amount of money needed for each endeavor. For example, construction blueprints and an art-ist's sketch of the chapel were put on display so people could see them and sponsor the project. If there is no ongoing project, I was told, a temple risks ultimately disappearing. Arun, the artist who painted the chapel murals, said that Luang Pho had assured him that "the temple will never be poor; if we keep moving the temple forward, people will always donate." Being part of one project engages participants in other projects. It is like buying a piece of land then putting buildings on it.

Second, even though all the money raised is deposited into a single account, merit-making activities are organized as if there were separate accounts. For example, the chapel's four donation boxes were all labeled "donation" in English. However, the boxes were labeled in Thai, "Taking care of the water and electricity bill," "Taking care of the temple's general spending," "Buying land to expand the temple," and "Money for the monks' food." I did not realize the importance of itemization until I compared the total amount each box generated over a period of several years. The box to pay the water and electricity bills received more money than the other three. I asked why. One person said, "A person will have a brighter future and greater prosperity by donating money to pay for the electric bill." Another said, "You want to give something back to the temple, because you have used the water and electricity. Otherwise, bad luck will follow you." Giving the boxes different captions reveals a conscious effort to market to Thai and non-Thai patrons.

The itemization strategy prompts people to sponsor particular projects. While the chapel was being built, the cost to build the bathrooms, elevator, and other items was posted. Different parts of the chapel carried different cultural meanings. As a result, about $100,000 was donated to build the bathrooms, but not one penny for the elevator. This occurred because of a folk belief that one accumulates greater merit by building bathrooms. Providing facilities to enable people to relieve themselves, a symbolic release of suffering, is a right act. In contrast, an elevator does not bear such meaning, in part because chapels in Thailand typically are one-story structures.

The third strategy is to reconfigure merit making to adjust to the new social conditions in the United States. When Wat Thai had only a few dozen members, everyone was welcome to offer food to the monks. In those days, the monks sometimes did not receive enough to eat, especially on weekdays, and had to buy food from nearby take-out restaurants. Nowadays, however, as the number of temple visitors has grown—and especially at big events—the monks cannot possibly consume all the food people wish to give. The solution? Canned food,

Figure 5.1. Repackaging, 2005. (Photograph by the author.)

which the monks seldom eat but which can be easily stored and used as a symbolic offering over and over again, is sold at the temple.

Some of the most innovative ideas for fundraising come from the monks. One example was creating wall plaques out of the $100 bills that Queen Sirikit had donated to Wat Thai. Than Gabriel told me that Maha Aphai, the handy monk, came up with the idea and designed the plaques. Maha Aphai placed the $100 bill in the center of the frame and surrounded it with five powerful images: a photograph of Queen Sirikit taken when she was visiting Wat Thai, her royal logo, a Buddhist symbol inscribed in a sacred ancient Khmer language, a picture of a high-ranking monk, and a picture of the chapel's foundation stone (Figure 5.1). The twenty framed $100 bills were used to make merit twice: first by the queen who donated them, then by the practitioners who purchased the plaques for $500 apiece. Thus, the queen's $2,000 was turned into $10,000. As Than Gabriel noted, "The plaques only cost $2. Low cost, high return."

Some reconfigurations reflect middle-class taste. For example, during Thai New Year in April 2009, the temple organized the release of doves, instead of sparrows, the bird typically released in Thailand. According to the Buddha's teachings, releasing life is a righteous act.

In the United States, releasing doves adds a new meaning: connecting Buddhism with peace. The monks and laypeople are aware that releasing doves is a reenactment not a real release, like freeing sparrows in Thailand, because the doves return to their trainers. Nevertheless, they are willing to join together to perform as a cosmopolitan Buddhist community.

Before the birds or fish are freed, merit makers hold a white string that passes through the crowd and touches the bird cage or the fish container. The purpose is to make sure that the monks' blessings pass on to every being. The moment that the birds fly into the sky or the fish swim into the lake, the monks chant in Pali. "The words of the chants, little understood by the laity[,] . . . are considered powerful in themselves; they are words of the Buddha, they embody his power, and the recitation of them brings effects" (Tambiah 1968: 101–102). Moreover, making merit is combined with preserving the environment. Before fish are released at a lake in a nearby park, great care is taken to ensure that the fish are compatible with the indigenous species.

To release a life, one needs to pay the price set by the organizer: $29 for a dove and $9 for a fish. It is worth noting that these prices end in nine. In Thai, "nine" linguistically implies "making progress in all directions" (*kaona kaolang*). The organizers tap into this popular notion of lucky numbers. To make merit and perhaps to court good fortune, the major sponsor, a restaurant owner, donated $1,399.99 in 2009. The total raised by releasing fish and birds for that year was $5,415.99 of which Wat Thai donated $2,400 to the park.

The fourth strategy is typified by reifying Thainess to downplay the economic aspects of merit making. In the 1990s, a brochure listed fundraising as one of the reasons for holding Classical Night once a year.[6] Since the early 2000s, however, fundraising as a goal has been omitted from the brochure. Instead, Classical Night has been promoted as a "showcase of Thai culture" and to "strengthen the cultural bond" between Thai Americans and the United States, as well as to honor Thailand's king and queen.[7] Sponsors—primarily restaurants, entrepreneurs, realtors, doctors, importers, financial advisers, and travel agencies—were categorized in the program as gold or silver supporters, depending on the amount of money pledged. In the 2000s, Classical Night typically raised $14,000–$15,000 in a single evening.

The fifth strategy is to inscribe inexpensive items with symbolic meaning and sell them as objects for merit making on the temple grounds. This approach is an old practice in Thailand and other Southeast Asian Buddhist countries, but it is new in the United States. For example, three sticks of incense along with a finger-size candle and a few gold leaves sell for $5. The three sticks of incense symbolize the Buddha, the Dharma, and the Sangha. The candle represents enlightenment, and the gold leaves honor Buddha's teachings. A $10 offering package includes a spool of thread, needles, pencils, and more gold leaves. The thread indicates a long life; needles symbolize intelligence; a pencil indicates the ability to learn; and the ten pieces of gold leaf, each about one inch square, are used to gild the Buddha statue. A $50 package contains a robe, canned food, soap, envelopes, laundry detergent, tea, aspirin, toothpaste, and the like. The most expensive gift basket sells for $150 and includes $50 in cash. The price for a gift basket is higher than its actual cost. However, most people appreciate the convenience and would give the money to the temple anyway. These gift baskets are rarely opened but rather are resold over and over again. This process, again, shows that participants and monks are rational actors; they simultaneously are influenced by and act on merit making.

Each merit maker sometimes acts as a performer and sometimes as a member of the audience. Some give without mentioning it to anyone, believing that merit making to impress others can become an attachment rather than a liberation. Others carefully calculate how much to give and which project to sponsor to gain maximum merit in return. Luang Pho keeps track of attendance figures, how much money the temple raises at each event, and what needs to be improved or changed the next time.

Money is empowering. As Wat Thai becomes prosperous, it attracts more visitors and merit makers, and it can give more back to the larger society and to those in need. Every year, the temple donates money and supplies to a homeless shelter and to a Head Start program at a nearby elementary school. The donations are timed to arrive on the birthday of Thailand's king, Bhumibol Adulyadej. In other words, the temple is simultaneously supporting local institutions and making merit for the Thai monarch. Immediately following the terrorist attacks of September 11, 2001, Wat Thai members sold red ribbons to raise money to help those who suffered from the attack. Neighbors, regardless of their faiths, came to pray at the temple. The community also raised more than $15,000 for post-disaster relief after the Indian Ocean earthquake and tsunami of 2004 and conducted a ritual to transfer merit to those who had died. Mayors and other local officials took part in the ritual to pay respect to those who had lost their lives. Combining compassion, professional management techniques, and growth-oriented capitalist practices with merit making works at Wat Thai.

Making Food, Making Merit: Food as Identity and Social Glue

Merit making is not limited to giving money, food, medicine, and goods but also includes volunteer work such as teaching classes at the temple school and cooking and selling food at the food court. Although the food court is open for only a few hours on Sundays, preparation takes many hours.[8] Operating the food court on this scale requires a cadre of dedicated volunteers and enormous amounts of time, compassion, and commitment. The volunteers come from a wide range of professions, from homemakers and engineers to entrepreneurs and nurses. Among them are several members of the Parent-Teacher Association (PTA). Sometimes husbands and wives or mothers and daughters form teams. In 2012, Alan, the Hispanic Catholic; Michael, a Chinese Filipino engineer; and Matthew, a Farang engineer, formed a crew to cook Thai barbeque. A few former *dekwat*, or "temple boys," who temporarily lived at the temple and assisted the monks, joined them during the Thai New Year celebration, the biggest fundraising event at Wat Thai. However, the backbone of the food court is a core group of women who cook month after month, year after year (Figure 5.2).

Suwanna, who stated, "This temple is open to everyone, including cats and dogs," began cooking at the food court after she was widowed in 2006. She described working at the food court as "*marathon* cooking." To prepare for the two-day celebration of Thai New Year, Suwanna bought supplies on a Thursday in April 2009. On Friday, she soaked twenty-five packages of dried rice noodles, peeled and deveined buckets of ice-cold shrimp, chopped tofu, washed bean sprouts, squeezed lemons, and ground peanuts, the various ingredients of her specialty, Pad Thai (stir-fried noodles). While preparing the food, she prepared herself physically by wearing a full back brace to withstand the heavy lifting and the long hours of standing. She played Thai music as she worked, chatted with other volunteers, and greeted acquaintances who stopped by. On Saturday, she cooked and sold food from 8:00 A.M. to 4:00 P.M. Her Pad Thai was in such demand that people waited in line

Figure 5.2. Preparing food, 2012. (Photograph by the author.)

for an hour. That evening, she had to shop for the next day. On Sunday, she started cooking and selling the Pad Thai even earlier. In two days, she raised $1,319. Suwanna could easily have written a check for more than this amount, because she often made big donations.

Such marathon cooking sessions are a shared experience. Kamala explained the labor involved in barbecuing pork:

> You have to do a lot of preparation. I ordered the pork. I brought all the pork over here [to the temple]—50 pounds, 100 pounds, sometimes 150 pounds. I had to come early from San Jose, never later than 5:00 A.M. Light the fire, the propane. Burn the charcoal. I can burn the charcoal in two minutes. By 9:00 A.M., I had to have a lot of it done or at 10:00 A.M. people would have to stand in line. Boy, I was tired. My hands smelled like barbeque. My whole body smelled like barbeque. But I was in a good mood. I made money for the temple.

She did this not just on one occasion but for eight years. Moreover, she never asked to be reimbursed for her expenses. Similarly, Yok, who sponsored the mural on her birthday, volunteered at the food court for more than a dozen years. Her Farang husband, Phillip, did not know how to cook Thai food but helped load and unload supplies and ran errands when Yok needed something. For the Thai New Year celebration in 2009, the couple began preparing Thai desserts a week in advance, ultimately raising $3,155.

The PTA was allotted several cooking stalls because the school needed money to pay for musical instruments and dance costumes for the students, health insurance for the teachers from Thailand, and so on. Some parents volunteered every weekend; other parents pitched in when they could. At first, Doi dropped her daughter and son off at the temple school, then left. After a while, she said, she questioned herself: "They [the volunteer teachers and food court cooks] have their own lives, right? But they dedicate every single Sunday to the students." Doi began working as a substitute teacher. Later, she was elected president of the PTA and volunteered at the food court. Now she prepares food every Saturday and sells it on Sunday. Her husband, a computer engineer, maintains the computers at Wat Thai and serves on the board of directors. Their daughter and son go to the temple to take classes and play with friends. Doi's mother-in-law, who has offered food to the monks every Wednesday for many years, sometimes joins them. The whole family spends Sunday at the temple.

Natee, the registered nurse who sent her daughter, Muay, to a Catholic school, has been cooking at the food court almost every Sunday since 1992, the year her daughter attended the temple school. In 2006, Muay, by then a student at the University of California, San Diego, said, "My mom loves to cook. She sells food for the temple to raise money, and she gets to gossip with all the parents. I'm sure she enjoys it. I know she loves the temple or she wouldn't be doing this. Especially now she wouldn't be doing this since I am gone. I know some parents: when their kid leaves, they leave, too. This does not affect my mom. Isn't that amazing?" Natee does love to cook and chat, but most of all, she loves the children. I saw her at the temple checking on the kids running around, calling them "my child" in Thai, and making sure they had eaten lunch. The board of directors has acknowledged Natee more than once as parent of the year and rewarded her with her own parking space. In 2012, during the celebration of the queen's birthday, Natee was cooking at her station as usual. "How is your daughter?" I asked. "She is now a nurse practitioner in New York," Natee replied. "She is doing better than me." Her voice was loud, and she was proud.

Donating their labor and skills also allows these volunteer cooks to articulate their regional identities via their dishes. Each cook specializes in one or two dishes. Volunteers from southern Thailand often prepare coconut-milk dishes with green, yellow, or red curry. Northern-style food tends to be hot and sour. Ethnic Lao from Isan often cook barbecued chicken, papaya salad, and sticky rice. Ethnic Thai and Chinese from central Thailand make noodles known as *kuitieo*, Pad Thai, and other stir-fried dishes. Of course, there are exceptions. Natee, who was from southern Thailand, made an excellent southern Chinese-style porridge with shrimp, garlic, and cilantro. I have seldom tasted such delicious porridge. She revealed to me that she had learned to cook Chinese dishes because her husband was from Hong Kong.

On Sundays, many Thais meet friends and eat at the food court. The cooking smells; the sound of green papaya, cherry tomatoes, and peanuts being pounded in a mortar with a pestle and of pork sizzling on the grill; and the colors of the vegetables being stir-fried all remind them of home. The volunteers often switch back and forth between English and their mother tongue, joke with one another, and exchange bites of dishes they have prepared. *Sanuk*, a Thai word for fun, often is evoked to express their mood while eating and working at the food court.

At Wat Thai, food is often used as a medium through which to connect and communicate with people. When military personnel studying the Thai language at the Defense Language Institute Foreign Language Center in Monterey, California, went to Wat Thai to experience Thai culture, they were invited to eat Thai food. So were students and teachers from a German-American International School in San Mateo. Neighbors are invited to a "Thank You" party to eat, discuss their concerns, and make suggestions. In other words, whether a visitor is a soldier or a student or a neighbor, he or she is made to feel at ease through food.

Thai food attracts diners who come to the temple to eat "authentic" but inexpensive Thai food.[9] Dining under a canopy of giant trees next to the chapel, among a cheerful crowd of people speaking many different languages enhances the community atmosphere. For a while, the Internet-based urban guide Yelp ranked the food court as the top Thai

restaurant in the region. The board of directors tries to balance raising money with maintaining the character of the temple. One director
posted a correction on Yelp clarifying that Wat Thai is a "Buddhist
temple, *not* a restaurant."

The food court has unexpectedly provided a window of opportunity for Thai food lovers to explore the temple. After a big meal, some
diners walk around the temple and peek at the mural inside the chapel
or talk to the monks. They rarely experience nervousness or intimida-
tion that some first-time temple visitors might. The food court brings
people together and serves as a gateway to Wat Thai. Most important,
the food court has sustained the temple and the temple school.[10]

Patronage through Transnational Merit Making

Distance is no longer an obstacle for making merit. In fact, giving can
be conducted anywhere. Thailand's King Bhumibol offered Buddha
statues to Wat Thai in Los Angeles and to Wat Dhammaram in Chicago in the 1970s. Although no overseas Thai temple has royal status,
the king still gives royal robes to distinguished overseas Thai temples
at the end of Buddhist Lent each year. Through giving, the king reinforces his image as the biggest patron of Thai Buddhist temples. Other
members of the royal family are patrons of Thai American temples,
as well. Queen Sirikit visits overseas temples when she tours abroad.
Since 1994, Princess Bhansawali Kitiyakara has visited Wat Thai several times and made merit by sponsoring a chapel mural and cooking
and selling shark fin soup at the temple to *thambun*. She also played
a decisive role in helping Wat Thai receive a royal robe from the king
in 2004. The Thai royal family goes to great lengths to promote Thai
Buddhism and to connect with overseas Thais while simultaneously
making merit for themselves. Similarly, high-ranking monks and political figures, including Chavalit Yongchaiyudh, a general and former
prime minister (1996–1997), made merit at Wat Thai. Thaksin Shi-
nawatra, another former prime minister (2001–2006), never visited, but
he donated $2,000 via his former teacher, a member of Wat Thai. Wat
Paknum, a royal temple in Bangkok, not only provided financial support to Wat Thai and other overseas temples but also established Wat
Mongkoltepmunee in Philadelphia as its branch.

Just as these rich and powerful elites have made merit in the United
States, some members of Wat Thai have contributed money to those

in need in Thailand, participating in a kind of a merit-making circle. Every spring, the temple holds a communal merit-making ritual, *Phapa* Solidarity, to raise money for the education of young monks at a temple in Bangkok now headed by Maha Aphai. *Phapa* literally means "clothes forest." Nowadays, the *phapa* has been transformed into a handmade money tree that is decorated with currency of different denominations.[11] Such a configuration allows even those without much money to make merit and display their generosity.

Luang Pho also raises money for his home village in Isan. His village is made up of approximately 225 households of about 1,400 people, two Buddhist temples, one elementary school, and two small stores. Only about half the population, mostly seniors and children, reside in the village. The others live and work in Bangkok or in another urban area, a common phenomenon in Isan.

In 2007, I visited his village to study the effects Wat Thai's donations have had on the lives of the villagers. I quickly learned that the education fund (588,000 baht) has had a great impact on students, teachers, and families. (Over the past thirty years, the exchange rate has fluctuated between 20 baht and 35 baht to the U.S. dollar. In November 2014, the rate was about 32.85 baht to the dollar.) According to the principal, the fund is used for many purposes, such as improving the facilities, granting scholarships, offering low-interest loans to teachers and staff, and financing the lunch project. The lunch project feeds about 130 elementary school students daily, based on a budget of 800 baht a day, providing one or two dishes to go with the rice the children bring from home. Teachers and students plant vegetables and raise chickens to insure a steady food supply. Scholarships for middle-school through college-age students are not taken from the education fund; instead, they are provided separately by members of Wat Thai. The goal of these student scholarships, which range from as little as 100 baht to as much as 50,000 baht, is to give every child in the village a chance to acquire higher education.

Certain funds are designed to meet the particular needs of the villagers. To insure that the money will last and benefit future generations, only the interest, not the principal, is spent on projects, such as improving the reliability of the electricity supply and renovating a medical clinic. To raise living standards, the "Occupation Development for Housewives" fund (120,000 baht) provides no-interest microloans to enable women to buy material to weave cotton and silk textiles and mats to sell, thus providing much-needed cash for their households. The fund for planting trees has grown from 70,000 baht to 96,800 baht due to interest earned. Planting trees involved almost everyone in the village. For the first few years, the students watered the trees by hand to ensure their survival. Now the once tiny trees are thriving.

By far the most money, however, has been spent to renovate the village's primary Buddhist temple. Building a temple is, indeed, perceived as the most meritorious act and a good investment. Suwanna donated 5.5 million baht for the construction as a way to transfer merit to her parents and her deceased Farang husband. (A few "rich widows," I was told, generously gave money to Wat Thai as a way to transfer their merit to a deceased Farang husband, regardless of whether he was a Buddhist). Just as the monarchy is the patron of overseas Thai, members of Wat Thai are patrons of these villagers.

A Happy Business

Merit making might seem paradoxical: One gives to be detached from the material world, but giving requires having accumulated material wealth. Merit makers, as we have seen, are caught between a desire for detachment to reduce suffering and a longing to accumulate merit for future lives. This apparent contradiction makes my point: Everyday messy Buddhist practices are shaped by capitalist socioeconomic systems and Buddhist cultural logic. Capitalist practices—marketing, reconfigured forms of fundraising, sophisticated management techniques, and letting money make money effectively—strengthen rather than weaken merit making.

The synthesis of Buddhist and capitalist practices allows money to flow in the blink of an eye between Thailand and the United States to meet the demands of long-distance merit making. The circulation of resources connects Thais across national borders. Nevertheless, religious capital gained from merit making, royal robes, honorary Buddhist titles, or awards granted by the Thai state carry limited significance outside Wat Thai, let alone being convertible into symbolic capital. Converting economic capital into religious capital in Thailand can be read as a form of resisting the inconvertibility of religious and symbolic capital in American society.

The phrase "happy business," coined in English by Luang Pho, distinguishes merit making from a business involved in providing goods or services in exchange for money. The term highlights the tension between the yearning for happiness and the need for money to prove one's piety and support the temple. A person who gives generously is considered a good Buddhist. A monk who raises money for the temple is perceived as a good monk. A resourceful temple is considered a good temple, as it can provide space for people to practice, heal, relax, and better develop a sense of well-being. Without financial and material support and an entrepreneurial spirit, Buddhist temples could not operate; practitioners would have no place to go to confirm their moral worth, and monks would have no food, robes, medicine, and shelter.

As social agents, the participants—Thais and non-Thais, laypeople and monks—continuously build their temple and their community. The board of directors serves as a liaison between people of different faiths and cultures. Monks have developed their business acumen to engage with participants and the existing capitalist system. The volunteers at the food court nurture not only the monks and the students but also the patrons who enjoy Thai cuisine. Collectively, they rearticulate who they are to a new audience who is not familiar with or prejudiced against their practices.

Furthermore, through giving, elderly participants gain hope that family problems may be solved; volunteers who teach, cook, clean, and repair the temple feel rewarded as the temple community continues to prosper. Through giving, the monarchy reinforces its power and former sex workers are redeemed. Giving and doing things for others make participants happy. When one has nothing to give, one has a hard time demonstrating one's moral worth to the community and has little hope of being reborn higher in a future life. Merit making, to a certain extent, camouflages class privilege.

Merit making is conducted within complex webs of regulations and relationships. It is simultaneously a spiritual and economic practice, and it articulates both reciprocity and emotion. Merit making—a forum for translating economic capital into religious capital and for displaying class status and moral worth—becomes part of a cultural and religious struggle, both for the individual and the community. Perhaps in the near future, accepting offerings may no longer be misread as "living off of charity."

6

Shaping and Performing
Thai American Identities

I am Thai, though I was born and raised in a foreign land.
As I continue to thrive, day in and day out, people ask me who
    I am.
Yellow skin, pretty face, small body, thin waist.
Neither black nor white.
Generous and kind.
They say I am a good person.
Wherever in the world I may live, my blood is Thai.
Even though I may be far away from my motherland,
I take pride in being Thai.
Deeply loyal to the nation, the religion, and the king.
I will do good deeds, accumulate virtue, and live up to what it
    means to be a Buddhist.

"I Am Thai" (*Chan ben khunthai*), the song quoted above, is taught and sung at many overseas Thai temples.[1] It refers to Thailand as the "motherland." Good behavior, "yellow skin," and "[Thai] blood" are depicted as markers of being "Thai" and "Buddhist." The self-evident aspect of identity is informed by an ideology in which the nation, Buddhism, and the monarchy are viewed as the "three pillars" of Thai society. The lyrics were written by Prapasri Siha-ompai, a professor at Chula and a founder of the Teaching Thai Language and

Culture Abroad Program.[2] Since 1983, the Teaching Abroad Program has trained professional educators who volunteer to teach for a year or for a summer at Thai temple schools in the United States.[3] The curriculum developed by the program corresponds with the elementary school curriculum in Thailand, which is known for "its ideological and moralistic content, with a steady stress on gratitude and obligation" (Mulder 1997: 64). Temple schools become key sites for cultivating a sense of belonging and affection for Thailand. Meanwhile, the National Council on Social Welfare of Thailand has invited overseas students to perform Thai classical dance and music at national celebrations to raise money for the royal family's charity projects. Students are also encouraged to participate in Thailand's "Return to the Motherland" campaign (Teachout 2005: 13). Operating an overseas temple school is a transnational venture, supported by parents, volunteer teachers, and the temple community as well as Thai authorities.

The joint aim of the temple school and the Teaching Abroad Program is to integrate these youth into what Benedict Anderson (1983) has called an "imagined community." By "imagined," Anderson means that people who define themselves as "members of even the smallest nation will never know most of their fellow-members, meet them, or even hear of them, yet in the minds of each lives the image of their communion" (Anderson 1983: 15). Such a community is created and reinforced through the media, the Internet, museums, maps, and so forth. In particular, "through that language, encountered at mother's knee and parted with only at the grave, pasts are restored, fellowships are imagined, and futures dreamed" (Anderson 1983: 140).

Language plays a crucial role in bonding young students with the Thai community. Learning Thai *body language*, I suggest, is as important as linguistic ability. Body techniques are imposed by authorities (Mauss 1979: 109). For example, *waiing*—bringing the hands to a prayer-like gesture—is the most common body gesture for greetings, thanks, apologies, and good-byes. Appropriate social manners become objects of enforcement and monitoring by the Thai state, schools, and parents. Knowing how to use body language, in responding to one's standing within the social hierarchy, expresses cultural identity.

In "The Mindful Body," Nancy Scheper-Hughes and Margaret Lock (1987: 7) show the relationships between different kinds of bodies. They suggest three "separate and overlapping" realms of bodies: first, the "individual body," or the learned body-self (Mauss 1979); second, the "social body, referring to the representational uses of the body as a natural symbol with which to think about nature, society, and culture"; and third, the "body politic," regarding the control, regulation, monitoring, and management of bodies (Foucault 1979, 1980; Turner 1980). The mindful body captures the interconnection of the three different bodies, just as the body politic regulates the social body and shapes the individual body (Scheper-Hughes and Lock 1987: 8).

The Wat Thai temple school socializes youngsters and reproduces culturally appreciated individuals compatible with both American and Thai social bodies and teaches the youngsters how to act and *become* Thai Americans. In analyzing the process of how these youths are both self-making and being made, I consider the extent to which the temple school shapes their bodies and identities through "fun" activities—singing songs, dancing, and playing music—along with language drills, practicing body language, and learning Buddhist ethics. Second, I examine how youth reconcile Thai and American cultural expectations by performing their identities contextually. The tension between parent and child is not just generational but also tension between two social bodies. Similar to their parents and teachers, Thai American youth engage with not one but two clusters of cultural principles and arrays of regulations. These young Thai Americans, I suggest, are not docile receptacles of Thai cultural knowledge because they work both with and against Thai cultural principles. By selectively including some aspects of Thai practices and excluding others, teaching, learning, and practicing become a performance of Thai American identity.

The Organization of the Temple School

Temple participants refer to the school as *rongrian wat* (temple school) or just *rongrian* (school) in Thai. However, when they switch to English, they refer to it as Sunday school. To avoid the unwanted connotations of Sunday school, I refer to it as "the temple school" or just "the school." The stated goal of the temple school is "to teach and promote the Thai language, Thai art, and Thai culture as well as Thai customs to Thai youth and those who are interested."[4] However, in practice, more is going on than this. Achan Prem, who founded the temple school with Apinya (the first principal), said: "We need to *make* them proud to say, 'I am a Thai American.' We need to make them understand that being a Thai American is not something to be ashamed of.

It is something to be proud of. . . . That is why the school teaches not just the Thai language, but [also] Thai traditions, Thai history, where we come from and what we should be proud of for being Thai. *We want them to understand their ethnic group and the ethnic values that can be added to American society as a whole*" (emphasis added). Achan Prem hoped that "Thai tradition and history" would take hold in the United States so that others would be aware of the existence of Thais. Apinya stated that the school tries to "help the kids to stick together and to have their own network. Also, if it is possible, we want them to help Thailand." Achan Prem and Apinya, like many Thais I knew, emphasized the importance of cultivating Thai American identity among these youths.

The temple school is open to children (kindergarten to high school age) and adults. Most children are American-born Thai and "half Thai"; most adults are Farang interested in learning the Thai language. The number of students fluctuates throughout the year from a few dozen to more than a hundred. Some students are coerced by their parents into attending; others love to come. Some drop out after one or two years. Others attend the temple school for fifteen years or longer, from age five to when they go off to college and even during their college years if they live nearby.

The academic year is divided into spring, summer, and fall semesters. The school normally holds five or six classes each semester, organized by proficiency level. The class schedule and curriculum have been modified over the years. At present, the school begins with an assembly, followed by Thai language classes on Sunday mornings. Cultural classes, which include dance and music, are offered on Sunday afternoons. (Some music and dance students rehearse on Friday nights and Saturdays, especially when a performance is coming up.) Buddhist ethics is offered once a month. Summer school focuses primarily on teaching the Thai language.

The temple school is led by a volunteer principal. Since 1983, all but two of the principals have been women. The principal and the abbot recruit new teachers, Thai and non-Thai. For example, when Sabrina, the Farang who attended rituals to practice meditation, was recruited to teach Buddhist ethics, her immediate response was "You need a Thai person [to teach the class]." Luang Pho persuaded her. "When our children go to school, they're all Westerners doing the teaching," he said. "They need to see that Westerners do participate in

Buddhism, and they need to have good role models, both Thais and Westerners."

Over the years, teachers have come from four main sources. Some are local volunteers, mostly Thai immigrants; other are monks who teach meditation and chanting; Farang who teach Buddhist ethics; and six to eight junior and senior professional teachers whom Wat Thai annually receives from the Teaching Abroad Program.[5] The junior teachers—often one language instructor, two music teachers, and one dance instructor—teach during the fall and spring semesters.[6] The senior teachers usually teach the Thai language, songs, games, and handicrafts in the summer.[7] These local volunteers, monks, Farang, and the overseas teachers form the backbone of the temple school.

In short, the temple school has changed from depending on locals to having professional teachers come from Thailand, from free to charging a fee, and from informal to formal.[8] The chain of volunteer teachers has never been broken. "We all have the same goal: We want our children to be bilingual [and not to] forget our culture," one parent said. The following discussion is about how the Teaching Abroad Program trained teachers before sending them to the United States.

Teacher Training: Reproducing Thainess

In Thai society, teachers are regarded as *maephim khong chat*. The word *mae* means "mother"; *phim* means "print"; and *chat* means "nation." It is hard to translate the phrase precisely into English. However, it is clear that teachers are projected as role models who *mold* future Thai subjects. Thai authorities pay great attention to the quality of the teachers who are sent to overseas temples.

According to Professor Penchan, the director of the Teaching Abroad Program, whom I interviewed in 2007, the main goal of the month-long orientation program is to train these teachers to instill Thainess in their students. Experts in various fields are invited to give lectures.[9] The director of one of Thailand's preeminent dance and music troupes lectured on Thai dance and music, mapping out the interconnections among dance, music, Thainess, and history. A martial arts instructor demonstrated basic techniques of Muay (Thai kickboxing), which is considered *the* Thai sport. An etiquette expert was invited to teach elegant manners. Teachers have to practice a complex set of bodily techniques, such as showing respect via the *wai*, genu-flecting, sitting, and walking with poise in response to different social situations and hierarchical orders. "One has to *feel* it and express that feeling through the act. You pay respect to someone and you smile," said Professor Vatsana, who was in charge of teaching Buddhism and social manners for the program. Teachers are urged to teach body language according to a national standard, even if they habitually use body language incorrectly themselves. The training connects Thai music, dance, and social manners with Thainess, which is perceived as stable, distinctive, and exclusive.

The training program requires the teachers to live at a Buddhist temple for about a week. Each day is packed with activities from 5:00 A.M. to 9:30 P.M. Teachers are encouraged to eat vegetarian food to deepen their understanding of the notion of not taking life. They are given instructions on how to interact respectfully with monks, because living at a temple will be a new experience. The teachers also practice silent meditation so they will have a rudimentary understanding of it, in case the monk who teaches meditation needs assistance. Professor Vatsana advised the teachers to "endure" the pain of sitting meditation and be mindful of whatever they do. "Most of them were not used to doing silent meditation or being mindful when they sit, walk, and eat," she said.

The program attempts to mold these teachers into refined Thai cultural ambassadors. The teachers are also evaluated at the end of each spring semester by Chula faculty members sent to the United States.[10] These volunteer teachers' minds and bodies are carefully monitored and regulated, just like those of their students.

Parents: The Driving Force of the Temple School

In 2012, Luang Pho estimated that about half of the parents of the students at the temple school were engineers. The parents are chiefly interested in helping their children become bilingual and bicultural. Many parents find that the temple provides a much more inviting environment than home for their children to study. Thomthong, a teacher of English as a Second Language who suffered downward class mobility in the United States, volunteered at the school. "I really wanted my children to know Thai, but I could not teach them by myself, because they won't listen to me," Thomthong said. "When they came to the temple, they had new friends and played together. They went to class for a little while, learning the alphabet, learning the vowels, and then learning the grammar. Then they came out and played again. And then they had some snacks. That's fun for them. See?"

It was a shared belief that students would absorb Thai values just by being at the temple. Yui, a Thai Muslim who married a Russian American, said in an interview, "When I told my daughter what to do in the Thai way and she said, 'Mama, I'm *not* Thai, I'm *American*,' I felt kind of hurt." She coaxed her daughter into going to the temple. At the same time, Yui volunteered as a teacher and eventually served for three years as the temple school's principal.

Persuading teenagers to attend the temple school sometimes creates tension between parents and children (Cheah 2011: 105–106; Numrich 1996: 97). Some parents are afraid that if they do not take their children to the temple school early on, later in life they may not go at all. Jelena, a female software engineer and the temple school's principal from 2008 to 2010, pointed out, "It is much easier to teach children when they are young. When the vine is getting old, it is harder to bend it." One former student reflected that "taking classes from such a young age anchored within me beat, rhythm, and visual learning—all things I know I could not live without today."[11]

Parents invest a lot of time and energy in the temple school. Ludda, another software engineer who served as principal from 2000 to 2004, said, "If I want my kids to succeed, I have to put in the time." Her daughter attended from kindergarten until she graduated from high school. She learned to speak fluent Thai and performed classical Thai dance. Ludda took great comfort in the fact that her daughter had close Thai friends. "If anything happens, they look out for each other," she said. "That's what you gain by being in this community."

The Parent-Teacher Association has become a valuable resource for the school. Before the PTA was established in 1998, individual parents assisted the teachers informally, making copies, donating paper and pencils, bringing snacks for the students, and babysitting the children of the parent who taught the class. Now the PTA provides formal and systematic support to the school and teachers. In addition to raising money, it helps the principal organize weekly activities. Doi, the head of the PTA in 2007 and a devoted food court volunteer, told me that a dossier was assembled for each student with contact and registration information, just as a medical clinic does for its patients. Parents receive timely reminders to assist children with homework assignments, such as reciting the Thai alphabet, doing language drills, writing, singing, and chanting. The PTA also organizes American holiday celebrations. On Easter, students hunt for eggs on the temple grounds. For Valentine's Day, students write valentines in Thai to their parents or grandparents. Apinya organized a Christmas party so the students could sing Christmas carols and receive presents from Santa Claus; and some years Doi decorated a Christmas tree in the multipurpose hall. "You know, not all of the Thai families who come here are Buddhists," she said with a smile. "We are kind of open-minded Buddhists." Again and again, the theme is inclusion rather than exclusion.

A good education, taking pride in being Thai, and being bilingual are key elements of the legacy that the Wat Thai community wishes to pass on to these youths who are expected to learn and then pass these elements on to the next generation. Middle-class parents can afford to spend more time with their children and have more resources with which to cultivate their Thai identity and spark their curiosity than parents who must struggle to make ends meet.[12] Mary Yu Danico found a similar result in her study about the 1.5 generation becoming Korean American in Hawaii: Children from middle-class families tended to express "more pride in being Korean than the working-class Korean Americans" (Danico 2004: 185). The middle-class parents are motivated by their social trajectory, higher education, and class taste to cultivate their children's cultural identity and help them accumulate educational, social, cultural, and linguistic capital.

Morning Assembly

Every Sunday at 9:30 A.M., the students gather in front of the chapel to pledge allegiance to the flags of Thailand and the United States. Thailand's flag, like Old Glory, is red, white, and blue. The students learn that red represents the blood of the nation; white represents the purity of Buddhism; and blue represents the monarchy. The flag symbolizes the Thai tripartite national identity—the nation, Buddhism, and the monarchy. After singing and exercising, the students enter the chapel, sit in front of the principal Buddha statue, and chant four short texts in Pali:

HOMAGE TO THE BUDDHA
Homage to Him, the blessed one, the holy one, the self-enlightened one [thrice].[13]

HOMAGE TO THE TRIPLE GEM
Homage to Him, the blessed one, the self-enlightened one.
Homage to the Dharma, the noble doctrine well preached by the blessed one.
Homage to the Sangha, the noble Bhikkhus of the blessed one.[14]

HONOR PARENTS
Homage to our parents who gave us life. We appreciate all the comfort, love and kindness given by those who raised us. By the power of speaking these truths, may happiness be mine.[15]

HONOR TEACHERS
Homage to all great teachers who give us art and goodness; teachers who give us wisdom and who teach that evil is bad and that goodness is no crime. By the power of speaking these truths, may a victory blessing be mine.[16]

Initially, the students have no idea what they are chanting. They just memorize the words and repeat them back. Over time, many get the idea that one has to respect the Buddha and the monks and that one should honor parents and teachers—the former, who gave life and love, and the latter, who teach how to distinguish good from bad. Several parents mentioned to me in passing that their adult children can still chant even a decade after having left the temple school.

The chanting is followed by a short Dharma talk and meditation. At the session I attended, Maha Singtong asked the youngsters to sit up straight on the floor, close their eyes, cross their legs, and rest their hands on their knees. Then he spoke in a low, gentle voice: "*Sabai, sabai*" (easy or contented). He continued, "*Sabai, sabai chai* [heart], *sabai, sabai kai* [body], *sabai, sabai rian* [learning]." The sound of his voice was soothing. He repeated it. Finally he ended, saying, "If you meditate for a minute, your heart will be *sabai* for an hour; if you meditate for an hour, your heart will be *sabai* for a day."

Learning the Thai Language, Dance, and Music

Teaching youngsters how to speak Thai, use Thai body language, play Thai music, and perform Thai dance becomes a means of reproducing Thai cultural identity. Thai history, nationalism, cultural values, and Buddhist ethics are deeply embedded in the teaching of these subjects. Being able to switch between Thai and English and to act with appropriate politeness and proper manners are viewed as crucial social markers for becoming Thai American.

Language

The process of teaching the Thai language is continuously and vigorously informed by Thai national ideologies. Nipapon, a summer teacher, made sure that, if nothing else, the students remembered that "Thai" means "free"; that Thailand is the "only Southeast Asian country never to be colonized"; and that "written Thai has more than a seven-hundred-year history—longer than the history of the United States." (She did not mention the impact that Western powers have had on Thailand—for example, the effects of Thailand having signed the Bowring Treaty with Great Britain in 1855.)[17] In addition, Nipapon wore a Thai silk dress to help students "develop an appreciation for Thai beauty." She admitted that she rarely wore silk dresses when she taught in Bangkok. Her performance revealed her effort to plant the seeds of ethnic nationalism in her young charges.

Learning to speak, read, and write Thai requires a lot of practice. The teachers try to make it fun. Beginners memorize the Thai alphabet by solving puzzles, playing games, telling stories, watching videos and slides, and collaborating on projects. The teachers have created a reward system to encourage learning. One summer teacher spent her own money to buy Thai pottery toys to use as prizes in her classes. Jelena, the principal, shared with me her observation that the child of an intermarried couple might speak more fluent Thai than the child of a Thai couple, because fluency often is related to practicing Thai at home. After a few years of training, some students can read a Thai newspaper, although their vocabulary may be limited. Many students, though, find learning dance and playing music more fun than studying the Thai language.

Dance

In the dance classes, the teacher often makes the point that Thai dance is the jewel of Thai culture and a great source of national pride. Thai classical dance consists of 108 basic movements, each of which has a specific meaning. Dancers are required to remain erect from the neck to the waist, moving up and down, stretching to the rhythm, by bending at the knees. Such body movements and postures are considered graceful and elegant.

Hands and fingers are viewed as vehicles for conveying a wide range of meanings and emotions. A proficient Thai female dancer is able to bend her fingers toward the back of her hand at a seemingly impossible angle. Dance teachers trained students to make their fingers "speak." Pachanee, the dance teacher, asked her students to soak their hands in warm water every day and then flex their fingers backward while counting to five, and gradually increasing it. Some students gave up. Others were willing to endure the pain.

Dancing makes them realize how much practice and dedication are required to execute what appears to be a simple and easy gesture. Such a realization is translated to other things they do. Achara reflected that learning Thai dance profoundly shaped her life. "Thai classical dance requires focus, flexibility and grace—attributes that I try to bring into my everyday life practice. The dance instills modesty and respect—humility . . . not only to my teachers and peers, but to everyone around me," she said. "The monks, teachers, and parents infused good traits and characteristics that I will take with me throughout my adulthood. . . . I am blessed to have had help from the temple community in shaping my experiences during my childhood and young adult life."[18]

Student dancers are also taught to *wai* the headdress and say "*kho khama*," an extremely polite phrase for "excuse me," before donning the headdress. In addition, before each performance, everyone follows the Thai custom of performing a *waikhru* ceremony to pay respect to performance deities and seek their blessings for the performance. These culturally meaningful rituals introduce the students to the "Thai way" through dancing.

Thai classical dance is flavored by gender ideologies. Body gestures are used to express the male "I" and the female "I." When a dancer plays a male role, hands, fingers, feet, elbows, and torso are all used to express a sense of sturdiness and masculinity—for example, walking bowlegged and striding outward. A dancer playing a female role expresses her femininity through gentler body language, walking with dainty grace, one foot placed across the other. A Thai audience understands the story being depicted by the dancers' hand gestures, finger movements, and stances. I concur with Penny Van Esterik's insight that the "model of Thai gender identity is body based" (Van Esterik 2000: 202).

Moreover, the students learn about the historical relationship between Thailand and its neighboring countries through dance and music.[19] In studying Ramakien drama, perhaps the best known classical art form in Thailand, students are exposed to a mix of different elements that originated in southern Thailand, Java, and Indonesia. They perform dances that portray the lives of the hill-tribe people. In practicing the dance Plengchinkhim Yai, they learn about Chinese music, because the dance was composed during the Ayutthaya era (1350–1767), when many Chinese came to Siam as traders. In practicing the Farang Rumthao dance, the students come to realize that King Rama IV accommodated Western ideals in Thai dance by integrating its slower motion with more rapid Western movements. Thus, Thai dance and songs carry a great deal of social and historical significance.

Music and Songs

Through playing music, students learn that everything is in a state of ceaseless change; life is evanescent; and everything is impermanent. Music teaches students qualities of grace, balance, and clarity. Some students gradually internalize the Buddhist values and Thainess taught in these classes. For instance, the following excerpt is from the poem "Thai Music," written by Max when he was about twelve years old:

> Thai music is:
> Bliss to my ears.
> Thai music is:
> Very relaxing.
> Thai music is:
> The paintings on a wall.
> Thai music is:

The rhythm of the heart
Thai music is:
The essence of culture.[20]

Over time, Max transformed his love for music into love for Thailand.

While learning to play Thai instruments, new students sometimes carelessly toss the bamboo hammer dulcimer mallets to the floor. The teachers tell students to pay respect to their instruments because of a belief that "a teacher is located inside the instrument" (*mikhru yunai khruang*). The instrument symbolizes knowledge and authority. Students are prohibited from stepping over a musical instrument, regardless of how crowded the classroom or a stage may be. Through such discipline, the students become aware of the similarities and differences between Thai and American notions of music and musical instruments.

At Wat Thai, songs are often used to build a bond between the students and Thailand. To celebrate Thailand's National Mother's Day, students sing "The Value of a Mother's Milk" to express gratitude to the queen and to their own mothers. At Classical Night and on the king's birthday, the students sing Thailand's national anthem and the royal anthem together with the adults. Affection and respect for the monarchy and the nation are emphasized through learning and singing these songs. Wat Thai's anthem, written by the author of "I Am Thai," is another form of reifying temple identity. The following is an excerpt:

Thai temple, Thai temple, Thai temple,
Center for peace and happiness.
Honorable Sangha, O honorable Sangha.
Your teachings lead us to wisdom.
Small children come here and learn about Thailand.
Kind-hearted adults gather as a community.
Mighty Wat Thai, O Wat Thai.
Distinguished Thai temple for these United States.
Thai temple, Thai temple, Thai temple,
Center for peace and happiness.
Honorable Sangha, O honorable Sangha.
Your sermons lead us to wisdom.

Just as drops of rain nourish the land,
Bringing abundance and letting plants flourish.
So let us come together and support our temple.
Let us come together and support this wholesome place,
So that future generations may continue in faith.[21]

The anthem describes the temple as a wholesome refuge of peace and center of happiness, and associates the monks with wisdom and the adults with kindness. The youngsters are taught not only to identify with the temple but also to fulfill their obligation of supporting the temple.

These students perform at community and cultural events such as the City of Sunnyvale Fit and Fun Fair, the Asian-American Festival, the Vietnamese American Festival, and the Chinese New Year celebration (Figure 6.1). They and their teachers serve as cultural ambassadors, helping to connect the temple with other communities. As the youngsters grow into adults, many come to realize that the temple school had a great impact on their lives. "Becoming a performer has molded me into the person that I am today," one reflected. "It has made me more diverse and motivated than I was before."[22]

Figure 6.1. Thai dance, 2008. (Photograph by the author.)

Learning the Thai Social Order
through Body Language

Many youngsters find performing a *wai* or using the proper "I" in Thai to show respect challenging because such practices conflict with their notion of being equal and of being individuals in American society. "I" in English often is self-centered rather than relationship-centered; an individual body tends to be seen as an autonomous individual. As Scheper-Hughes and Lock (1987: 16) put it, "The Western conception of *one* individual, *one* self effectively disallows or rejects social, religious, and medical institutions predicated on ethnopsychologies that recognize as normative a multiplicity of selves."

In Thai, "I" is always expressed in relation to others. There are multiple ways to say "I." When a teacher talks to her students, she refers to herself as *khru* (teacher); when she talks to a monk, she refers to herself as *yom* (a humble layperson); when she talks to her parents, she calls herself *luk* (child). She uses different kin terms, such as *mae* (mother), *pa* (aunt), *phi* (elder sister), *nong* (younger sister), *nu* (younger one), and *lan* (grandchild) when referring to herself according to the relationship she has with the person whom she is addressing. In giving a public speech, she may refer to herself as *khapachao*, a formal and gender-neutral "I." In answering questions, she may switch to *dichan*, a gendered "I." Thus, expressions of "I" are not only multiple but also fluid; the "I" exists in the context of interactions, relating to status, age, gender, formality, and degrees of intimacy and familiarity. The plural "I" organizes the flow of everyday life and conveys politeness, which often is reified as being Thai. However, youngsters who grow up in the United States often find "I" in Thai, as defined and expressed through a hierarchical social order, baffling.

Using "I" appropriately in Thai requires knowledge of Thai cultural principles such as *kalatesa*, which refers to an awareness of how to talk, act, and dress appropriately in time and space (Van Esterik 2000: 36, 39). To help students develop a new sense of self, teachers and parents teach them to practice Thai body language. For example, when one *wais* a monk or a Buddha image, one raises one's hands to a point at which the thumbs are at the middle of the eyebrows and the index fingers touch the edge of the scalp while one's head and body are bent. When one *wais* seniors, the thumbs slightly touch the nose, and the index fingers touch between the eyebrows. When one *wais* someone of

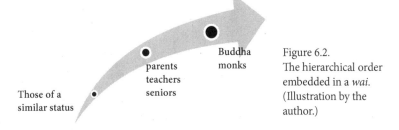

Figure 6.2.
The hierarchical order
embedded in a *wai*.
(Illustration by the
author.)

Figure 6.3. How to *wai* a monk and a teacher, 2010. (Photograph by the author.)

equal standing, the hands are held at chest level (Figure 6.2). In other
words, the higher the hands are held, and the more the body is lowered,
the more respect one has offered.

A classroom poster provided students a visual image of how to *wai*
properly (Figure 6.3). The top right illustrates the three steps it takes for
a girl to *wai* a monk, the figure standing at the center of the poster. At
the top left, the poster shows gender-specific body gestures for *waiing*
the monk: A girl must bend her knees; a boy does not. At the bottom
right, boys and girls lower their heads less when they *wai* a teacher
because a teacher has a lower position than a monk in Thai society.

Figure 6.4. *Waiing,*
using the body
from head to toe,
2006. (Photograph
by the author.)

Waiing, similar to speaking Thai or performing dance, teaches the students a sense of Thai femininity and masculinity via body language. This process confuses the kindergartners. I witnessed a boy imitate the girl next to him, and vice versa. Moreover, *waiing* often is presented as central to Thai etiquette. "You are Thai. You have to do it like this," one teacher said. Since a *wai* carries great social significance, teachers patiently instruct students over and over, hand by hand (Figure 6.4). Teachers and parents become distressed when a young child forgets to *wai* a teacher or a monk. Some claim that they can tell whether a child has attended the temple school just by seeing how he or she *wais.* *Waiing* serves as an apparatus for regulating the students' bodies, minds, and emotions.

Struggling between Two Clusters of the Body Politic

Thai American youth have been socialized to think of themselves as free individuals and to believe that everyone is equal. Suree, who associated *thambun* with paying debts owed, found it very difficult to teach her students, age ten to sixteen, to show gratitude and pay back what they owe their parents. Her notion of reciprocity often clashed with her students' notion of equality. "When I said parents and children are not equal and children *owe* their parents, immediately the entire class of fifteen kids [said], 'What? Not equal? *What?*'" Suree said. "It is so wrong to them. Some teenage students argue, 'I didn't ask to be born. Since they chose to bear me, then they owe me. They owe me food and everything.'" What appears to be a clash between teacher and students is actually the clash of two different social bodies. Suree blamed American schools, which teach that "everyone is equal, an individual has to earn respect, and you have to prove it. So [the student] starts thinking, 'Well, why am I *waiing* the *phra* [monk]? Why am I *waiing* the teacher? This is stupid.' Then the student starts to think that the whole *waiing* culture thing is disgusting or ridiculous."

Suree believed that children had a moral obligation to their parents, teachers, and monks, and to pay respect to social hierarchies and demonstrate obedience. Her perception of the Thai social order significantly informed her teaching. Sutama Bhikkhuni, however, felt sympathy for the students. Drawing from her own cross-cultural experience, she knew it was difficult for the youngsters to act on an ethical regulation that was in conflict with a value emphasized in American society. "If you impose on them, that's going to make them unhappy, and it is not going to help them," she said. "I didn't try to teach Buddhist morality as a kind of external form. [Instead, I] approached it from their experiences about what makes them feel good." Sutama Bhikkhuni used positive reinforcement as the means for regulation.

For some young people, it is extremely frustrating when what is considered normal conduct in the United States is considered rude in Thailand. Especially at a small school, students will wait for teachers to descend stairs to avoid rising above them, which can be interpreted as a lack of respect. This sense of vertical space is unfamiliar to those who grow up in the United States. Mary, who was born in California but attended junior high school in Thailand, recalled, "Once my teacher was sitting in her chair grading my paper, and I stood next to her. I got in trouble for that. She said, 'Why are you doing this? Where are your manners? This is not appropriate.' I'm like, 'Oh, gosh—I'm sorry. I didn't know those things.' I had that happen a lot, because I was always standing around, because I didn't know what to do."

Mary knew how to mimic but found it difficult, especially when she visited Bangkok as a college student. "I just feel uncomfortable when I meet adults, because I don't know how to *wang tua* [place myself]," she said. "Sometimes I forget to *wai* them. They give me a look, and I *wai* them. My Dad [a microbiologist] will tell his friends, 'Oh, she just came from the United States,' so they'll know it's not that I'm rude."

Showing the precise degree of expected respect requires cultural knowledge and the ability to read power relationships. Rosa, who was born in the United States, was confused about how to interact with her Farang Thai language teacher at the University of California, Berkeley. "When I go to her office hour, I'm not sure what I should do," she said. "For one thing, she is Caucasian, but she is very aware of Thai culture. I don't know how to act." Reconciling the mismatch was challenging. At the same time, she said, "I *do* act differently in America toward American adults and Thai adults. Very differently. With Thai adults, I'm always having to lower myself and show them a lot of respect." She learned the rules—it was safer to offer a lot of respect than to offer too little.

I have personally witnessed the struggles of Thai American youths in this area. Usually, Thai American college students interact with me as they would with any other non-Thais. But when students realize that I speak Thai, they often *wai* me. Once a student jumped up from a sofa and pulled me up from the floor in the middle of our conversation, even though I kept saying that sitting lower than she was did not bother me. The power of the Thai body politic could be keenly felt at that moment.

Not just the American-born but also those born in Thailand who came to the United States as teenagers have difficulties performing appropriately. Kayai—who was sent from Bangkok to attend ninth to twelfth grade at a private boarding school in the United States—experienced a different kind of cultural shock. Kayai came from an elite family: His maternal grandfather had been the chief of police in Singapore and his paternal grandfather had served as prime minister of Thailand. While his parents lived in London and Bangkok and worked as international financiers, he went to school in the United States. At first, Kayai was surprised by the "equal" relationship between students and teachers. "One day, the teacher brought in a hot cup of coffee and put it down on his desk," he said. "A girl said, 'Ohhh,' then went up and grabbed his cup and drank some coffee, and he didn't mind. I thought, 'Wow, what is going on?' Another example: I was in class, and a teacher was walking into the room. Another student came from behind and jumped on the teacher's back. The teacher just carried him into the classroom. I thought, 'That is very interesting.'"

The familiar Thai hierarchical order between teacher and student suddenly disappeared from Kayai's gaze. The teacher-student relationship that he saw in these examples was informal and friendly. As his appreciation for this new kind of relationship increased over the years, he began feeling more uncomfortable with some of the Thai values with which he was brought up:

> A lot of the time, I struggle with Thai culture and aspects of Thai society—blind respect, for example. I want to respect people because of merit, because of their character. But in Thailand, generally speaking, if the person is older than you, that's all it takes. Just because of age, title, just because of position, you have to be respectful. So what if he is a teacher if he is not a *good* teacher? And also, excuse me, so what if he is a monk if he is not a *good* monk? Thai people will not question that. It is very difficult to go against the stream that way. I think that was my worst struggle with Thai culture. I would like to treat people at the same level. I respect them through the way I treat them, not by how I address them.

Kayai's transnational encounter and American education made him question Thai cultural principles—for example, reflexively paying respect to the elderly and to monks. The Thai cultural logic of *waiing* ceased to be self-evident. He began to believe not that one should be granted respect automatically because of preexisting social conditions but, rather, that one should earn respect. The shift had an impact on him. When he visited his family in Bangkok, he sometimes forgot to say *khrap*, as a junior man is required to do at the end of a sentence, to show respect: "My dad feels very uncomfortable. He says to me, 'If you're going to forget to say *khrap*, speak English.' His main point was that . . . he does not want his son to go out and speak to older people and forget to say it. It's a bad reflection on the family. Parents are very afraid that people will say that. So they are very concerned about that." Neglecting or forgetting to *wai* or to say *khrap* is a matter of class respectability.

Kayai, who was born in Bangkok, and Mary, who was born in California, traveled to opposite ends of the world to make sense out of two distinctive body politics. Both found performing what was expected of them emotionally difficult, yet they had to for the sake of maintaining their families' class respectability. After many years of struggling, Kayai, who was a college student when I interviewed him, came up with a new strategy. "I've got to learn to *play the game*," he said. "Now I act the way they feel that I should act. There are people in Thailand who feel that just because they are older, they should be given a degree of respect. So I give them this degree of respect. In turn, the relationship I have with them is non-conflicting. It is a way to avoid conflict."

Kayai, who spoke central Thai perfectly and had been trained to use Thai body language to express his Thai and class identity, ironically used these very skills to subvert the cultural meanings invested in his acts. He "played the game" at an advanced level. He conveyed precise respect outwardly but refused to feel it. In this way, he could live without conflict within the Thai social body.

His transnational experiences made him rethink his identity. "I will not say that I am just Thai American but that I am not this or that," he said. "I think my life should be a process of building an identity rather than just trying to search for one. I am trying to create one." He believed that his identities would further unfold after he graduated from college: "I will be doing business that will take me across national boundaries. It's a global economy. If you are ambitious, it is not possible to limit yourself within one border. I might have a home; I might feel a country is a home, but I would also like to feel that *the world is my home*." Kayai spoke these last few words slowly and with deliberate emphasis. He was determined to go beyond national borders and open himself to the world. His "home," where he belonged, was still uncertain. But he wanted to embrace the world. He saw himself as an autonomous individual, free of social constraints.

In comparison, Mary felt torn between two homes. "I don't know where I should call home, America or Thailand, because I think half of my life is there and half of my life is in America," she said. "That is the hardest thing for me. I feel the most like I'm being a Thai when I'm in the United States. I feel the most like I'm being an American when I'm in Thailand." Mary was conflicted because both homes attempted to monopolize her loyalty; neither encouraged her to develop multiple belongings. In everyday life, she felt more attached to one home at one moment, but then, at another moment, she felt more attached to a different home. Engaging with two social bodies becomes part of who these youths are. The "I" becomes transnational.

Transnational Performances

On several occasions, the National Council on Social Welfare of Thailand invited student musicians and dancers from Wat Thai and other Thai temples in New York, Chicago, and Washington, DC, to perform in Bangkok. "Tour activities are organized around three key institutions: the monarchy, Buddhism, and the nation-state. They represent our national identity, so we want the students to understand them," said Somporn Thepsithar, vice-president of the National Council on Social Welfare of Thailand and coordinator of the Thai American youth tours to Thailand. The tour was usually scheduled to coincide with special occasions, such as the anniversary of the king's accession to the throne or the king's or queen's birthday. It is probably not the excellence of the performance per se but the fact that the performers are Thai American youth that fills the Thai nation with pride and conforms to a reified notion of Thainess.

From the moment their jet touched down in Thailand, these youths and their chaperones were treated like VIPs.[23] They were provided with army buses and a police escort to avoid Bangkok's notorious traffic jams. Since the participants came from different states, they were purposely mixed together in the buses to give them the chance to get to know one another. Despite jet lag, they rehearsed vigorously, for they understood the importance of performing live on Thai television. Sometimes a princess would attend the concert and have her picture taken with the students. Emily, who went on the 1996 tour, said, "Here [in the United States] it really does not matter that much if you mess up, because people won't know what you did wrong. But when you went [to Thailand] they would probably know."

Between rehearsals and the performance, the students met with dignitaries, including the prime minister, military officials, and famous monks. According to Somporn, the prime minister often found time to take a picture with the students and encouraged them to act as informal "ambassadors" (*tut*) and to come back to Thailand and help build the country once they grew up.

In addition to meeting officials, they visited iconic national institutions. The tour usually included excursions to the royal palaces, the National Museum and the Royal Thai Army Museum, ancient capitals, Constitution Hall, several famous Buddhist temples, and Chula. These young performers felt that they were special. Nancy, who had a

Thai mother and a German father, took pride in touring one palace. "There were signs that said 'Keep Out' and 'Do Not Enter.' We got to do something that people who live there would probably never get to do," she said. Opportunities were granted from the top down to help the students absorb Thai history, bond with their ancestors' home, and take pride in being Thai.

Multiple Belongings and a Hybrid "I"

Today, for those who spent much of their childhood at the temple, the Thai nation, the monarchy, and Buddhism are no longer abstract ideas. Instead, they are realized in the language that they speak, the songs that they sing, the chanting that they recite, the body language they have learned to use, the musical instruments that they play, and the communities with which they engage. Constructing the Thai cultural identity of these youth has been one of Wat Thai's major organizational concerns.

Recently, American-born youngsters have started to take up positions of leadership at the temple. In 2011, Tom, a twenty-three-year-old special education teacher who was born in Silicon Valley, was recruited to be the principal of the temple school under the mentorship of two senior members. He called Wat Thai his home and used affectionate kinship terms such as "uncle" and "aunt" to refer to other members. The temple was where he made friends and learned to read and write Thai, to chant in Pali, and to play Thai musical instruments. Tom saw himself as different from the previous school principals because he grew up at Wat Thai. He tried to take a nuanced approach. In 2012, he helped to organize a summer camp for Thai American youth—Buddhists and Christians—in Northern California to explore the meanings of being Thai American.

Seventeen-year-old Supansa, who had been accepted to the University of California, Santa Cruz, said that she appreciated how the temple had helped her "find out who I am. . . . I am proud to say that I can read and write Thai, perform the classical art of Thai dancing, and am a Thai Buddhist . . . because I was comfortable with myself as a Buddhist I had much to offer my fellow classmates."[24] Similarly, Max, who later became president of the Thai American Student Association at the University of California, Davis, said, "The temple offered me opportunities to meet the princess, the prime minister, the head monks, everything like that. It just really makes me feel connected to everything back in Thailand."

Eighteen-year-old Brian, who was also going to attend the University of California, Davis, said, "Over the years, I have managed to attain the position of Thai American Youth Association vice-president and participate in such activities as the martial art of Thai kickboxing, classical Thai dancing, and the musical art of the *khim* [hammered dulcimer]. Not only has the temple allowed me to acquire a great deal of knowledge of Thai culture, traditions, and language. It also has given me the chance to make new friends in the Thai community. . . . I have learned a lot about discipline [and] the importance of having self-respect and determination."[25] Gratitude is expressed; bonds have been forged; and multiple belongings have been cultivated.

At the Classical Night concert in 2006, Dan happily announced that many of the graduating high school seniors in the temple orchestra had been accepted at top-tier universities. "We are proud of our temple, our Thai community, and our students," he said. In 2012, Sulak, the president of the board of directors, proudly told me that more than 90 percent of the temple school students went on to major universities and that many earlier graduates were already working in the fields of medicine, law, engineering, and finance. The temple community helps produce talented American citizens. The accomplishments of these youths reflect well on their middle-class families and community.

Many youngsters have been shaped by two social bodies simultaneously and become Thai Americans and members of the transnational Thai community. During the weekends and in the summer, they sing the Thai national anthem, speak Thai mixed with English, play Thai music, practice Thai dance and body language, and celebrate Thai and American national holidays. During the week, they speak English, watch movies with their friends, sing popular songs, and play sports such as baseball and soccer, like the rest of their cohort at the regular American school. Sometimes in a single day they switch back and forth between Thai and American activities. They often modulate between a self-centered "I" and an "I" expressed in relation to others. The hybrid "I," at times, works with one particular kind of body politic; at other times, it resists or even works against it. Sometime it is hard to say what "Thai" is and what "American" is as the two are mixed and become one. The young people have developed multiple, shifting, inconsistent, and fragmented identities. They conduct cultural performances onstage and off in the United States and in Thailand. They are Thai, American, and Thai American all at once.

7
Conclusion

Interaction, Interdependence, and Transformations

On January 6, 2011, I took a group of monks and volunteer teachers from Wat Thai to visit Red Rock Canyon in Las Vegas. A few Farang hikers raised their hands with the palms pressed together in a prayer-like gesture to show respect to the monks. On two separate occasions, young backpackers asked to take a picture with the monks as if they were celebrities. No one confused monks with kung fu masters or pot smokers. Such encounters brought home to me how much America has changed over the past thirty years, even though Buddhism is still marginalized. The United States has become home to virtually every existing Buddhist school and lineage in the world. Not only do more people have access to the practice of Buddhism, but practitioners of various Buddhist schools and sects separated geographically in Asia, have more chances to intermingle here.

Scholars who have surveyed American Buddhism have come up with a variety of terms/categories, such as "two Buddhisms," "three Buddhisms," "White Buddhism," "ethnic Buddhism," "baggage Buddhism," "export Buddhism," "import Buddhism," and "elite Buddhism." To develop a more detailed map, Jeff Wilson (2009a: 844–845, 2012) suggests that we pay attention to "regionalism." The debate over these categories has dominated the discourse on American Buddhism. I contend that focusing exclusively on difference diminishes the effects of interdependence and interconnections among various social and religious groups and omits too much of significance.

On the basis of long-term research that I conducted at Wat Thai, I suggest that *webs of interconnections*—between shared goals and different practices, between the local and the global, between Buddhism and capitalism, between ethnic minority and majority, and between immigrants and their homelands—matter as much as ethnic, racial, class, gender, and religious differences in the formation of American Buddhism. Differences and sameness are always in dialogue; they are contingently involved with local, national, and transnational power relationships. Paying attention to the dialogue in process and to the juxtaposition of ever- changing ideologies and practices allows us to analyze clusters of differences and webs of connections that underscore the heterogeneity of American Buddhism.

The demographic and cultural heterogeneity at Wat Thai exists at many other American temples, though at a different degree and scale.[1] Wat Thai therefore can serve as an empirical case study. Wat Thai challenges the dominant discourse that equates community with ethnic minority as it includes people of different ethnicities, races, and faiths. Forging class alliances becomes a community strategy for negotiating the racial hierarchical order and achieving visibility as middle class. Social interactions, intermarriages, and the experience of working together have made some Whites more sensitive to racial discrimination and their White privilege. Volunteering at the temple, for the Whites, becomes a way to combat racism and make use of their expertise and connections for the community. Having served at the temple for over a decade, Dan takes pride in being "a Thai with an American face" while keenly aware of the perceived mismatch between his racial and cultural identities. Ethnic Chinese, Lao, Phunoi, and Sikhs who migrated from Thailand tend to downplay their ethnicity at Wat Thai. For them, it is far more relevant to emphasize Thai cultural identity than their ethnic identity—especially to those who know little about them. Emphasizing Thai identity becomes a way to express solidarity and avoid further marginalization. They, together with ethnic Thai, follow this path in response to social pressure to articulate their Thai cultural identity to gain recognition and establish their social standing in the United States. Members of other ethnic groups from Asia join Wat Thai for religious and other reasons. Thus, Wat Thai should not be likened to an ethnic haven because the temple includes the perspectives and practices of both minorities and the majority. Scrutinizing human diversity and exploring interconnectedness help us capture the pluralistic characteristics of American Buddhism and America itself.

Probing the formation of the Wat Thai community enables us to appreciate the process of boundary crossings and the refashioning of Americans and American Buddhism. Boundaries can be bent, twisted, and redrawn depending on the conditions at a given moment. The participants transcend the boundaries between traditional and modern, between spirituality and materiality, between East and West, and among different religions. On the one hand, they do not hesitate to reify Thai culture; on the other hand, they selectively integrate different cultural symbols that are meaningful to them. The monks not only construct sacred Buddhist space but also cross the boundaries between sacred and mundane as needed. The creation of the Wat Thai community and the physicality of the chapel become a way to say, in spatial form, "We are here. We are different, but we are Americans, too."

Many of the temple members consider practicing Buddhism a form of exercising their American citizenship. For people of color in particular, building a temple becomes a citizen-making, class-making, place-making, and community-making project. They learn the value of equality, democracy, and interdependence in the process of creating the temple power structure, the community, the school, and the food court. By refusing to be stigmatized as "takers" or as cult members, they confront prejudice and inequality and demonstrate that they are worthy American citizens.

Webs of dynamic religious and family relationships are continuously being reproduced. A good example is Terry, a Farang Catholic who was ordained temporarily as a monk. He was not shy about performing his Buddhist identity and, in so doing, came to the realization that comprehending Buddhism made him better appreciate his Catholic faith. His self-identification and performance as a monk complemented the diversity-making in a predominately Thai Buddhist monastic community that embraced him and taught him the Dharma and monastic codes. The meaning of his religious endeavor was not limited to the spiritual realm. His ordination strengthened his bond with his Thai wife and especially with his Thai mother-in-law, who considered his ordination an expression of filial piety and a way to make merit for her. This example reveals the juxtaposition of the perspectives and affiliations of people with different faiths and positions.

Crossing religious and ethnic boundaries is a part of messy daily practices. People at Wat Thai maintain the boundaries not through isolation but, rather, through cooperation, which enables them to articulate who they are and to construct flexible relationships with other people. It becomes more and more difficult to find anyone who always thinks and acts within his or her cultural box along ethnic, racial, and class lines. We live extremely complicated lives because we move in many different circles and many different people are important to us for many different reasons. For example, a Thai Buddhist woman attends Sunday services at a Christian church with her Farang husband and takes him with her to a Buddhist temple. The couple maintains their plural affiliations because religion constitutes only one aspect of their conjugal relationship. The racial categories and different faiths that they bring to their family do not push them apart. Instead, they oblige the couple to communicate, compromise, and appreciate what each can contribute to the relationship. Having two faiths is not a "burden" but a "gift," as Chuck put it earlier. People have an amazing capacity to forge bonds even as they hold different political positions, speak different languages, have different faiths, prefer different foods, and so on. Such connections disrupt the prevailing ethnic Buddhist–White convert paradigm and challenge the equation ethnicity equals community equals culture.

The same can be said of Natee and her husband, devout Buddhists who sent their only daughter to a Catholic school, and Yui, an observant Thai Muslim who coaxed her teenage daughter into attending the temple school. They show us how contingent and temporal religious differences are through the different weighing of priorities and interests at different times in their lives. Indeed, identity is scarcely consistent or fixed. Immigration and becoming Thai American contribute to further loosening the coherence of their religious and cultural identities. Identity formation is thus a complex, fluid, and many-sided process whose outcome is hard to predict.

At Wat Thai participants find space to develop multiple paths for practicing spirituality. For some, doing whatever the temple community needs is a path to achieving well-being; the well-being of an individual is seen as intertwined with the community. For some, chanting or being mindful about everything one does is practicing spirituality. For others, practicing generosity is a way to seek freedom from suffering and a path to a better rebirth. For still others, practicing meditation is a spiritual journey. The ability to battle ego or insecurity is viewed as a path to enlightenment. Paths or activities may look different, but they are underscored by a shared inspiration. These numerous paths do not just illustrate a wide range of approaches in pursuing the same goal; they also challenge the idea that Buddhism can be reduced to meditation.

Spirituality is practiced while engaging with many facets of social life. On the surface, a monk sitting in the lotus position meditating in front of a Buddha statue and a monk slicing papaya at the food court are engaged in separate domains. These monks, however, challenge the assumption of the division between the mundane and the sacred. For example, the Smiling Monk regarded eating a bowl of alms food—whatever was offered—as practicing detachment. Maha Ampon drove a car to go shopping at Costco during his residence in Silicon Valley, but after returning to his temple in Bangkok he walked barefoot with eyes cast downward to receive alms food on the street. Neither monk separated worldly from spiritual activities or drew a line between traditional and modern, because each believed that everything he did was connected to his spiritual journey.

Diversity at Wat Thai is entangled within clusters of socioeconomic activities, institutional regulations, and power relations. Even though Buddhist teachings emphasize impermanence and detachment from the material world, a Buddhist organization must deal with money and negotiate American legal regulations, Buddhist moral codes, and culturally specific principles. While many meditation centers charge fees—like a health club—to cover the costs of the services and to pay instructors, Wat Thai does not charge fees but taps into the practice of merit making to raise money. The difference between the administration of Wat Thai and a typical meditation center is more style than substance; each handles money in a configuration compatible with its own cultural logic. Furthermore, an abbot, like a chief executive officer, has to stay within a budget and make ends meet, create projects so that the temple flourishes, and organize participants with different personalities and skills to work together as a team.

At the national level, bits and pieces of Buddhism have been integrated into American popular culture and the market economy. Numerous enterprises (including casinos and nightclubs) appropriate the vocabulary and images of Buddhism to promote their products and businesses. They contribute to commercializing Buddhism. Individuals with some level of interest in Buddhist philosophy may not just read books written by the Dalai Lama and practice meditation but also drink Awake tea, eat Dharma pizza, snack on Organic Zen cranberry cereal, and order Enlightened smoothies, as well as incorporate statues of Buddha into their home decor. The marketplace thus drowns out a key Buddhist doctrine: Life is suffering, and this suffering is caused by craving and attachment to transient things. (An examination of the effects of material culture, money, psychology, and individualism on Buddhist practitioners would be a worthwhile project.)

Moreover, Buddhist practices are informed by dynamic gendered power relationships. When a woman fights for the right to be ordained as a monk and to conduct rituals as a form of practicing her spirituality, she prompts a broad spectrum of responses, including acceptance, partial inclusion, and outright rejection. She challenges not just the patriarchal order in the monastic community but also gender inequality in Buddhism. Thai and non-Thai women share a great deal in their practice of Buddhism. More Thai and Farang women than men practice meditation at Wat Thai. Gender differences cross ethnic and racial lines. Women make significant contributions by working in the kitchen, fundraising, serving on the boards, and overseeing and teaching at the temple school. Without the women's participation and leadership, Wat Thai would be a very different community.

Social interactions among the participants open many possible doors for learning and for change. Transnational monks teach different styles of meditation and introduce notions of space and cosmology. Thai food sold at temples enriches the American palate and serves as an entry to Thai culture. The youngsters—trained in temple schools—do not just perform dance and music. They also establish cultural clubs and ethnic associations at colleges and universities throughout the United States. Many take with them the values that they learned at the temple and apply them to everything they do. A few, after college, have gone to teach or work with nonprofit organizations in Thailand. As one put it, "I must say that I would not be in Thailand had I not set foot in the temple those many years ago."[2] These American-born youngsters have become Thai Americans through the persistent cultivation of their parents, teachers, temple community, and Thai authorities. Moreover, as immigrants become Americans, some Whites identify with Thais. They claim multiple identities because of the numerous relationships they have forged and cultural meanings they have absorbed. They, Thais and non-Thais, are engaged in a dialectic with the

American nation-state, empowered or limited by it; at the same time, they are reproducing and changing it. The idea of Americanization as timeless and homogeneous is an ideology rather than a practice.

The world is shrinking; the local and the global increasingly are interconnected and dependent on each other. Participants, whether at a temple in California, Illinois, Massachusetts, or Virginia, rarely just think and act locally. Some Whites never travel to Asia or even outside their home state (Wilson 2012: 11). Nevertheless, beliefs, symbols, and meditation styles travel and circulate, which transforms these rarely traveled people into members of a Zen meditation group or a Tibetan Buddhist group. They no longer rely on face-to-face interactions but stretch their religious practices and relationships by communicating across space and time. Such a journey requires no passport or visa. If we examine a Buddhist temple from only an American-centered perspective and dismiss such interconnectedness, we will miss many important contingent ties that the participants have forged.

Furthermore, religious bonds can be tapped by the nation-state. Religious connections between immigrants and the country they came from are as important as their political and economic ties because religious affiliations can be mobilized to serve economic and political causes. Thus far, we have learned only how Asian immigrants—Filipinos, for example—forge strong socioeconomic and political bonds with the country they left behind.[3] Wat Thai demonstrates how its long-distance religious and educational ties with Thailand help to mobilize resources and reconstruct Thainess. The process of reterritorializing Buddhism is dialectically shaped and reshaped by local and transnational regimes.

In short, we need to keep in mind that people are simultaneously agents and subjects. Various forms of self-making and being made capture a wide range of relationships and tensions among individuals and institutional power structures. Multiple ways of self-making and being made constitute and energize this community. The participants at Wat Thai make the temple community, but the community also makes them.

Notes

Chapter 1

1. Following Thai usage, I use *wat* and "temple" to refer to the entire temple complex; "chapel" refers to the most important building in the complex.

2. Wat Thai of Silicon Valley is a pseudonym. When it was founded in 1983, Wat Thai was the eleventh Thai Buddhist temple in the United States. As of March 2014, 162 Thai American Buddhist temples were recognized by the Council of the Thai Bhikkhus in the United States and monastic authorities in Thailand.

3. Mahayana is sometimes called the Great Way or the Northern School. Its liturgical language is Sanskrit. Most Mahayana followers are concentrated in China, Japan, and Korea. They tend to believe in many Buddhas and bodhisattvas and are known for a much more liberal reinterpretation of the teachings of the Buddha than Theravada Buddhists. Theravada Buddhism, sometimes called the Elder Way or the Southern School, is widely practiced throughout Southeast Asia. Followers attempt to remain "true" to the historical Buddha's teachings and believe in one Buddha. In addition, achieving enlightenment often is regarded as an individual matter (Keown 2000; LaFleur 1988).

4. Racial and ethnic categories are social constructions. I use "race" and "ethnicity" as folk categories. In the public discourse, race tends to be associated with observable phenotypic traits, while ethnicity is viewed a cultural classification that includes language, religion, and other cultural elements. I concur with the view that while race does not exist biologically, it certainly does exist socially. Both racial and ethnic identities are articulated through interaction and contrast, and they are performative, never stable, sometimes overplayed and sometimes downplayed, depending on context.

5. In *The Future of Us All*, Roger Sanjek (1998) depicted such a situation in New York City.

6. Thailand's Office of National Buddhism under the Ministry of Culture funds accomplished overseas temples. Wat Thai has received such funding since 1994.

7. See "The Pluralism Project at Harvard University: Statistics by Tradition," available at http://www.pluralism.org/resources/statistics/tradition .php#Buddhism (accessed April 14, 2014).

8. As of 2012, there are approximately 17.3 million U.S. residents of Asian descent, and about 14 percent (2.4 million) of them self-identify as Buddhist. Thus, if there are 4 million American Buddhists, more than 50 percent are Asian Americans. See http://projects.pewforum.org/2012/07/18/religious-affiliation- of-asian-americans-2/asianamericans_affiliation_2 and http://www.census .gov/newsroom/releases/archives/facts_for_features_special_editions/cb12-ff09 .html (both accessed April 14, 2014).

9. We do not know exactly what the human Buddha taught 2,500 years ago, because what "he taught was preserved in memories of generations of his followers, not to be written down until some four centuries after his death" (Lopez 2001: 7).

10. A few scholars acknowledge the existence of middle-class Asian immigrants (Cadge 2005; Cheah 2011; Chen 2008; Numrich 1996). Nevertheless, class is rarely used as an analytical category in studying Asian immigrants.

11. See http://pewresearch.org/pubs/1434/multiple-religious-practices- reincarnation-astrology-psychic (accessed April 14, 2014).

12. The Buddhist Church of America and Soka Gakkai International are known for attracting a diverse assortment of followers (Fields 1998: 197; Fronsdal 1998: 169; Machacek 2001: 78; Tanaka 1999: 10).

13. See also Teresa Watanabe, "A Boost for Thai Town," *Los Angeles Times*, August 3, 2008, available at http://www.latimes.com/news/local/la-me-thai- town3-2008aug03,0,5187708.story?track=rss (accessed May 5, 2014).

14. A few scholars resist the idea of Americanization, as it had already taken place when Buddhism arrived in America (Gregory 2001: 248; Hori 1998: 77; Moriya 2010: 112–113, 128). Peter Gregory (2001: 248, 251–252) points out that "the concept of 'Americanization' might be problematic" because Buddhists of all different stripes have gathered in one place for the first time. Thomas Tweed (2011: 20) coined the term "translocative" to capture multiple movements, positions, and relations in studying Buddhism. Jeff Wilson (2008, 2009b) addresses the impact of Buddhist practices in Asia on current practices in the United States.

15. *Program for Thai Youth in the United States in Celebration of the Thai Queen's 72nd Birthday* (Bangkok: privately printed [in Thai], n.d.).

16. The female monastic order is believed to have been founded by the Buddha some 2,500 years ago and to have flourished for more than 1,000 years in India and Sri Lanka (LaFleur 1988: 17, 50, 52). Nevertheless, the order lay dormant for about 1,000 years, until the late 1990s, when Sri Lankan monks

ordained female monks and restored the line of Bhikkhuni: Atiya Achakul-wisut, "A Path Less Travelled," *Bangkok Post*, April 17, 2001, available at http://www.budsas.org/ebud/ebdha220a.htm#2 (accessed May 5, 2014); D. Amarasiri Weeraratne, "Revival of the Bhikkhuni Order in Sri Lanka," *The Island* (Colombo, Sri Lanka), April 4, 1998, available at http://www.buddhanet.net/nunorder.htm (accessed May 5, 2014); Xuan 2008.

17. Monastic service is believed to transform a "raw" man into a "mature" one, although the length of service can vary considerably (Keyes 1987: 36).

Chapter 2

1. "Thai American Interesting Facts," available at http://thailand-usa.com/statistics/thai-american-facts-and-information-thais-in-america-americans-in-thailand (accessed April 14, 2014).

2. The massacre was a crackdown on university students and protesters who were demonstrating against the return to Thailand of Thanom Kittikachorn, a corrupt right-wing dictator. As many as three hundred people were shot and killed.

3. See U.S. Department of Justice 1978: table 6.

4. From 1966 to 1973, more than forty thousand U.S. troops, on average, were stationed in Thailand, mostly on Air Force bases (Correll 2004: 5).

5. The percentages were 52.6 percent in 1980, 53.6 percent in 1990, and 48.7 percent in 2000, according to Danielle Hidalgo and Carl Bankston (2011: 88).

6. See U.S. Census Bureau, 2010 American Community Survey, Three-Year Estimates (2006–2010), Selected Population Tables, Population Group: Thai Alone or in Any Combination, using American FactFinder, available at http://factfinder2.census.gov (accessed August 18, 2012).

7. For 1980–2000, see Hidalgo and Bankston (2011: 88); for 2010, see U.S. Census Bureau, Age Groups and Sex: Census Summary File 2, using American FactFinder, available at http://factfinder2.census.gov (accessed August 28, 2012).

8. These statistics are based on U.S. census data pulled from American Community Survey five-year sets accessible through the Integrated Public Use Microdata Series (IPUMS) project.

9. The number of undocumented Thai migrants (160,000) was estimated on the basis of 237,583 Thai Americans recorded in the 2010 U.S. Census and an estimate that nearly 400,000 Thais live in the United States: Kavi Chongkit-tavorn, "What Is the Value of a Thai Passport?" *The Nation*, December 12, 2011, available at http://www.nationmultimedia.com/opinion/What-is-the-value-of-a-Thai-passport-30171681.html (accessed May 14, 2014).

10. U.S. Census Bureau, Thai Alone or in Any Combination, Table S0201, available at http://factfinder2.census.gov (accessed February 20, 2013).

11. U.S. Census Bureau, American Community Survey 2010, San Mateo and Santa Clara Counties. See also Joint Venture, *2012 Index of Silicon Valley*, 14, available at http://www.jointventure.org/images/stories/pdf/2012index.pdf (accessed April 18, 2014).

12. U.S. Census Bureau, 2010 American Community Survey, One-Year Estimates, Selected Population Profile in the United States, using American FactFinder, available at http://factfinder2.census.gov (accessed July 28, 2012).

13. "Dancing Angeles: Touring Thailand's 77th Province," September 23, 2007, available at http://www.experiencela.com/calendar/eventmore.asp?key=15059 (accessed April 14, 2014).

14. U.S. Census Bureau, Census 2010, American FactFinder, Total Population, 2006–2010 American Community Survey Selected Population Tables, "Thai alone or in any combination" available at http://factfinder2.census.gov (accessed August 10, 2012).

15. U.S. Census Bureau, Thai Alone or in Any Combination, available at http://factfinder2.census.gov (accessed July 28, 2012).

16. U.S. Census Bureau, 2006–2010 American Community Survey, Selected Population Tables, Sex by Educational Attainment for the Population 25 Years and Over, using American FactFinder (county data are for Thai alone or in any combination), available at http://factfinder2.census.gov (accessed July 28, 2012).

17. Ibid.

18. Asian Americans have long been part of the labor force in Silicon Valley. From the mid-nineteenth century to the mid-twentieth century, Asian Americans worked the gold fields, built the railroad lines, picked crops from the fields, and worked on cannery assembly lines (Pellow and Park 2002: 39–49). Most were low-skilled laborers. In the early 1980s, as the computer industry began replacing the canning industry, young, well-trained, well-educated Asian immigrants were attracted to the area. Today, locals still joke that "Silicon Valley is built on ICs," which refers not to integrated circuits but to Indian and Chinese engineers (Saxenian 1999: v–vi).

19. Quoted in Mike Swift, "Other Tongues Overtaking English as Language Spoken in Majority of Santa Clara County Homes," *San Jose Mercury News*, December 7, 2007, 3.

20. Rona Marech, "Of Race and Place," *San Francisco Chronicle*, May 17, 2002, available at http://sfgate.com/cgi-bin/article.cgi?file=/chronicle/archive/2002/05/17/EB49066.DTL (accessed May 14, 2014).

21. Tracey Kaplan, "Growing Group Changes Bay Area," *San Jose Mercury News*, December 12, 2004, 1, available at http://www.ncvaonline.org/D_1-5_2-136_4-249_5-40_6-1_17-6_14-2_15-2/#GROWING_GROUP_CHANGES_BAY_AREA (accessed May 14, 2014).

22. Joint Venture, *2012 Index of Silicon Valley*, 4.

23. Ibid., 14.

24. Ibid., 4.

25. Les Christie, "Six-Figure Zip Codes," *CNN/Money Online*, November 18, 2004, 2, available at http://money.cnn.com/2004/11/15/real_estate/mil_life/richestzipcodes (accessed May 5, 2014).

26. At Wat Philadelphia, where Wendy Cadge did her research, the abbot

was the decision maker even when his health was failing. In 2012, in Las Vegas, the abbots of two Thai temples appointed all of the board members.

27. "Bay Area Temple" is a pseudonym.

28. Thomas Fuller, "Monks Lose Relevance as Thailand Grows Richer," *New York Times*, December 18, 2012, available at http://www.nytimes.com/2012/12/19/world/asia/thai-buddhist-monks-struggle-to-stay-relevant.html?pagewanted=2&_r=0 (accessed April 18, 2014).

29. Quoted in *30th Anniversary of Wat Thai*, privately printed, 2013, 206, in my possession.

Chapter 3

1. "Buddhist Temple Intrudes on Town," *Times Daily*, February 11, 1984, 81, available at http://news.google.com/newspapers?nid=1842&dat=19840211&id=O3koAAAAIBAJ&sjid=QcgEAAAAIBAJ&pg=2230,2138835 (accessed May 5, 2014).

2. See also Annysa Johnson, "Proposed Buddhist Temple in Greenfield Expected to Draw Opposition," *Journal Sentinel*, September 9, 2012, 1, available at http://www.jsonline.com/features/religion/proposed-buddhist-temple-in-greenfield-expected-to-draw-opposition-it6pd25–168970256.html (accessed May 14, 2014); Nick Keppler, "Buddha in Suburbia," *Fairfield Weekly*, July 24, 2008, available at http://www.buddhistchannel.tv/index.php?id=70,6852,0,0,1,0 (accessed April 12, 2014); Martine Powers, "Buddhist Temple Causes Stir in Lowell: Neighbors Complain of Noise and Code Violations," *Boston Globe*, October 5, 2011, 1, available at http://www.bostonglobe.com/metro/2011/10/04/lowell-residents-odds-with-buddhist-temple/qSoxt7dhG322WT148hytxO/story.html (accessed May 5, 2014); Yi Xian, "Do Americans Discriminate against Chinese Buddhism?" *Nanfang Daily* [in Chinese], September 21, 2010, available at http://watchingamerica.com/News/70073/do-americans-discriminate-against-chinese-buddhism (accessed May 5, 2014), translation by Michelle Deeter, edited by Stefanie Carignan.

3. Paul Engstrom, "Buddhists, Neighbors Are Not at Peace," *San Jose Mercury News*, April 18, 1984, 1.

4. Quoted in ibid., 8.

5. If a temple does not have a chapel, the principal Buddha statue will reside within the *wihan*.

6. According to Stanley Tambiah (1970: 21), "South is of neutral value." However, people I interviewed did not agree. This controversy means that the meanings ascribed to directions are not singular.

7. See "Thailand Related Information," available at http://umich.edu/~thailand/resources-thailand-info.htm (accessed May 20, 2014).

8. "Three Worlds of Buddhist Cosmology," pamphlet [in Thai], n.p., 7, in my possession.

9. This statue was cast in Bangkok and blessed by Luang Pho's preceptor.

Chapter 4

1. See *The World Factbook*, available at https://www.cia.gov/library/publications/the-world-factbook/geos/th.html (accessed April 18, 2014).

2. Currently, there are six Bhikkhunis at Songdhammakalyani Monastery in Nakhonpathom, Thailand (Rasicot 2007).

3. A small number of monks, especially those who belong to the Dhammayut sect, eat just one vegetarian meal a day.

4. Thai Theravada Buddhism is divided into two sects: Mahanikay and Dhammayut. Such a distinction continues in the United States. Each sect has established its own council in the United States: the Council of the Thai Bhikkhus for Mahanikay and the Dhammayut Order for Thammayut. However, both are under the leadership of the Supreme Sangha Council of Thailand. Wat Thai belongs to the Mahanikay sect.

5. A Thai monk has to meet three criteria to serve overseas: He must have been ordained as a monk for at least five years; he must hold a bachelor's degree; and he must have no visible tattoos. Each monk must also pass a qualifying examination.

6. The master's degrees were in the fields of social welfare, literature, computer science, and Asian studies.

7. A few decades ago, a monk could live in rural Thailand without having to touch money. He could find shelter when he traveled because almost every village had a temple. In remote areas with no temples, a monk could stay in a public space such as a forest.

8. The Thai government currently pays a salary of 1,500 baht (less than $50) a month to monks who achieve level-nine expertise in Pali, a financial reward for having attained the highest level of Pali proficiency.

9. "Part Three: The Exhortation Chapter," *The Patimokkha: The Bhikkhus' Code of Discipline*, 2009, trans. Thanissaro Bhikkhu (Valley Center, CA: Metta Forest Monastery, 2009), available at http://www.vipassana.com/canon/vinaya/bhikkhu-pati-part2.php (accessed May 18, 2014).

10. This was the only time I was ever asked not to take a picture at Wat Thai.

11. "Part Three."

12. Aree Chaisatien, "Women in Buddhism: Planting the Seed of Peace," *The Nation*, October 5, 2001, available at http://www.budsas.org/ebud/ebdha220a.htm#6 (accessed May 5, 2014).

13. Cat food is purchased with the money made from recycling.

14. *Buddhist Monastic Code I: The Patimokkha Training Rules Translated and Explained,* trans. Thanissaro Bhikkhu (Valley Center, CA: Metta Forest Monastery, 2009), available at http://www.accesstoinsight.org/lib/authors/thanissaro/bmc1.pdf (accessed April 20, 2014).

Chapter 5

1. In China and Taiwan, for example, capitalist activities are conducted through personal connections, gifts, and favors, creating what is called *guanxi* (networking) capitalism (Blim 2000: 28).

2. "Dana-Giving" (Samyuta Nikaya 1.33), in *Merit: A Study Guide,* trans. Thanissaro Bhikkhu, June 7, 2009, available at http://www.accesstoinsight.org/lib/study/merit.html (accessed June 18, 2009).

3. This method is now commonly used. To save the cost of the plaques, one temple in Las Vegas painted the names directly on the wall.

4. Magha Puja Day is celebrated in February, honoring the day that 1,250 monks from all different places came to pay homage to the Buddha. Thai New Year is celebrated in April. Visakha Puja Day, in May, commemorates the day the Buddha passed away. In July, there is a celebration of the beginning of Buddhist Lent. In August, the queen's birthday is celebrated as Mother's Day. Sard Thai, in September, is a day to dedicate merit to ancestors and loved ones who have passed away. In October, the end of Buddhist Lent is celebrated and the robes-giving ritual, or Kathin, is held. Loy Krathong is organized in November. Participants float small rafts as a way to pay respect to the goddess of water and bring about good luck. The king's birthday is celebrated in December.

5. In October, Kathin and King Rama V Memorial Day are celebrated together.

6. Thai Classical Night programs, 1993–1995, 1998–1999.

7. Ibid., 2002–2007.

8. The food court was officially open on Sundays from 11:00 A.M. to 2:00 P.M. People started lining up to buy food around 10:00 A.M., and some were still there eating after 3:00 P.M.

9. As of 2012, a full meal could be purchased for about $11: $6 for a main dish, $3 for desserts, and $2 for drinks.

10. The city closed the food court in December 2012. There is a sense of loss: no more fragrant Thai curry smell, no sounds of shredded green papaya being pounded into salad, no more lines of foodies purchasing mouth-watering Pad Thai. Wat Thai is not the first temple to have its food court shut down by the city. Many food courts have been closed because of neighbors' complaints about the noise, concerns about hygiene, and, most often, parking problems. When these issues are ironed out, temples, such as Wat Thai Los Angeles and the BA Temple, reopen their food courts. The future of Wat Thai's food court was unknown as this book went to press. Nevertheless, food continues to play a significant role in the practice of generosity, compassion, and merit making. Volunteers cook rice at the temple; almsgivers bring homemade food to offer to the monks. The monks carry an alms bowl and receive whatever people offer: rice, green papaya salad, spicy *larb*, salty fish, mango with sticky rice, and so on, all mixed together. The monks eat on the platform in the chapel; laypeople eat together—sitting or standing around an ornamental fountain—like a big potluck party. I observed

Natee and Doi on March 30, 2014, as usual, tirelessly working at a small cooking station, feeding the temple school students and teachers. No one is required to pay, but everyone puts money into a nearby donation box.

11. Both robes and money trees are offered at a *Phapa* Solidarity.

Chapter 6

1. Prapasri Siha-ompai, Wat Thai Summer School Sports brochure [in Thai], 1998, 19, in my possession; my translation, edited by Amdee Vongthongsri.

2. According to Luang Pho, the sending of professional teachers from Thailand was initiated by the abbots of Thai temples in Los Angeles and Chicago. In response, Professor Prapasri launched the Teaching Abroad Program at Chula.

3. Recently, the Teaching Abroad Program has been expanded to include other English-speaking countries.

4. Wat Thai Temple School program, 1992, in my possession.

5. From 1983 to 1986, the school was completely dependent on parents and volunteers. The temple school first had access to teachers from the Teaching Abroad Program in 1987. The junior teachers are given free round-trip airline tickets. The temple also gives them a small amount of pocket money. Summer school teachers receive their regular salary as government employees.

6. Junior teachers are new Chula graduates.

7. Senior teachers come from schools throughout Thailand. They teach classes from 9:00 A.M. to 3:00 P.M. four or five days a week for ten weeks for the summer school.

8. Wat Thai's annual Classical Night, one of the most popular events, did not begin until 1993. The Student Council was formed in 1999.

9. The program helps the teachers address practical issues, too. An American embassy officer teaches them how to deal with problems at the airport. Apinya, who retired and moved to Thailand, has been invited to Chula to instruct teachers on how to live and work at a temple in the United States.

10. In addition to evaluating the teachers from Thailand, Chula faculty members present the students with certificates of completion.

11. *30th Anniversary of Wat Thai*, 310.

12. Not all middle-class parents pay close attention to their children's education. Some parents do not speak Thai at home or help their children practice speaking Thai.

13. Wat Thai School chanting text brochure, 2005, 19, in my possession.

14. Ibid., 14.

15. Ibid., 16.

16. Ibid., 17.

17. In 1855, the Bowring Treaty was negotiated between Siam and Great Britain. It opened Thailand up to trade and Western influence. Similar agreements between Thailand and other nations—notably, Japan and the United

States—soon followed. Although these treaties cost Thailand a considerable measure of legal and fiscal autonomy, they also saved the country from the military invasions and colonial subjugation other Southeast Asian countries suffered.

18. *30th Anniversary of Wat Thai*, 294.

19. Wat Thai classical dance program, 1993, 6–18, and Wat Thai Classical Night program, 1994, 7–23, in my possession.

20. The poem "Thai Music" was published in the Wat Thai Summer School brochure in 2001.

21. My translation, edited by Amdee Vongthongsri.

22. *30th Anniversary of Wat Thai*, 310.

23. Thai officials, especially Somporn, prepared an itinerary far in advance. After arriving in Thailand, the youngsters' chaperones coordinated with the officials. They paid attention to every detail, including not feeding the students uncooked food because "the kids have a Farang's stomach."

24. Wat Thai Classical Night program, 1993, 5, in my possession.

25. Ibid., 1994, 5.

Chapter 7

1. For example, Virginia has relatively few Asians and fewer Buddhists. Nevertheless, Ekoji Buddhist Sangha in Richmond—a multidenominational Buddhist temple that stands in the middle of evangelical Protestant churches— is a good example of religious and cultural heterogeneity (Wilson 2012).

2. *30th Anniversary of Wat Thai*, 299.

3. A few scholars have extensively discussed such economic bonds (Basch, Schiller, and Szanton-Blanc 1994: 226–228, 240, 248; Espiritu 2003: 70–97).

Glossary

1. Access to Insight, ed., "The Eight Precepts: *Attha-sila*," *Access to Insight (Legacy Edition)*, November 30, 2013, available at http://www.accesstoinsight .org/ptf/dhamma/sila/atthasila.html (accessed May 11, 2014).

2. Access to Insight, ed., "The Five Precepts: *Pañca-sila*," *Access to Insight (Legacy Edition)*, November 30, 2013, available at http://www.accesstoinsight .org/ptf/dhamma/sila/pancasila.html (accessed May 11, 2014).

3. See Keown 2000: 45.

4. See Rahula 1974: 45–46.

5. Access to Insight, ed., "The Ten Precepts: *Dasa-sila*," *Access to Insight (Legacy Edition)*, November 30, 2013, available at http://www.accesstoinsight .org/ptf/dhamma/sila/dasasila.html (accessed May 11, 2014).

Glossary

Achan. Teacher.

Bhikkhu. Male monk.

Bhikkhuni. Female monk.

Bot. Chapel; considered the most sacred space in a Buddhist temple as the result of a purification ritual.

Chaokhun. Honorific title granted by Thailand's king to 704 distinguished monks.

Dharma. The teachings of the Buddha.

The Eight Precepts. To refrain from (1) destroying living creatures; (2) taking that which is not given; (3) sexual activity; (4) incorrect speech; (5) intoxicating drinks and drugs which lead to carelessness; (6) eating at the forbidden times; (7) dancing, singing, music, going to see entertainments, wearing garlands, using perfumes, and beautifying the body with cosmetics; and (8) lying on high or luxurious sleeping places.[1]

Farang. A Thai term often referring to White people, regardless of their ethnic or cultural differences.

The Five Precepts. To refrain from (1) destroying living creatures; (2) taking that which is not given; (3) sexual activity; (4) incorrect speech; and (5) intoxicating drinks and drugs which lead to carelessness.[2]

The Four Noble Truths. (1) Life is suffering; (2) suffering is caused by craving; (3) suffering can have an end; and (4) there is a path that leads to the end of suffering.[3]

Karma. Everything is believed to be connected and all actions have consequences. Karma can be positive or negative depending on the sum of the merits and demerits one has accumulated. It keeps people bound to a cycle of births and rebirths.

Khuam pen thai. Thainess.

Kuti. Residence building for monks and novices.

Maha. Honorific title for a monk who has passed at least the first three levels (out of nine) of expertise in Pali.

The Noble Eightfold Path. (1) right understanding; (2) right thought; (3) right speech; (4) right action; (5) right livelihood; (6) right effort; (7) right mindfulness; and (8) right concentration.[4]

Pali. The ancient scriptural and liturgical language of Theravada Buddhism.

Sabai sabai. Easy or contented.

Sala. A multipurpose hall.

Sangha. Community of monks (some temples in the United States include lay practitioners).

Somdet. Honorific title granted by the king to nine of the highest-ranking Thai monks who form the Supreme Sangha Council of Thailand.

The Ten Precepts. The same as the Eight Precepts with the division of rule 7 into two rules—(7) to refrain from dancing, singing, music, going to entertainments and (8) to refrain from wearing garlands, using perfumes, and beautifying the body with cosmetics—and the addition of rule 10, to refrain from accepting gold and silver (money).[5]

Thambun. Doing good, making merit; the transfer of economic capital into religious capital.

Than. A term for showing respect; also refers to a monk who does not have expertise in the first three levels of Pali.

Vinaya. The monastic disciplinary code.

Wai. Bringing the hands to a prayer-like gesture used for greetings, thanks, apologies, and good-byes.

Wat. Temple.

Wihan. A large hall used for worship and rituals but whose space is not purified.

References

Altman, Dennis. 2001. *Global Sex*. Chicago: University of Chicago Press.

Ama, Michihiro. 2010. "The Legal Dimensions of the Formation of Shin Buddhist Temples in Los Angeles." In *Issei Buddhism in the Americas*, ed. Duncan Ryuken Williams and Tomoe Moriya, 65–86. Chicago: University of Illinois Press.

Andaya, Barbara Watson. 2002. "Localising the Universal: Women, Motherhood and the Appeal of Early Theravada Buddhism." *Journal of Southeast Asian Studies* 33 (1): 1–30.

Anderson, Benedict. 1983. *Imagined Communities: Reflections on the Origin and Spread of Nationalism*. London: Verso.

———. 2012. *The Fate of Rural Hell: Asceticism and Desire in Buddhist Thailand*. Calcutta: Seagull.

Anderson, Carol S. 2013. "The Possibility of a Postcolonial Buddhist Ethic of Wealth." *Buddhist-Christian Studies* 33:139–152.

Appadurai, Arjun. 1991. "Global Ethnoscapes: Notes and Queries for a Transnational Anthropology." In *Recapturing Anthropology: Working in the Present*, ed. Richard G. Fox, 191–210. Santa Fe, NM: School of American Research Press.

———. 1996. *Modernity at Large: Cultural Dimensions of Globalization*. Minneapolis: University of Minnesota Press.

Asai, Senryo, and Duncan R. Williams. 1999. "Japanese American Zen Temples: Cultural Identity and Economics." In *American Buddhism: Methods and Findings in Recent Scholarship*, ed. Duncan Ryuken Williams and Christopher S. Queen, 20–35. London: Curzon.

Atkinson, Jane M., and Shelly Errington, eds. 1990. *Power and Difference: Gender in Island Southeast Asia*. Stanford, CA: Stanford University Press.

Bao, Jiemin. 2005. *Marital Acts: Gender, Sexuality, and Identity among the Chinese Thai Diaspora*. Honolulu: University of Hawai'i Press.

Barth, Fredrik. 1969. "Introduction." In *Ethnic Groups and Boundaries: The Social Organization of Culture Difference*, ed. Fredrik Barth, 1–38. Boston: Little, Brown.

Basch, Linda Green, Nina Glick Schiller, and Cristina Szanton Blanc. 1994. *Nations Unbound: Transnational Projects, Postcolonial Predicaments, and Deterritorialized Nation-States*. Langhorne, PA: Gordon and Breach.

Baumann, Gerd. 1996. *Contesting Culture: Discourses of Identity in Multi-ethnic London*. Cambridge: Cambridge University Press.

Blim, Michael. 2000. "Capitalisms in Late Modernity." *Annual Review of Anthropology* 29:25–38.

Bloom, Alfred. 1998. "Shin Buddhism in America: A Social Perspective." In *The Faces of Buddhism in America*, ed. Charles S. Prebish and Kenneth K. Tanaka, 31–48. Berkeley: University of California Press.

Bonilla-Silva, Eduardo. 2012. "The Invisible Weight of Whiteness: The Racial Grammar of Everyday Life in Contemporary America." *Ethnic and Racial Studies* 35 (2): 173–194.

Borchert, Thomas. 2011. "Monastic Labor: Thinking about the Work of Monks in Contemporary Theravada Communities." *Journal of the American Academy of Religion* 79 (1): 162–192.

Bourdieu, Pierre. 1984. *Distinctions: The Social Judgment of Taste*. Cambridge: Cambridge University Press.

———. 1987. "What Makes a Social Class? On the Theoretical and Practical Existence of Groups." *Berkeley Journal of Sociology* 32:1–18.

Bowie, Katherine A. 1998. "The Alchemy of Charity of Class and Buddhism in Northern Thailand." *American Anthropologist* 100 (2): 469–481.

Brah, Avtar. 1987. "Women of South Asian Origin in Britain: Issues and Concerns." *South Asia Research* 9 (1): 39–54.

Cadge, Wendy. 2005. *Heartwood: The First Generation of Theravada Buddhism in America*. Chicago: University of Chicago Press.

Cate, Sandra. 2003. *Making Merit, Making Art*. Honolulu: University of Hawai'i Press.

Chan, Sucheng. 1991. *Asian Americans: An Interpretive History*. Boston: Twayne.

Cheah, Joseph. 2011. *Race and Religion in American Buddhism*. Oxford: Oxford University Press.

Chen, Carolyn. 2008. *Getting Saved in America: Taiwanese Immigration and Religious Experience*. Princeton, NJ: Princeton University Press.

Choi, David Y., Dong Chen, and Woo Jin Lee. 2010. "Asian American-Founded Ventures in Silicon Valley: Challenges, Strategic Partnership, and Performance." *Journal of Enterprising Culture* 18 (4): 355–375.

Clark, Peter Yuichi. 2003. "Compassion among Aging Nisei Japanese Americans." In *Revealing the Sacred in Asian and Pacific America*, ed. Jane Naomi Iwamura and Paul Spickard, 43–65. London: Routledge.

Clifford, James. 1986. "Partial Truths." In *Writing Culture: The Poetics and Politics of Ethnography*, ed. James Clifford and George E. Marcus, 1–26. Berkeley: University of California Press.

Cohen, Stephen S., and Gary Fields. 2000. "Social Capital and Capital Gains: An Examination of Social Capital in Silicon Valley." In *Understanding Silicon Valley: The Anatomy of an Entrepreneurial Region*, ed. Martin Kenney, 190–217. Stanford, CA: Stanford University Press.

Coleman, James W. 1999. "The New Buddhism: Some Empirical Findings." In *American Buddhism: Methods and Findings in Recent Scholarship*, ed. Duncan Ryuken Williams and Christopher S. Queen, 91–99. London: Curzon.

Coningham, R.A.E., K. P. Acharya, K. M. Strickland, C. E. Davis, M. J. Manuel, I. A. Simpson, K. Gilliland, J. Tremblay, T. C. Kinnaird, and D.C.W. Sanderson. 2013. "The Earliest Buddhist Shrine: Excavating the Birthplace of the Buddha, Lumbini (Nepal)." *Antiquity* 87 (338): 1104–1123.

Constable, Nicole. 2003. *Romance on a Global Stage: Pen Pals, Virtual Ethnography, and "Mail Order" Marriages*. Berkeley: University of California Press.

Conze, Edward. 1975. *Further Buddhist Studies: Selected Essays*. Oxford: Bruno Cassirer.

Correll, John T. 2004. *The Air Force in the Vietnam War*. Arlington, VA: Aerospace Education Foundation.

Danico, Mary Yu. 2004. *The 1.5 Generation: Becoming Korean American in Hawaii*. Honolulu: University of Hawai'i Press.

Darlington, Susan M. 2009. "Translating Modernity: Buddhist Response to the Thai Environmental Crisis." In *TransBuddhism: Transmission, Translation, and Transformation*, ed. Nalini Bhushan, Jay Garfield, and Abraham Zablocki, 183–208. Amherst: University of Massachusetts Press.

Davids, T. W. Rhys, and Caroline A. F. Rhys Davids. 1951. *Dialogues of the Buddha, [Part 2] Translated from the Pali of the Dīgha Nikāya*. London: Luzac.

Desbarats, Jacqueline. 1979. "Thai Migration to Los Angeles." *Geographical Review* 69 (3): 302–318.

Doane, Woody. 2003. "Rethinking Whiteness Studies." In *White Out: The Continuing Significance of Racism*, ed. Ashley W. Doane and Eduardo Bonilla-Silva, 4–18. New York: Routledge.

Douglas, Thomas J. 2003. "The Cross and the Lotus: Changing Religious Practices among Cambodian Immigrants in Seattle." In *Revealing the Sacred in Asian and Pacific America*, ed. Jane Naomi Iwamura and Paul Spickard, 159–175. London: Routledge.

Eck, Diana L. 2001. *A New Religious America: How a "Christian Country" Has Now Become the World's Most Religiously Diverse Nation*. New York: HarperSanFrancisco.

Eisenlohr, Patrick. 2012. "Media and Religious Diversity." *Annual Review of Anthropology* 41:37–55.

Eriksen, Thomas Hylland. 2010. *Ethnicity and Nationalism: Anthropological Perspectives*. London: Pluto.

Espiritu, Yen Le. 2003. *Home Bound: Filipino American Lives across Cultures, Communities, and Countries*. Berkeley: University of California Press.

Falk, Monica Lindberg. 2007. *Making Fields of Merit: Buddhist Female Ascetics and Gendered Orders in Thailand*. Seattle: University of Washington Press.

Fields, Rick. 1994. "Confessions of a White Buddhist." *Tricycle* 4 (1): 54–56.

———. 1998. "Divided Dharma: White Buddhists, Ethnic Buddhists, and Racism." In *The Faces of Buddhism in America*, ed. Charles S. Prebish and Kenneth K. Tanaka, 196–206. Berkeley: University of California Press.

Footrakoon, Orapan. 1999. "Lived Experiences of Thai War Brides in Mixed Thai-American Families in the United States." Ph.D. diss., University of Minnesota, Minneapolis.

Foucault, Michel. 1979. *Discipline and Punish: The Birth of a Prison*, trans. Alan Sheridan. New York: Vintage.

———. 1980. "Body/Power." In *Power/Knowledge: Selected Interviews and Other Writings 1972-1977*, ed. Colin Gordon, 55–62. New York: Pantheon.

———. 1984. *The Foucault Reader*, ed. Paul Rabinow. New York: Pantheon.

Frankenberg, Ruth. 1993. *White Women, Race Matters*. Minneapolis: University of Minnesota Press.

Franklin, John Hope, and Alfred Moss Jr. 1994. *From Slavery to Freedom: A History of African Americans*. New York: Alfred A. Knopf.

Fronsdal, Gil. 1998. "Insight Meditation in the United States: Life, Liberty and the Pursuit of Happiness." In *The Faces of Buddhism in America*, ed. Charles S. Prebish and Kenneth K. Tanaka, 163–182. Berkeley: University of California Press.

Fuengfusakul, Apinya. 1993. "Empire of Crystal and Utopian Commune: Two Types of Contemporary Theravada Reform in Thailand." *Sojourn* 8 (1): 153–183.

Giddens, Anthony. 1990. *Consequences of Modernity*. Stanford, CA: Stanford University Press.

Gilroy, Paul. 1991. "It Ain't Where You're From, It's Where You're At: The Dialectics of Diasporic Identification." *Third Text* 5 (13): 3–16.

Gregory, Peter N. 2001. "Describing the Elephant: Buddhism in America." *Religion and American Culture: A Journal of Interpretation* 11 (2): 233–263.

Gupta, Akhil, and James Ferguson. 1992. "Beyond 'Culture': Space, Identity, and the Politics of Difference." *Cultural Anthropology* 7 (1): 6–23.

———. 1997. "Culture, Power, Place: Ethnography at the End of an Era." In *Culture Power Place*, ed. Akhil Gupta and James Ferguson, 33–51. Durham, NC: Duke University Press.

Hacking, Ian. 1990. "Making Up People." In *Forms of Desire*, ed. Edward Stein, 69–88. New York: Garland.

Hale, Grace Elizabeth. 1999. *Making Whiteness: The Culture of Segregation in the South, 1890–1940*. New York: Random House.

Hall, Stuart. 1990. "Cultural Identity and Diaspora." In *Identity: Community, Culture, Difference*, ed. Jonathan Rutherford, 222–237. London: Lawrence and Wishart.

———. 1995. "New Cultures for Old." In *A Place in the World? Places, Cultures and Globalization*, ed. Doreen Massey and Pat Jess, 175–213. Oxford: Oxford University Press.

Hanks, Lucien. 1962. "Merit and Power in the Thai Social Order." *American Anthropologist* 64:1247–1261.

Hannerz, Ulf. 2010. "Diversity Is Our Business." *American Anthropologist* 112 (4): 539–551.

Harris, Cheryl I. 1993. "Whiteness as Property." *Harvard Law Review* 106:1707–1791.

Harvey, David. 1993. "From Space to Place and Back Again." In *Mapping the Future*, ed. Jon Bird, Barry Curtis, Tim Putnam, George Robertson, and Lisa Tickner, 3–29. London: Routledge.

Hershock, Peter D. 2012. *Valuing Diversity: Buddhist Reflection on Realizing a More Equitable Global Future*. Albany: State University of New York Press.

Hickey, Wakoh Shannon. 2010. "Two Buddhisms, Three Buddhisms, and Racism." *Journal of Global Buddhism* 11:1–25.

Hidalgo, Danielle, and Carl L. Bankston III. 2011. "The Demilitarization of Thai American Marriage Migration, 1980–2000." *International Migration and Integration* 12:85–99.

Hori, Victor Sogen. 1998. "Japanese Zen in America: Americanizing the Face in the Mirror." In *The Faces of Buddhism in America*, ed. Charles S. Prebish and Kenneth K. Tanaka, 49–78. Berkeley: University of California Press.

Hurst, Jane D. 1992. *Nichiren Shoshu Buddhism and the Soka Gakkai in America: The Ethos of a New Religious Movement*. New York: Garland.

Inda, Jonathan, and Renato Rosaldo. 2002. "Introduction: A World in Motion." In *The Anthropology of Globalization: A Reader*, ed. Jonathan Inda and Renato Rosaldo, 1–36. Malden, MA: Blackwell.

Ishii, Yoneo. 1968. "Church and State in Thailand." *Asian Survey* 8 (10): 864–871.

———. 1986. *Sangha, State, and Society: Thai Buddhism in History*. Translated by Peter Hawkes. Honolulu: University of Hawai'i Press.

Iwamura, Jane Naomi. 2010. *Virtual Orientalism: Asian Religions in American Popular Culture*. Oxford: Oxford University Press.

Jindra, Michael. 2014. "The Dilemma of Equality and Diversity." *Current Anthropology* 55 (3): 316–334.

Jones, Charles Brewer. 2007. "Marketing Buddhism in the United States of America: Elite Buddhism and the Formation of Religious Pluralism." *Comparative Studies of South Asia, Africa and the Middle East* 27 (1): 214–221.

Kangvalert, Wasana. 1986. "Thai Physicians in the United States: Causes and Consequences of the Brain Drain." Ph.D. diss., State University New York, Buffalo.

Kapleau, Philip. 2000. *The Three Pillars of Zen*. New York: Anchor.

Keown, Damien. 2000. *Buddhism: A Very Short Introduction*. Oxford: Oxford University Press.

Keyes, Charles F. 1971. "Buddhism and National Integration in Thailand." *Journal of Asian Studies* 30 (3): 551–568.

———. 1978. "Political Crisis and Militant Buddhism in Contemporary Thailand." In *Religion and Legitimation of Power in Thailand, Laos, and Burma*, ed. Bardwell L. Smith, 147–163. Chambersburg, PA: Anima.

———. 1984. "Mother or Mistress but Never a Monk: Buddhist Notions of Female Gender in Rural Thailand." *American Ethnologist* 11 (2): 223–235.

———. 1987. *Thailand: Buddhist Kingdom as Modern Nation-State*. Boulder, CO: Westview.

———. 1989. "Buddhist Politics and Their Revolutionary Origins in Thailand." *International Political Science Review* 10 (2): 121–142.

Kieschnick, John. 2003. *The Impact of Buddhism on Chinese Material Culture*. Princeton, NJ: Princeton University Press.

Kingshill, Konrad. 1976. *Ku Daeng—The Red Tomb: A Village Study in Northern Thailand*. Bangkok, Thailand: Suriyaban.

———. 1991. *Ku Daeng—Thirty Years Later: A Village Study in Northern Thailand, 1954–1984*. Monograph Series on Southeast Asia, special report no. 26. Center for Southeast Asian Studies, Northern Illinois University, DeKalb.

Kirsch, A. Thomas. 1975. "Economy, Polity, and Religion in Thailand." In *Change and Persistence in Thai Society*, ed. G. William Skinner and A. Thomas Kirsch, 172–196. Ithaca, NY: Cornell University Press.

———. 1977. "Complexity in the Thai Religious System: An Interpretation." *Journal of Asian Studies* 36 (2): 241–266.

———. 1978. "Modernizing Implications of Nineteenth Century Reforms in the Thai Sangha." In *Religion and Legitimation of Power in Thailand, Laos, and Burma*, ed. Bardwell L. Smith, 52–65. Chambersburg, PA: Anima.

———. 1985. "Text and Context: Buddhist Sex Roles/Culture of Gender Revisited." *American Ethnologist* 12 (2): 302–320.

Kitiarsa, Pattana. 2012. *Mediums, Monks, and Amulets: Thai Popular Buddhism Today*. Seattle: University of Washington Press.

Klima, Alan. 2004. "Thai Love Thai: Financing Emotion in Post-Crash Thailand." *Ethnos* 69 (4): 445–464.

Knodel, John. 2012. *The Future of Family Support for Thai Elderly: Views of the*

Populace. Research Report 12–779. Population Studies Center, Institute for Social Research, University of Michigan.

Krittayapong, Jirah. 2012. "Robin Hood in the Land of the Free? An Ethnographic Study of Undocumented Immigrants from Thailand in the U.S." Ph.D. diss., Ohio University, Athens.

Kwon, Okyun. 2003. *Buddhist and Christian Korean Immigrants: Religious Belief and Socioeconomic Aspects of Life*. New York: LFB Scholarly Publishers.

LaFleur, William R. 1988. *Buddhism: A Cultural Perspective*. New York: Prentice Hall.

Lamphere, Louise, ed. 1992. *Structuring Diversity: Ethnographic Perspectives on the New Immigration*. Chicago: University of Chicago Press.

Layman, Emma. 1976. *Buddhism in America*. Chicago: Nelson-Hall.

Lee, Chong-Moon, William F. Miller, Marguerite Gong Hancock, and Henry S. Rowen. 2000. "The Silicon Valley Habitat." In *The Silicon Valley Edge: A Habitat for Innovation and Entrepreneurship*, ed. Chong-Moon Lee, William F. Miller, Marguerite Gong Hancock, and Henry S. Rowen, 1–15. Stanford, CA: Stanford University Press.

Lewis, Nantawan Boonprasat. 1997. "Thai." In *American Immigrant Cultures: Builders of a Nation*, vol. 2, ed. David Levinson and Melvin Ember, 883–887. New York: Simon and Schuster and Prentice Hall International.

Liechty, Mark. 2003. *Suitably Modern: Making Middle-Class Culture in a New Consumer Society*. Princeton, NJ: Princeton University Press.

Lipsitz, George. 1998. *The Possessive Investment in Whiteness: How White People Profit from Identity Politics*, rev. ed. Philadelphia: Temple University Press.

Lopez, Donald S. 1998. *Prisoners of Shangri-La: Tibetan Buddhism and the West*. Chicago: University of Chicago Press.

———. 2001. *The Story of Buddhism: A Concise Guide to Its History and Teachings*. San Francisco: HarperCollins.

———. 2013. *From Stone to Flesh: A Short History of the Buddha*. Chicago: University of Chicago Press.

Machacek, David W. 2001. "Immigrant Buddhism in America: A Model of Religious Change." *Nova Religio* 5 (1): 65–85.

Makalani, Minkah. 2003. "Rejecting Blackness and Claiming Whiteness: Antiblack Whiteness in the Biracial Project." In *White Out: The Continuing Significance of Racism*, ed. Ashley W. Doane and Eduardo Bonilla-Silva, 81–94. New York: Routledge.

Mason, Andrew. 1999. "Population and Economic Growth in East Asia." East-West Center Working Papers, Population Series, no. 88–25.: East-West Center, Honolulu.

Massey, Doreen. 1993. "Politics and Space/Time." In *Place and the Politics of Identity*, ed. Michael Keith and Steve Pile, 141–161. New York: Routledge.

Mauss, Marcel. 1979. *Sociology and Psychology: Essays*. London: Routledge and Kegan Paul.

McDaniel, Justin. 2011. *The Lovelorn Ghost and the Magical Monk: Practicing Buddhism in Modern Thailand*. New York: Columbia University Press.

McIntosh, Peggy. 1989. "White Privilege: Unpacking the Invisible Knapsack." *Peace and Freedom Magazine*, July–August, 10–12.

McLellan, Janet. 1999. *Many Petals of the Lotus: Five Asian Buddhist Communities in Toronto*. Toronto: University of Toronto Press.

Mills, Mary Beth. 1999. *Thai Women in the Global Labor Force: Consuming Desires, Contested Selves*. New Brunswick, NJ: Rutgers University Press.

Moriya, Tomoe. 2010. "'Americanization' and 'Tradition' in Issei and Nisei Buddhist Publications." In *Issei Buddhism in the Americas*, ed. Duncan Ryuken Williams and Tomoe Moriya, 110–134. Chicago: University of Illinois Press.

Morreale, Don, ed. 1988. *Buddhist America: Centers, Retreats, Practice*. Santa Fe, NM: John Muir.

———, ed. 1998. *The Complete Guide to Buddhist America*. Boston: Shambhala.

Morris, Rosalind. 2000. *In the Place of Origins: Modernity and Its Mediums in Northern Thailand*. Durham, NC: Duke University Press.

Morrison, Toni. 1992. *Playing in the Dark: Whiteness and the Literary Imagination*. Cambridge, MA: Harvard University Press.

Muecke, Marjorie A. 1984. "Make Money not Babies: Changing Status Markers of Northern Thai Women." *Asian Survey* 24:459–470.

———. 2004. "Female Sexuality in Thai Discourses about *Maechii* ('Lay Nuns')." *Culture, Health and Sexuality* 6 (3): 221–238.

Mulder, J. A. Niels. 1969. "Merit: An Investigation of the Motivational Qualities for the Buddhist Concept of Merit in Thailand." *Social Compass* 16 (1): 109–120.

———. 1997. *Thai Images: The Culture of the Public World*. Chiang Mai: Silkworm.

Nattier, Jan. 1998. "Who Is a Buddhist? Charting the Landscape of Buddhist America." In *The Faces of Buddhism in America*, ed. Charles S. Prebish and Kenneth K. Tanaka, 183–195. Berkeley: University of California Press.

Nguyen, Cuong Tu, and A. W. Barber. 1998. "Vietnamese Buddhism in North America: Tradition and Acculturation." In *The Faces of Buddhism in America*, ed. Charles S. Prebish and Kenneth K. Tanaka, 129–146. Berkeley: University of California Press.

Niland, John R. 1970. *The Asian Engineering Brain Drain: A Study of International Relocation into the United States*. Lexington, MA: Heath Lexington.

Nissara Horayangura. 2005. "Old Pillar, New Possibilities: What the Revival of the Bhikkhuni Sangha Contributes to Thai Women and Society." Master's thesis, Chulalongkorn University, Bangkok.

Numrich, Paul David. 1996. *Old Wisdom in the New World: Americanization in Two Immigrant Theravada Buddhist Temples*. Knoxville: University of Tennessee Press.

———. 1998. "Theravada Buddhism in America: Prospects for the Sangha." In *The Faces of Buddhism in America*, ed. Charles S. Prebish and Kenneth K. Tanaka, 147–162. Berkeley: University of California Press.

———. 2003. "Two Buddhisms Further Considered." *Contemporary Buddhism* 4 (1): 55–78.

O'Connor, Richard A. 1993. "Interpreting Thai Religious Change: Temples, *Sangha* Reform and Social Change." *Journal of Southeast Asian Studies* 24 (2): 330–339.

Ohnuma, Reiko. 2005. "Gift." In *Critical Terms for the Study of Buddhism*, ed. Donald S. Lopez, 103–123. Chicago: University of Chicago Press.

Omi, Michael. 2001. "Foreword." In *The Sum of Our Parts: Mixed-Heritage Asian Americans*, ed. Teresa Williams-Leon and Cynthia L. Nakashima, ix–xii. Philadelphia: Temple University Press.

Omi, Michael, and Howard Winant. 1986. *Racial Formation in the United States: From the 1960s to the 1980s*. New York: Routledge and Kegan Paul.

Ong, Aihwa. 1999. *Flexible Citizenship*. Durham, NC: Duke University Press.

———. 2003. *Buddha Is Hiding*. Berkeley: University of California Press.

Ortner, Sherry. 1998. "Identities: The Hidden Life of Class." *Journal of Anthropological Research* 54:1–17.

———. 2003. *New Jersey Dreaming: Capital, Culture, and the Class of '58*. Durham, NC: Duke University Press.

Padgett, Douglas. 2000. "'Americans Need Something to Sit On,' or Zen Meditation Materials and Buddhist Diversity in North America." *Journal of Global Buddhism* 1:61–81.

Pellow, David Naguib, and Lisa Sun-Hee Park. 2002. *The Silicon Valley of Dreams: Environmental Injustice, Immigrant Workers, and the High-Tech Global Economy*. New York: New York University Press.

Perreira, Todd LeRoy. 2008. "The Gender of Practice: Some Findings among Thai Buddhist Women in Northern California." In *Emerging Voices: The Experiences of Underrepresented Asian Americans*, ed. Ling Huping, 160–182. New Brunswick, NJ: Rutgers University Press.

Pirsig, Robert. 1974. *Zen and the Art of Motorcycle Maintenance*. New York: William Morrow.

Potter, Sulamith. 1977. *Family Life in a Northern Thai Village*. Berkeley: University of California Press.

Prebish, Charles S. 1979. *American Buddhism*. North Scituate, MA: Duxbury.

———. 1993. "Two Buddhisms Reconsidered." *Buddhist Studies Review* 10 (2): 187–206.

———. 1999. *Luminous Passage: The Practice and Study of Buddhism in America*. Berkeley: University of California Press.

Prothero, Stephen. 1996. *The White Buddhist: The Asian Odyssey of Henry Steel Olcott*. Bloomington: Indiana University Press.

Queen, Christopher S. 1999. "Introduction." In *American Buddhism: Methods and Findings in Recent Scholarship*, ed. Duncan Ryuken Williams and Christopher S. Queen, xiv–xxxvii. London: Curzon.

Rahula, Walpola. 1974. *What the Buddha Taught*. New York: Grove.

Rasicot, Cindy. 2007. "Visiting the Venerable Dhammananda." *Sawadee Magazine*. Available at http://talkinghearttoheart.org/parenting-adopted-teens/visiting-venerable-dhammananda. Accessed May 14, 2014.

Rātchabandittayasathān. 1968. *Romanization Guide for Thai Script*. Bangkok, Thailand: Royal Institute.

Reynolds, Craig J. 1991. "Introduction: National Identity and Its Defenders." In *National Identity and Its Defenders, Thailand, 1939–1989*, ed. Craig J. Reynolds, Monash Papers on Southeast Asia, 1–40. Melbourne: Center of Southeast Asian Studies, Monash University.

Reynolds, Frank E. 1978. "Legitimation and Rebellion: Thailand's Civic Religion and the Student Uprising of October, 1973." In *Religion and Legitimation of Power in Thailand, Laos, and Burma*, ed. Bardwell L. Smith, 134–145. Chambersburg, PA: Anima.

Ringis, Rita. 1990. *Thai Temples and Temple Murals*. Oxford: Oxford University Press.

Rosenberg, Larry, and David Guy. 1998. *Breath by Breath: The Liberating Practice of Insight Meditation*. Boston: Shambhala.

Rothenberg, Paula S., ed. 2002. *White Privilege: Essential Readings on the Other Side of Racism*. New York: Worth.

Sacks, Karen Brodkin. 1994. "How Did Jews Become White Folks?" In *Race*, ed. Steven Gregory and Roger Sanjeck, 78–102. New Brunswick, NJ: Rutgers University Press.

Saeng, Chandra-nga. 2002. *Buddhism and Thai People*. Bangkok, Thailand: Mahamajut Buddhist University and Institute of Buddhist Missions Overseas.

Sanitsuda Ekachai. 2001. *Keeping the Faith: Thai Buddhism at the Crossroads*. Bangkok, Thailand: Bangkok Post.

Sanjek, Roger. 1998. *The Future of Us All: Race and Neighborhood Politics in New York City*. Ithaca, NY: Cornell University Press.

Saxenian, Annalee. 1999. *Silicon Valley's New Immigrant Entrepreneurs*. San Francisco: Public Policy Institute of California.

Scheper-Hughes, Nancy, and Margaret Lock. 1987. "The Mindful Body: A Prolegomenon to Future Work in Medical Anthropology." *Medical Anthropology Quarterly* 1:6–41.

Schopen, Gregory. 1997. *Bones, Stones, and Buddhist Monks: Collected Papers on the Archaeology, Epigraphy, and Texts of Monastic Buddhism in India*. Honolulu: University of Hawai'i Press.

———. 2004. *Buddhist Monks and Business Matters: Still More Papers on Monastic Buddhism in India*. Honolulu: University of Hawai'i Press.

———. 2005. *Figments and Fragments of Māhāyana Buddhism in India: More Collected Papers*. Honolulu: University of Hawai'i Press.

———. 2009. "The Buddha as a Businessman: Economics and Law in an old Indian Religion." The 106th UCLA Faculty Research Lecture. Available at http://www.youtube.com/watch?v=3GeZGFvbDzo. Accessed May 14, 2014.

Seager, Richard. 1999. *Buddhism in America*. New York: Columbia University Press.

Shinagawa, Larry H., and Gin Yong Pang. 1996. "Asian American Panethnicity and Intermarriage." *Amerasia Journal* 22 (2): 127–152.

Smith-Hefner, Nancy. 1999. *Khmer American*. Berkeley: University of California Press.

Snodgrass, Judith. 2009. "Discourse, Authority, Demand: The Politics of Early English Publications on Buddhism." In *TransBuddhism: Transmission, Translation, and Transformation*, ed. Nalini Bhushan, Jay Garfield, and Abraham Zablocki, 21–41. Amherst: University of Massachusetts Press.

Somekawa, Ellen. 1995. "On the Edge: Southeast Asians in Philadelphia and the Struggle for Space." In *ReViewing Asian America: Locating Diversity*, ed. Wendy L. Ng and Gary Y. Okihiro, 33–47. Pullman, WA: Washington State University Press.

Spiro, Melford E. 1966. "Buddhism and Economic Action in Burma." *American Anthropologist* 68 (5): 1163–1173.

Suh, Sharon A. 2004. *Being Buddhist in a Christian World: Gender and Community in a Korean American Temple*. Seattle: University of Washington Press.

Suzuki, Shunryu. 1970. *Zen Mind, Beginner's Mind*. New York: Walker/Weatherhill.

Swearer, Donald K. 1995. "A Modern Sermon on Merit Making." In *Buddhism in Practice*, ed. Donald S. Lopez, 399–401. Princeton, NJ: Princeton University Press.

Tambiah, Stanley J. 1968. "Literacy in a Buddhist Village in North-east Thailand." In *Literacy in Traditional Societies*, ed. Jack Goody, 86–131. Cambridge: Cambridge University Press.

———. 1970. *Buddhism and the Spirit Cults in North-East Thailand*. Cambridge: Cambridge University Press.

———. 1976. *World Conqueror and World Renouncer: A Study of Buddhism and Polity in Thailand against a Historical Background*. Cambridge: Cambridge University Press.

———. 1978. "Sangha and Polity in Modern Thailand: An Overview." In *Religion and Legitimation of Power in Thailand, Laos, and Burma*, ed. Bardwell L. Smith, 111–133. Chambersburg, PA: Anima.

———. 1984. *The Buddhist Saints of the Forest and the Cult of Amulets: A Study in Charisma, Hagiography, Sectarianism, and Millennial Buddhism*. Cambridge: Cambridge University Press.

———. 1985. *Culture, Thought, and Social Action: An Anthropological Perspective*. Cambridge, MA: Harvard University Press.

Tanaka, Kenneth K. 1999. "Issues of Ethnicity in the Buddhist Churches of America." In *American Buddhism: Methods and Findings in Recent Scholarship*, ed. Duncan Ryuken Williams and Christopher S. Queen, 3–19. London: Curzon.

———. 2007. "The Individual in Relation to the Sangha in American Buddhism: An Examination of 'Privatized Religion.'" *Buddhist-Christian Studies* 27:115–127.

———. 2011. "Dramatic Growth of American Buddhism: An Overview." *Dharma World* 38:4–9.

Taylor, James L. 1993. *Forest Monks and the Nation-State: An Anthropological and Historical Study in Northeastern Thailand*. Singapore: Institute of Southeast Asian Studies.

Teachout, Stephanie J. 2005. "Thai Language Maintenance in New York City: Wat Thai and the Preservation of Thai Identity." In *Languages, Communities, and Education*, 9–16. New York: Society for International Education.

Thongchai Winichakul. 1994. *Siam Mapped: A History of the Geo-Body of a Nation*. Honolulu: University of Hawai'i Press.

Thongthiraj, Rahpee. 2003. "Unveiling the Face of Invisibility: Exploring the Thai American Experience." In *The New Face of Asian Pacific American Numbers, Diversity and Change in the 21st Century*, ed. Eric Lai and Dennis Arguelles, 102–104. San Francisco: Asian Week and Asian American Studies Center Press, University of California, Los Angeles.

Traweek, Sharon. 1988. *Beamtimes and Lifetimes: The World of High Energy Physicists*. Cambridge, MA: Harvard University Press.

Truong, Thanh-Dam. 1990. *Sex, Money and Morality: Prostitution and Tourism in Southeast Asia*. London: Zed.

Tsomo, Karma Lekshe. 2009. "Global Exchange: Women in the Transmission and Transformation of Buddhism." In *TransBuddhism: Transmission, Translation, and Transformation*, ed. Nalini Bhushan, Jay Garfield, and Abraham Zablocki, 151–165. Amherst: University of Massachusetts Press.

Turner, Terence. 1980. "The Social Skin: Bodily Adornment, Social Meaning and Personal Identity." In *Not Work Alone. A Cross-Cultural View of Activities Superfluous to Survival*, ed. Jeremy Cherfas and Roger Lewin, 112–140. London: Temple Smith.

Tweed, Thomas A. 1999. "Nightstand Buddhists and Other Creatures: Sympathizers, Adherents, and the Study of Religion." In *American Buddhism: Methods and Findings in Recent Scholarship*, ed. Duncan Ryuken Williams and Christopher S. Queen, 71–90. London: Curzon.

———. 2011. "Theory and Method in the Study of Buddhism: Toward 'Translocative' Analysis." *Journal of Global Buddhism* 12:17–32.

Tworkov, Helen. 1991. "Many Is More." *Tricycle* 1 (2): 4.

U.S. Department of Justice. 1978. *Immigration and Naturalization Annual Reports 1968–1977*. Washington, D.C.: U.S. Government Printing Office.

Van Esterik, Penny. 1992. *Taking Refuge: Lao Buddhists in North America*. Monographs in Southeast Asian Studies. Tempe: Arizona State University Press.

———. 1996. "The Politics of Beauty in Thailand." In *Beauty Queens on the Global Stage*, ed. Colleen Ballerino Cohen, Richard Wilk, and Beverly Stoeltje, 203–216. London: Routledge.

———. 1999. "Ritual and the Performance of Buddhist Identity among Lao Buddhists in North America." In *American Buddhism: Methods and Findings in Recent Scholarship*, ed. Duncan Ryuken Williams and Christopher S. Queen, 57–68. London: Routledge.

———. 2000. *Materializing Thailand*. New York: Berg.

Vertovec, Steven. 1997. "Three Meanings of 'Diaspora' Exemplified among South Asian Religions." *Diaspora* 6 (3): 277–299.

———. 2007. "Super-Diversity and Its Implications." *Ethnic and Racial Studies* 30 (6): 1024–1054.

———. 2010. "Depicting Diversities: Editorial Introduction." *Diversities* 12 (1): 1–3.

Wallace, Irving, and Amy Wallace. 1978. *The Two*. New York: Simon and Schuster.

Walsh, Michael J. 2007. "Efficacious Surroundings: Temple Space and Buddhist Well-being." *Journal of Religion and Health* 46 (4): 471–479.

Watts, Alan. 1957. *The Way of Zen*. New York: Pantheon.

Weisman, Jan R. 2001. "The Tiger and His Stripes: Thai and American Reactions to Tiger Woods's (Multi-) 'Racial Self.'" In *The Sum of Our Parts: Mixed-Heritage Asian Americans*, ed. Teresa Williams-Leon and Cynthia L. Nakashima, 231–243. Philadelphia: Temple University Press.

Wertheim, Willem F. 1965. "The Trading Minorities in Southeast Asia." In *East West Parallels: Sociological Approaches to Modern Asia*, ed. Willem F. Wertheim, 39–82. Chicago: Quadrangle.

Whittaker, Andrea. 1999. "Women and Capitalist Transformation in a Northeastern Thai Village." In *Genders and Sexualities in Modern Thailand*, ed. Peter Jackson and Nerida Cook, 43–62. Chiang Mai, Thailand: Silkworm.

Wildman, Stephanie M. 1996. *Privilege Revealed: How Invisible Preference Undermines America*. New York: New York University Press.

Williams, Duncan Ryuken, and Christopher S. Queen, eds. 1999. *American Buddhism: Methods and Findings in Recent Scholarship*. London: Curzon.

Wilson, Jeff. 2008. "'Deeply Female and Universally Human': The Rise of Kuanyin Worship in America." *Journal of Contemporary Religion* 3 (3): 285–306.

———. 2009a. "Mapping the American Buddhist Terrain: Paths Taken and Possible Itineraries." *Religion Compass* 3 (5): 836–846.

———. 2009b. *Mourning the Unborn Dead: A Buddhist Ritual Comes to America*. Oxford: Oxford University Press.

———. 2012. *Dixie Dharma: Inside a Buddhist Temple in the American South*. Chapel Hill: University of North Carolina Press.

Wiyada Thongmitr. 1979. *Khrua in Khong's Westernized School of Thai Painting*. Bangkok, Thailand: Akson Samphan.

Xuan, Fang. 2008. "Contemporary Buddhism: Theravada Buddhism, The National Women's Liberation Movement of the Inspection." *Hongshi* 91. Available at http://www.philosophyol.com/BBS/viewthread.php?tid=25320. Accessed November 18, 2009. [In Chinese.]

Yaeger, Patricia, ed. 1996. *The Geography of Identity*. Ann Arbor: University of Michigan Press.

Yang, Mayfair Mei-Hui. 2008. "Introduction." In *Chinese Religiosities: Afflictions of Modernity and State Formation*, ed. Mayfair Mei-Hui Yang, 1–42. Berkeley: University of California Press.

Yu, Henry. 2001. *Thinking Orientals: Migration, Contact, and Exoticism in Modern America*. Oxford: Oxford University Press.

Zehner, Edwin. 1990. "Reform Symbolism of a Thai Middle-Class Sect: The Growth and Appeal of the Thammakai Movement." *Journal of Southeast Asian Studies* 21 (2): 402–442.

Index

Jiemin Bao is a Professor of Anthropology at the University of Nevada, Las Vegas, and the author of *Marital Acts: Gender, Sexuality, and Identity among the Chinese Thai Diaspora.*